The Practice of Reality Therapy

Learning to Counsel with Choice Theory Psychology

For Doreen

Stalwart of CT

Brian

Brian Lennon

Use of the original Reality Therapy logo and terms Reality Therapy ® and Choice Theory®
by kind permission of Carleen Glasser.

DEDICATION

This book is dedicated to

William Glasser M.D.
Creator of Reality Therapy
and Choice Theory Psychology

for

his profound respect for the total independence of each human being
his persistence in always seeking more effective ways to help others
his courage in wading against the tides of unchallenged traditions
his fine sense of humour in telling jokes and laughing with us
the many good times we have had in his company
the enrichment he has brought to so many lives
his generosity in sharing his ideas with us
helping make the world a better place
always being himself

CONTENTS

Foreword

One of the last significant decisions William Glasser made before he died, was to appoint Brian Lennon, as the first chairman of the newly formed William Glasser International. Brian was chosen because he had consistently demonstrated the responsible leadership skills necessary for the role and he had a superior understanding of the Reality Therapy and Choice Theory Psychology that has now become the Glasser legacy. These traits are readily apparent in the pages of this excellent book, *The Practice of Reality Therapy.*

This book provides the reader with a fresh new look at Glasser's work from the perspective of a master teacher, and an effective practitioner of Reality Therapy, combined with the originality of a creative story teller. Beginning with a clear and authentic explanation of Choice Theory, the author adds insights of his own and examples of how the theory provides a foundation for the practice of Reality Therapy.

Dr. Glasser referred to Choice Theory as a psychology. The subtitle of his book, *Choice Theory, is "A New Psychology of Personal Freedom".* Brian Lennon agrees with Glasser's view and defends his belief in the use of Psychology, as in Choice Theory Psychology, because the theory is about human behavior and that is what psychology does, theorize about human behavior. Theories are part of science, the first step towards researching and getting empirical support for views.

Take for example, Stimulus Response Psychology. It also theorizes about human behavior as being externally motivated by stimuli. In one of his lectures, Dr. Glasser called Ivan Pavlov, who got dogs to salivate at the sound of a bell, a very smart Russian. "Had Pavlov used cats," Glasser quipped, "he'd still be ringing the bell!"

Psychology is the science of the psyche, the science of the mind. Choice Theory Psychology theorizes about human behavior being internally motivated by genetic needs. In the case of Choice Theory there is a real explanation of human behavior and how the human mind works. That is why the integration of Choice Theory Psychology into the practice of Reality Therapy is so essential. This book uniquely addresses the effectiveness of combining the two together in helping people to better understand themselves and others. With a new awareness of their internal motivation to behave to fulfill basic needs, unhappy people can learn to evaluate their own behavior and make more effective choices that lead to happiness.

Almost every chapter in this book ends with a section called Ideas and Exercises. This is an experiential involvement in the learning process that provides opportunities to practice and integrate the skills presented in the book. Practicing counseling by participating in role-plays is one of the many exercises that help the learner actually use counseling skills in a safe environment and enjoy the process.

What motivates someone to want to help others? The sub-title of this book is "Learning to Counsel With Choice Theory Psychology". Since all we can give or get from one another is information, then help is information that the person on the receiving end may or may not perceive as helpful. Since the helper is also perceived as outside or external by their very nature of being the other and potentially controlling, the relationship is off to a rocky start.

One way to get through to a person who seeks or is sent to counseling is to deliver information to them that they will perceive as useful. Learning Choice Theory Psychology is the key to unlocking the mystery of reaching people and making a connection with them that is based on their needs not on some predetermined, external outcome. Once that kind of connection is made, counseling or helping can proceed. The information is allowed in and can now at least be heard.

This book is a valuable resource, full of Choice Theory based ideas for those in the helping professions who want to connect with and be heard by the people they are attempting to help. The ultimate goal is to help people help themselves. Given the information in this book, helpers can choose to become well equipped to share what they have learned with the people they want to help. An added benefit is, in the process, Choice Theory helpers have internalized and applied Choice Theory to their own lives.

What motivates someone to want to continue to help others? The short answer is success. As is well known, practice leads to success in any endeavor undertaken. The title of this book is *The **Practice** of Reality Therapy, Learning to Counsel with Choice Theory Psychology*. In it, Brian Lennon, offers a comprehensive guide to successful counseling and a bonus, the gift of learning how to change the only person's behavior you can change, your own.

Carleen Glasser
1st September 2019

Acknowledgements

At some stage in 1985 a guidance counselling colleague and friend, Arthur Dunne, told me that he was hoping to bring Dr. William Glasser, the founder of Reality Therapy to Ireland that summer. At the time I was tired of attending seminars that sometimes gave little return for a day missing from work. However this immediately sounded like a good investment of time although I knew little about the man and his ideas at that stage. I decided to go. It would turn out to be a very significant decision for me and my first word of thanks goes to Arthur for that special invitation.

Dr. Glasser followed his lecture by a week long introductory course in Reality Therapy and so I had the good fortune to begin my training with Dr. Glasser himself.

I remain indebted to my earlier training based on the teaching of wonderful counselling sources such as Carl Rogers, George Kelly and Violet Oaklander, all bright stars in my counselling sky.

In the following years, our training continued in the superbly competent hands of Suzy Hallock Bannigan and the late Richard Pulk. As we got to know more Reality Therapy faculty and members around the world, we benefitted from their friendship and expertise. They included: Naomi Glasser, Carleen Glasser, Larry Palmatier, Al Katz, Don O'Donnell, Bob and Terry Hoglund, Tom Smith, Bob Wubbolding, Nancy Muir Dees, Jeannette McDaniel, Jim Montagnes, Tom Parish, Marty Price, Jagoda Tonšić-Krema, Juan Pablo Aljure, Jean Suffield, Leon Lojk, Bob Sullo, Diane Gossen, John Brickell and very especially to the late Linda Harshman.

I owe a big debt of gratitude to my colleagues in the William Glasser Institute Ireland who have always engaged in the most profound discussions of Reality Therapy and Choice Theory: Jimmie Woods, Carmel Solon, Ken Lyons, Eileen Hearne, Arthur Dunne, Sr. Claire Sweeney and Marcella Finnerty.

In my work life I found St. Oliver's Community College, Drogheda very supportive of the guidance counselling role, work that was greatly enriched by my colleagues in the Institute of Guidance Counsellors. In schools, Community Training Workshops and Youthreach it was my privilege to share my days with a wonderful team of teachers and parents. Guiding and counselling teenagers gave me remarkable insights into the challenges they face and the amazing courage and tolerance they so often show. Some of their most wonderful successes are stories that cannot be told.

Good friends Professor Dermot Keogh and Dr. Enda McGovern gave me great encouragement throughout this process.

When it came to putting this book together, the gentle critical eye of Ken Lyons was greatly appreciated, aided and abetted by Aoife Lyons.

My Mum and Dad were my first teachers, the first to encourage any project I undertook and I am forever grateful for their love, creativity and inspiration.

If 1985 was a good year for me then 1973 was an even better one, the year Laura and I married. My studies, my career changes, my involvement in Reality Therapy, countless trips to conferences and courses and the time to put these pages together. None of these would have been possible without her unbelievable support and inspiration.

Introduction

It is impossible to understand another human being. The best we can do is to try to understand them. That is the special challenge for those who engage in counselling or indeed in a wide range of people-orientated careers. Since the main focus of this book is counselling and helping people improve their counselling skills, we will be paying particular attention to the understanding of human behaviour that provides the foundation for such work.

The aim of this book is to help people learn about the practice of Reality Therapy. Hopefully, it will help deepen your understanding of the theory that guides the therapy and of the various procedures that characterise Reality Therapy.

As a skill, counselling is required far beyond the professional therapist's office. Educators, parents, youth-workers, medical personnel, emergency intervention teams and many others will engage in a counselling role from time to time. What is especially interesting is that the theory of human behaviour offered in these pages will apply not only to counselling but to human life in general. It will shed new light on the way we run our relationships, on how we communicate with our children and on many different aspects of our lives. For these reasons the book reaches out to readers with very different needs:

- It explains a theory of human behaviour that challenges everyone to re-evaluate their lives.

- It elaborates an approach to counselling that relies on this theory.

- It breaks the practice of this counselling into manageable modules to help those who wish to learn how to apply the approach.

- It also details many general applications of the ideas in everyday life.

Although the author makes constant reference to counsellors and therapists, most of the ideas could be used by anyone in a helping role. The specific counselling approach explained in the book is Reality Therapy, created by Dr. William Glasser, and it is based on Choice Theory psychology, the framework he has evolved to explain human behaviour.

Hopefully those who are already familiar with a particular model of counselling will find this a useful introduction to Reality Therapy but the book will take it for granted that many readers have no previous training in counselling.

William Glasser

Since 1985 I have made Reality Therapy the theoretical and practical framework for my counselling and this book makes this its foundation. I fully acknowledge my indebtedness to   Dr. Glasser and his ideas.

Since he first published a description of his therapy in 1965 he has been a remarkable innovator in the area of counselling.   His dissatisfaction with the theories that were current during his training days inspired him to approach human problems in a new way.   His success soon attracted the attention of others.   As people sought him out for courses and lectures it became necessary for him to be more specific about both his practical approaches. In spite of the clarity and quality of his explanations I believe that Glasser's own demonstration therapy sessions will always communicate much more than his words and are an invaluable resource to those studying his approach.

At the present time Glasser's ideas are taught throughout the world and his Institute is active in all continents except Antarctica. He himself has been actively teaching his ideas until 2009 and he has been a regular invited guest at some of the world's leading psychotherapy conferences.

This book will summarise key ideas from Glasser and then will attempt to go beyond what he himself says by reading between the lines of his practice and probing deeper into his theory, teasing out new connections and implications. The author writes from a position of strong belief in Glasser's theories but is firmly convinced that they contain more implications that even Glasser himself is aware of or teaches. It is a regular comment from people completing the two year training in Reality Therapy that the ideas are beguilingly simple but remarkably profound and far-reaching in their implications.

This book, therefore, is not intended to be a mere summary of Glasser's views nor is it limited to being a "primer" for those who want to learn Choice Theory or Reality Therapy. A companion book published by the same author, "The Practice of Choice Theory Psychology" explores a variety of specific applications of Choice Theory and provides ideas for counselling a range of problems.

Opinion and Experience

A very big part of the book relies on the author's personal experience and this means that many of the ideas are personal opinions or observations rather than research conclusions. Accurate well-designed research is ultimately the only way to confirm what we believe to be true but, unlike extreme empiricism, I do not turn my back on other sources of knowledge. These have their very important place. Given the great difficulties in researching the efficacy of counselling it is inevitable that we rely more on observations, speculation and opinion until adequate research can support or counter the ideas.

The author has worked as a Guidance Counsellor with teenagers for a quarter of a century and for twenty of those years has used a Reality Therapy approach. The views offered in these pages come from the wide range of experience obtained in and out of the school context over those years, working as a counsellor and also as an Instructor in the William Glasser Institute (now "William Glasser International"[1]).

The Need for a Core Theory

It is very important for the anyone intending to work as a counsellor to become familiar with a wide range of theories and techniques. However, to be an effective counsellor I believe that the person must have identified a core theory to support the approach he or she[2] will use with clients. The counsellor may have assembled that theory from several sources and may have added his own variations on this. Whatever its origins, this core theory will form the backbone of that person's counselling.

On asking a counsellor, "What is your main approach?" I believe there should be a clear answer. The answer "I'm an eclectic" is not sufficient in itself especially if this implies the total absence of any central structure. I do not believe in a disjointed pick-and-mix approach to therapy. The counsellor needs some core sense of what he is doing, something that will help tie different strategies and

---

[1] www.wglasserinternational.org

[2] The English language has not yet caught up with gender equality making the use of pronouns "he" and "she" rather awkward. I will alternate gender pronouns and only occasionally resort to the cumbersome "he or she" phrase. Generally where I use "he" or "she", both genders are included.

techniques together and ultimately improve the quality of professional help the client receives.

Whatever method a counsellor adopts as central there are certain key questions that its theory needs to answer clearly:

1. How does this theory explain human behaviour? How does it answer the question, "Why do people do what they do?"
2. How does the theory define "problem behaviour"?
3. How exactly does counselling "help" the client according to this theory?

I will attempt to answer these three questions in the following chapters, the first in the chapter on "Choice Theory" and the other two in the chapter on "Reality Therapy and Choice Theory".

Using This Book

There are two main sections in the book and the first aims to establish the solid theoretical foundation of Reality Therapy and show how its practical aspects flow from Choice Theory psychology. It will introduce the key concepts and terminology of Glasser's approach to therapy.

The second section moves on to explore the skills required in the practice of Reality Therapy. The emphasis is on helping the reader understand the main components of this approach and there are exercises and guidelines about how to practise the component parts before integrating them into one's own counselling style. In fact the first chapter of this section explores the challenge of learning how to counsel and offers some guidelines about this complex process.

Most of the chapters of this book will have an extra section at the end entitled "Ideas and Exercises". This section has exercises to help in the learning or application of Reality Therapy in counselling or in everyday life. Counselling cannot be a self-taught skill and so many of the exercises throughout the book are intended to be used by supervisors and instructors who are helping others to become proficient in Reality Therapy.

Glasser's Choice Theory is more than a counselling theory. It extends to all human behaviour and if the counsellor is not aware of this broader application the counselling work will be less effective than it might be. For this reason the Ideas and Exercises section will also contain ideas about the application of Reality Therapy and Choice Theory to everyday life.

Because this book relies so heavily on an understanding of Choice Theory the reader is recommended to become familiar with the first section before reading the remainder. A familiarity with Glasser's main ideas and terminology will greatly enhance the reader's understanding of the later chapters.

Once a person has a core theory and approach it is even more possible to make effective use of a range of techniques from other sources and this book will certainly draw on materials from outside of Reality Therapy. Once the counsellor has identified a clear core theory as a foundation, a well-integrated eclecticism becomes possible and powerful.

Regarding the counselling examples used throughout the book, all clients and cases presented are in themselves fictitious. They are based broadly on the author's experience but no one example represents any specific real individual in the author's experience. The details are selected and presented in order to illustrate aspects of Reality Therapy.

The Purpose of Counselling

There is one other question that it is important to answer before evaluating any approach to counselling: What is the overall purpose of counselling?

Once we agree on a definition of this purpose, whatever skills and techniques we might use in counselling must contribute to it. Conversely, no matter how orthodox our techniques are, if they do not achieve the overall purpose, we may need to review our approach.

The purpose cannot be defined in terms of the techniques that we use to serve our purpose. We cannot say that our overall aim is to listen, to empathise or even to understand. These may be vital parts of the process but they are not the ultimate goals. My preferred wording is that the purpose of counselling is to help the client achieve a happier life. It is part of my belief system (and central to Choice Theory psychology) that the client is responsible for his or her own happiness and so, to achieve the purpose, I see my role is that of a consultant who helps clients help themselves.

Glasser's approach to therapy is more pro-active than some other client-centred schools of counselling. He takes initiatives in engaging with the client using Choice Theory to guide his exploration of the client's life. This high level of interaction with the client can surprise counsellors from other traditions but an evaluation of any therapy must ultimately be in terms of the purpose of therapy. Similarly, as counsellors (and we are always trainees), we can only evaluate our own practice well if we have clarified what we are trying to do in the first place.

Key Questions about Your Approach

At the very outset and before reading the remainder of this book it may be useful to ask yourself some of the above questions about your own approach to counselling? (If you are not yet a counsellor apply the questions to any area of your life where you work in a helping, parenting or teaching role to others.) Even if you are "eclectic" by choice, you still need a clear answer to the questions posed here.

1. How do you yourself explain human behaviour? In your opinion why do people do what they do? How important is the past, early upbringing, life experiences, present environment, learning?

2. How do you define "problem behaviour"? Is it defined in terms of deviation from the norm or normal? Is it caused by genetic or chemical factors? Can the weather be a cause? Can a person generate his or her own problems?

3. How exactly does counselling "help" the client? How much, if any, of our work should be passive listening, active listening, supporting, advising, lecturing, teaching, questioning, challenging, disclosing, planning?

Your Core Theory

If you are already involved in counselling or therapy you may find it helpful to answer these questions before proceeding.

1. What is your core theory?

2. Who are the main authors you choose to guide you?

3. What aspects of your core theory come from your own personal experience?

4. What other counselling theories do you find useful for additional ideas and techniques?

Your Theory and Your Life

1. To what extent does your current approach to helping others professionally impact on how you interact with people in everyday life? Should there be a connection?

2. How does your counselling or helping role influence other roles in your life, e.g., parent, friend, teacher, employer, worker?

THE THEORY

Choice Theory Psychology

In this chapter you will learn about:

- The core principles of Glasser's Choice Theory psychology
- The concept of internal control
- The role of the Basic Needs, physical and psychological
- The nature of motivation
- The part played by our perceptual system
- The concept of the "Quality World"
- The way our behaviour attempts to keep our needs in balance
- Our organised and creative behavioural systems
- The centrality of relationships in Choice Theory

Choice Theory psychology is relatively simple to explain but its implications for human life can take many years if not a lifetime to understand. In developing the ideas, Glasser's original intent was to establish his therapy on a firm theoretical footing. What he created as a result was not merely a theory of counselling but has become an explanation of human behaviour in general. Indeed it has such a direct relevance for the choices we make at every moment that it could be seen to have a strong existential dimension.

Glasser applies Choice Theory not only to his therapy but also to his ideas on education and management. In fact, from approximately the year 2000 onwards, the theory came more and more to the fore in his counselling leading him to focus on the teaching of mental health both inside and outside of formal counselling.

For Glasser, Choice Theory was to become a set of principles that could be applied directly to life as well as therapy. Bannister and Fransella observed that "in psychology, many of us behave as if 'theory' were like heaven – a fine place to go when the practical business of living is all over, but not a matter of much concern here and now."[3] Glasser, more a technician than a technologist, would not want his ideas to have this particular heavenly quality. For him theory is very much something to enlighten the practice. This is borne out by the fact that he has quietly moved some aspects of his ideas (such as "levels of perception") away from centre-stage, not because they were not valid but because they were not of great practical application in his view.

Choice Theory challenges many of the everyday assumptions we make about our own behaviour and that of the people in our worlds. It is deceptively simple on the one hand and surprisingly profound on the other. It began to form when Glasser first challenged what he was taught as a trainee psychiatrist in the early nineteen sixties.

Glasser originally explained his ideas using some of the language of traditional psychiatry in his very first book "Mental Health and Mental Illness" published in 1960. Five years later with the publication of "Reality Therapy" he was already using his own terms summing up his theory in a set of quite radical statements.

By 1981 he had discovered William Power's application of Control Theory to psychological phenomena[4] and found there a clear explanation of how and why we behave. By the end of the 90's he realised he had changed so many aspects of this theory to fit his own explanations that a new name was required and "Choice Theory" came into being as the definitive statement of his underlying belief system. It remains heavily indebted to William Powers'

---

[3] D. Bannister & Fay Fransella. *Inquiring Man*. Penguin Books Ltd., 1971.

[4] Powers, William. *Behavior: The Control of Perception*. New York: Aldine, 1973.

Control Theory but differs in important aspects such as the role of Basic Needs and Total Behaviour.

In the rest of this chapter I will examine the main tenets of Choice Theory and explore briefly the corollaries they give rise to. Taken together these will give the Choice Theory answer to the question posed in the introduction "Why do people do what they do?"

I am controlled from within.

Central to Choice Theory is the idea that I am controlled from within myself and not by outside stimuli. Once I acknowledge that I am controlled from within this has four important corollaries for us:

Only I can change me.

You can take me to the water but you cannot make me drink. You can keep me in school but you cannot make me think. All personal change will begin with the individual's willingness to change.

I am responsible for my own behaviour.

Some have misinterpreted this as meaning that I am to "blame" for what I do but Glasser's emphasis is on choice. If I am responsible for my behaviour it means I am choosing what I do and this in turn means I can choose something different. My control over my own behaviour is a liberating power and it is a characteristic of Reality Therapy that clients discover just how much control they have over the problems they brought to counselling.

Another confusion that people experience is that they assume choice is synonymous with awareness. In fact we make many choices in everyday life without full awareness of what we are doing. They are still our choices! Obviously, in counselling, the Reality Therapy practitioner will help the client become aware of his or her own choices so that it then becomes more possible to change them.

I cannot change other people.

This has enormous implications for our relationships. So many marriages and similar long-term relationships are seriously damaged, sometimes beyond repair, by attempts to change the other person. It would appear that the closer I draw to another person, the easier it becomes to confuse the delineation between the two persons. The result is that my attempts to improve myself become attempts to improve the other person and this ultimately is seen by the other as criticism or nagging, two of the most destructive behaviours for relationships.

There are, of course, situations where our goal appears to be to change someone else, as in education for example. However the Glasserian view is that whether we are in the counselling office, the home, the classroom or the workplace, we simply cannot change anyone else unless they want to change. It is not the educator's task to change others but to present ideas in such a way that the recipients want to change.

Other people cannot change me.

We often live according to the myth that other people can change us. We say "John makes me angry", "Mary makes my life a misery" and so on. We even believe that people can do this remotely: "the telephone drives me mad!" Glasser says we choose these behaviours. I choose my behaviour in regard to John, Mary or the telephone and by doing so I choose to be angry, miserable or mad. Only when we fully realise this can we begin to take responsibility for our own lives and begin to examine more effective choices for ourselves.

Even when a criminal puts a gun to my head and demands the keys of my car, it is still my choice to give them or not. Normally, of course, I would choose to do so in the interests of staying alive. In fact, all others can do is, as Glasser likes to say, "give me information". The criminal with the gun is giving me a lot of quite definite information about what he wants me to do but it is not control. I control me because it is I who decide what to do with the incoming information.

I rely on my own evaluation of my life.

If my control is internal then it is my evaluation of my internal world that determines whether or not I change. This introduces the very important Choice Theory concept of "self-evaluation". A major focus of Reality Therapy is in helping the client make a self-evaluation of his own life specifically in the problem area he has brought to counselling. Instead of offering the client an external evaluation of his or her life situation, the Reality Therapy practitioner will help that client tease out different aspects of the situation and then let the client reach his or her own conclusions about it.

I have basic needs.

At the very heart of my internal control is my set of basic needs, the ultimate driving force of my organism. Glasser lists these as five though he acknowledges that others may list a different number of needs and different titles for them:

Survival

This need refers to our genetic instruction to survive, not only as an individual but also as a species. As individuals we need health and safety, warmth and nourishment. As a species we need to reproduce. As we evolved and our larger brain capacity permitted the mind to develop we became aware of other needs that enhanced our survival chances and the very quality of that survival. Whereas we might see "survival" as mainly a biological need, the other needs could be classified as "psychological".

Love and Belonging

Having a strong relationship with those around us and belonging to a group greatly improves the quality of our survival both as individuals and as a species. This is a very important need insofar as we meet most of our needs through our relationships with others.

Power

This relates very closely to having a sense of control of our own lives. It does not mean power over others although many people try to satisfy it in this way and the result is serious conflict with their love and belonging needs. Power in the Choice Theory sense is associated with personal confidence and competence.

Freedom

This is the need to be unfettered, not to be controlled, to have the space to meet all our needs. It includes the freedom to express ourselves but also carries a responsibility to respect the freedom of others.

Fun

This is seen by Glasser as "the genetic reward for learning"[5]. It is part of our ongoing adaptation to the world we live in, always updating our need-satisfying skills.

---

[5] Glasser, William. *Choice Theory*. New York: HarperCollins, 1998.

What constantly motivates my behaviour is my basic needs.

My needs are internal and are constantly moving me to satisfy them. Seeing them as the driving force of my behaviour has a number of implications:

When a need is not fully satisfied I am motivated to behave in order to fulfil it.

Hunger is a very good example and it relates to the need for survival. When my body is short of food hunger signals reach the brain and begin to focus my behaviour on seeking food. The other needs work in a similar way each with its own specific feeling signals. Feeling lonely, helpless, trapped or bored relates to love and belonging, power, freedom and fun respectively.

When a need is satisfied I am motivated to behave in order to maintain it.

Once I get what I want the motivation to acquire changes to a motivation to keep. In simple terms, once I get a bowl of soup to satisfy my hunger I behave in order to enjoy it and not to spill it.

Insofar as my needs have a hierarchy, the need that is currently experiencing the greatest frustration becomes the strongest motivator at the present time.

Unlike Maslow's idea[6] of a fixed hierarchy, Glasser's view is that the rank order changes frequently according to the current state of frustration. Survival might appear to be permanently top of the list of needs but people have been known to give up their lives to satisfy the Love and Belonging need.

---

[6] A.H. Maslow. *Motivation and Personality.* New York: Harper, 1954.

Everyone seems to have the same needs but not necessarily the same ways of satisfying them.

Glasser admits that others may propose a different set of words to label the basic needs but generally it appears that people's basic needs are similar to those he describes.[7]   However, the ways people satisfy needs can vary a lot.   For example, the nature of shelter and food varies considerably around the globe although the basic need for survival they cater for remains the same.

The more immediate motivator of my behaviour is any discrepancy between what I want and what I have.

Whereas my Basic Needs are running in the deeper layers of my being, my thoughts are constantly interpreting these into realities I want to achieve. I am constantly sizing up my view of my real world to see how well I am getting what I want. I then behave to reduce the difference between what I have and what I want.

If I decide I want a new camera, one with very specific capabilities and accessories, it is because this object somehow or other satisfies one or more of my basic needs. It may be that I want to make a really good photographic report of my kid sister's wedding and so my relationship to her is a key factor.

In my current real world I note the shortfall in my finances compared with the advertised price of the camera.   Consequently I either modify the picture of what I want or I begin to behave to acquire the additional funds.

In the following paragraphs we will examine these processes in more detail.

---

[7] Jesús Miranda Páez. *Construct Validation of The Reality Therapy Model.* Unpublished Doctoral Thesis, University of Málaga, Spain. 2000.

I behave according to my present perceptions of the world.

The importance of perceptions is common to other authors such as Rogers[8], Kelly[9] and Powers[10]. All that we know comes through our perceptions and we behave in order to control this perceived world, our best estimate of what is real. This principle too has important corollaries:

I deal with my perceptions of the world, not the world itself.

What I take to be "real", what I believe to be happening depends totally on my perceptual system. This in turn will depend on where I am, what my senses can perceive, how well my senses are working, how my values system selects what I perceive, how I label what I observe and finally how my inner logic deals with the resulting perceptions.

My perceptions operate in the present.

It is possible that the past will help explain the present and we may even be able to learn lessons from the past but any problem we have exists in the here and now and so the solution will be in the here and now. In Reality Therapy it will be rare for the therapist to begin by exploring the past since the main focus of the counselling will be on the client's current perceptions. If there is any exploration of the past it is to clarify the present.

When your car has a puncture, to quote an example from Glasser, you normally prefer to have it fixed than to fill in a survey about how

---

[8] Carl Rogers. *Client-Centered Therapy.* Boston: Houghton Mifflin, 1951.

[9] George A. Kelly. *The Psychology of Personal Constructs (2 vols).* New York: W.W. Norton & Co., 1955

[10] William T. Powers. *Behavior: The Control of Perception.* Chicago: Aldine Publishing Co., 1973.

and where it happened. One important exception to this focus on the present is when the Reality Therapy practitioner explores the past for evidence of strengths that might be used in the present.

I cannot change the past.

This has important implications for personal living and for therapy and is a Choice Theory view that sets it apart from many other approaches to therapy. Glasser often comments that we cannot eat yesterday's dinner. He will not invite a client to re-live painful episodes from the past. If there is such a thing as "catharsis" it is in solving the problem in the present rather than in re-visiting yesteryear's pain. Revisiting the past can easily become a form of avoidance or can generate excuses for inactivity.

I may be able to change the present or future.

Indeed the only hope of change in my life is the present or future. Once I realise just how much control I have over my life then a new world of choices can open up to me in the present.

For another to interact effectively with me, he or she needs to try and understand my perceptual world.

No matter how well another human being can fathom my "personality" (that summary description of my behaviour as viewed from the outside), they will only ever really understand me insofar as they comprehend how I see the world. As I said in the first lines of this book, I believe that full understanding of another human being is in fact impossible. All we can do is try to get an insight into their perspective.

There is a joke about a psychologist who was about to chastise his son for cutting a worm in two. As he approached to scold his errant child he heard the boy whisper to the two wriggling pieces, "there, you're not alone anymore. Now you have a friend!" Although the worm might not appreciate it, the boy's intentions were noble and were based entirely on his perceptions of his world.

Obviously in counselling it becomes of paramount importance to attempt to understand the client's perceptual world. This world includes how the individual is perceiving the present situation and also what the client wants. These are both important as they govern the person's choice of behaviour.

I myself decide whom I will permit to probe my internal world.

If I control my own internal world then I can decide whom I will explain it to. I control the access. The trust required for me to open up to another person means that I must first add that person to my own internal world identifying him or her as a potentially satisfying person in my life. For this to happen Glasser says I must be "involved" with that person and so involvement becomes a key component of Reality Therapy.

The counsellor seeking this involvement will behave in such a way that the client will be able to see him as need-satisfying. As we shall see in the next paragraph, this means that the client takes the counsellor into what Glasser calls her "Quality World". It becomes important therefore for the counsellor to create this very special environment or relationship for counselling.

I behave according to a set of internal perceptions known as my "Quality World".

Over time I learn that certain persons, situations, objects, experiences and values appear to be satisfying to me. These become a very special sub-set of my perceptions because I perceive them to be need-satisfying. These are more than simply good memories; they are also blueprints for future satisfaction. They become my very own personal catalogue of ways to satisfy my needs and Glasser calls this the "Quality World". We have already referred to these when we spoke about "wants".

We do not normally live our daily lives thinking overtly about our basic needs themselves. Of course, this generalisation does not apply to those who have studied Choice Theory. Such students become prone to utterances such as "My need for power is a bit low at the moment". "Normal people" are more likely to spend time dwelling on the images from our Quality World, daydreaming about a holiday, some nice food, a close friend. These special pictures we carry in our Quality Worlds have certain characteristics:

Quality World pictures are perceptions.

No matter what in the real world may have contributed to the pictures in my Quality World, what I store internally is a set of perceptions and not external reality. For a long time I may have held the name of a new film in my Quality World because I have heard so many people sing its praises. I want to see this film. When I eventually get to see it in the cinema, motivated by that image in my Quality World, the reality may disillusion me and I promptly remove it from my Quality World. It is no longer one of my wants.

Quality World pictures can be of people, activities, objects or values.

In fact, anything I can want. I want to be close to a particular person. I want to visit Peru. I want a new boat. I want democracy. Our wants are the pictures in our Quality World.

The pictures in my Quality World are always "good" in my eyes.

This is an important concept and is easily misunderstood. The word "good" is very relative here. My pictures are not "good" because they are in my Quality World. Rather I put them into my Quality

World because I consider them good. It does not mean others will consider these pictures as "good" nor that they are good by any objective standard.

When I visit a new restaurant with a few friends and find it very need satisfying I then add it to my Quality World as a good place for dining with my friends. In my internal world that restaurant will carry a big plus sign for the foreseeable future.

My pictures are not necessarily need-satisfying in reality. I put them in my Quality World because I believe them to be satisfying but I could be mistaken – or they might be satisfying in the very short term only. This could be said about many drugs, especially alcohol. I may put it in my Quality World because I believe it gives me greater confidence!

A tragic aspect of the power of these inner pictures is that some people put horrific pictures into their personal albums, pictures of killing or harming others, for example. In the twisted logic of their lives they see these acts as "good" whereas the rest of the world may deem them totally evil.

If we hope to help people deal with ineffective, evil or illegal pictures in their Quality Worlds, we need to understand how and why they get them in the first place.

These pictures come from my personal and cultural experiences.

As I go through life I have direct pleasant experiences myself. Similarly I may adopt experiences from my surrounding culture or from the recommendations of friends. An apparently simple picture such as "a cup of tea" can have very different meanings in different cultures. We are offered and usually adopt very specific pictures about family and relationships from our own cultures. In Ireland "family" usually means the father-mother-child group whereas "familia" in Spain will extend all the way from grandparents to cousins.

The pictures are very specific.

If I claim that "Jazz" is in my Quality World it does not mean that I will automatically like everything from Bebop to Cool to Swing. Indeed, our tendency to be vague when expressing our wants gives rise to many interpersonal misunderstandings and, indeed, unwanted gifts. When you want to request something from another person you really need to state it in very specific terms because the picture you have in your head will be very specific.

Many of my pictures are difficult to change.

Once we make a definite decision to include somebody or something in our Quality World it can be quite hard but not impossible to remove it.

These pictures have their own internal logic.

Some time ago an accountant friend told me about a family of middle-aged brothers she needed to meet with to discuss their shared finances. They seemed to have some aversion to coming together and it was some time before she understood the internal logic of what was, as it happens, their shared Quality World. For them, the idea of coming together was not in their Quality World as it would involve leaving nobody at home to safeguard their life-savings stored in hard cash under one of the beds!

Asking people why they want something can often reveal a complex logic of interrelated wants. Without some understanding of that logic, their behaviour can appear quite mystifying and difficult to deal with.

My Quality World pictures are not necessarily good for me or others.

The fact that I believe something to be need-satisfying does not mean that it really will satisfy my needs. In like manner, the fact that I believe a particular behaviour is good does not mean that it will be seen as good by others. In fact, as already indicated, my Quality World pictures can be terribly destructive for myself and others.

Just as my Quality World may include a picture of myself graduating in civil engineering or buying a good book for my child it might equally carry a picture of me physically punishing a child "for his or her own good". It might even include acts of violence against those I see as my enemies or plans to overthrow a democratic government.

Somehow in my inner perceptions and the logic that holds them together I choose pictures that in each moment seem to be the best for me. It is this inner belief that can give frightening power to acts that the rest of the world may see as inherently evil.

My behaviour is the best indicator of what is really in my Quality World.

We behave according to the pictures in our Quality Worlds. I may know that smoking is bad for me and tell my friends that I really want to stop. However, if I am still choosing to smoke it is because it is in my Quality World. For some reason the picture of smoking is still more attractive to me than the picture of not smoking. I may not even be able to express why this is so.

I am constantly choosing behaviours to keep my needs in balance.

This is very similar to the biological notion of "homeostasis" or to the servo-mechanisms of engineering. Homeostasis is the natural balancing that goes on in living organisms. If my brain detects heat loss in my fingers it sends an extra blood supply to restore temperature levels. Servo-mechanisms have a similar function in engines and a simple example can be seen in the small metal vanes that help steady the motor in a music box. Glasser believes that human choice has a similar balancing function.

Just as physical dehydration will spur my brain into water-seeking behaviours, so too any form of psychological frustration will create a felt need and active search for whatever will satisfy it. After many hours doing serious work my fun need starts to run low.

These "fun-hunger pangs" take the form of feelings of boredom and weariness and send a clear message to the mind: "I need fun". One look at my cluttered desk and I perceive a major discrepancy between what I need and what I have before me. In my mind I begin a quick search for some Quality World picture that will fill the gap. I pick up the telephone and arrange a game of tennis with a friend. Even as we joke on the phone my fun needs are beginning to balance again.

In a general way my organism urges me to meet my needs.

When I am peckish I may visit the kitchen and prowl around looking for something to nibble. There is a constant flow of signals about the state of my needs and, where a need is running low, these signals are uncomfortable and may even be painful.

In a specific way my mind urges me to achieve my need-satisfying pictures.

I have a set of established ways of meeting certain needs such as playing golf several times a week to meet fun and friendship needs or I may enter the kitchen looking specifically for a packet of my favourite snacks.

I seek the pictures that meet the currently frustrated needs.

After a business trip away from home I might pick up the telephone and call around my friends to arrange a game of golf. Even without fully realising it I am restoring an imbalance in both my fun and my love and belonging needs. In my Quality World I want to be in contact with my friends; in my real world they are absent. So I choose a Quality World picture that will bring us together. My internal set of Quality World pictures is my personal formula for need satisfaction.

This self-regulatory process is an ongoing feedback loop.

Although we become more aware of this at times of greater frustration, this processing of phenomena is continuous. At a physical level we constantly adjust our posture to reduce discomfort. Our heart rate increases to deal with a potential threat. Our skin sweats to deal with over-heating. We decide we need a little break when we begin to tire. The core of the brain, the older part in evolutionary terms, looks after this biological balancing without conscious control from us.

The newer part of the brain evolved giving us the distinctly human attribute of the mind but Glasser claims it works in the same way. We constantly behave to keep our needs in balance. Somewhere in our mind we compare what we have with what we want and, on detecting a gap between these, the resulting frustration creates a negative feedback loop that aims at a reduction of this gap. If we receive positive feedback, that all is well and we are in fact getting what we want, then we simply behave to enjoy and maintain this.

My behaviour is my attempt to activate my pictures.

My behaviour is always my best attempt to meet my needs.

In my own very private internal logic everything I choose to do is, at that moment, my best attempt to meet my needs. If I thought I had a better choice I would take it. This Choice Theory idea offers a very positive view of human behaviour but does seem to present some contradictions. For example, I may be a "workaholic", doing lots of extra work putting my physical health at risk and straining family relationships. How could something so negative be a choice and how could it be described as my best choice at the time?

First of all we need to remember that a choice does not mean it is conscious. Although it may be difficult to do I could choose not to work extra hours and so it is a choice. But how could my inner logic favour something so gruelling as an excessive work schedule? One possibility is that there is a situation at home that I don't know how to deal with and it is easier to choose this form of avoidance.

Another possibility could be that many things have been going wrong for me in recent times but work gives me a strong sense of security I badly need just now. Yet another possible explanation is that I simply have not spotted the damage my over-working is generating.

This specific choice might not be pleasant but in my internal view of the world it somehow makes sense at this point in time. The logic we use to run our lives is not always clear-cut; sometimes it is quite fuzzy. Like the person who smokes in spite of knowing the health risks, I might not be able to explain my choice very easily. Somehow, in my internal logic, the balance in favour of making the choice is greater than the balance against it.

Normally I resort to organised behaviours.

When one of my needs is frustrated my own direct experience and vicarious experience through learning usually offers me a range of known options. If I need food I can try the refrigerator, the shop at the corner, a nearby restaurant or a friend's house. If I have been brought up in a jungle tribe my organised behaviours for getting food may be quite different. This organised behaviour system is not unlike a filing system of ideas for different situations, a personal resource I have built up and constantly turn to for solutions and ideas.

In special circumstances my creative system helps me develop new behaviours.

If my frustration is very big and my organised behavioural system has no solution to offer, my creative system may churn out some brand-new options. If I become hungry while camping miles from my usual sources of food I might decide to search for bird's eggs or eat insects, something I have never done before. For me this would be a creative behaviour. However, once I have used the new behaviour successfully I might then add it to my organised behavioural system for future use.

Such new behaviours may appear "crazy" or may even interfere with my physical health.

My hunger may be so great that, failing to find any bird's eggs, I may start screaming to the heavens in desperation. To the onlooker this would certainly appear somewhat "crazy" but to me it is simply a desperate attempt to change my situation. Of course, not all crazy behaviours are so ineffective! I may find that thumping the table in anger, originally a creative gesture, does in fact achieve the attention I need. In this case I will probably use the same behaviour again. Reflection on my behaviour might help me realise that although I do get the attention it is at the expense of relationships and respect.

I normally satisfy most of my needs through relationships.

Glasser has often joked that the only real problem we have is that others will not do what we want. In more recent adjustments to his ideas Glasser firmly puts relationships centre-stage and says, "the cause of the misery is always our way of dealing with an important relationship that is not working out the way we want it to."[11]   In a further refinement of this idea[12] Glasser emphasises that all we do that separates us from others creates problems for us since the need to relate to others is in our genes.

Everybody needs at least one significant relationship.

This theme first appeared in Glasser's writings in 1960[13] but was more clearly stated in 1972: "Involvement with at least one successful person is a requirement for growing up successfully, maintaining success, or changing from failure to success."[14]   As children, we learn mainly from adults and if good role-models are not available to us then our learning can be seriously impoverished.

Most long-term psychological problems are really relationship problems.

In Choice Theory Glasser identifies relationships as at the heart of people's problems. By 1999, when he published "Reality Therapy in Action"[15], he was recommending counsellors to seek the

---

[11] Glasser, William. *Choice Theory.* New York: HarperCollins, 1998.

[12] Address to the Annual William Glasser Institute Convention, Ottawa, Canada in July 2000.

[13] Glasser, William. *Mental Health or Mental Illness?* New York: Harper & Row, 1960.

[14] Glasser, William. *The Identity Society.* New York: Harper & Row, 1972.

[15] Later released in 2001 as *"Counseling with Choice Theory: The New Reality Therapy"*

relationship problem as the heart of most problems people bring to counselling. This is not limited exclusively to the quality of our relationships in terms of level of human warmth. It would extend equally to the expectations we believe others have of us. We live our lives in a world of relationships.

Those who do not have relationships in their Quality Worlds tend to use dangerous non-relational substitutes.

If people completely remove the idea of relationships from their Quality World then the pictures they use to meet their needs will also be devoid of relationships. They will not take other people's rights or feelings into account, for example, and this can give rise to many problems.

Glasser believes that this explains why people will resort to drugs, promiscuous sex and violence. These are apparent need satisfiers that do not involve relationships. They appear to offer fun, love and power but without relationship. Those who have been abused or have been reared in a world of shallow or non-existent relationships may very well shy away from true relationships and seek solace in the notorious trio of drugs, promiscuous sex and violence.

My behaviour is an inseparable totality of four components.

The reader will have already grasped the idea that Glasser sees all human activity as behaviour and that most of it is chosen by us in our ongoing attempt to meet our basic needs using our own special set of pictures to guide us. Taking this analysis of human behaviour one enormous step forward Glasser then explains that all behaviour has four inseparable components: acting, thinking, feeling and physiology.

When we describe these components in a given individual we might do this in a very narrow sense like a snapshot of the behaviour in a given moment (e.g. while sitting in the dentist's chair) or in a broader sense (e.g., my total behaviour at my place of work).

This idea of "Total Behaviour" is unique in Glasser's thought and one with very powerful implications for therapy. In a later chapter we will examine these implications but first we need to explain "total behaviour".

The four components are acting[16], thinking, feeling and physiology.

No matter what I "do" (the verb we generally use in popular language to describe behaviour), I am always changing the four components in some way.

I am responsible for all four of these.

Although we tend to think of having control and responsibility over what we "do", the physical ("acting") part of our behaviour, Glasser claims that this extends to the totality, to all four components. This means we have a responsibility for our feelings and physiology as well.

I tend to describe any particular behaviour by its most salient component.

Playing football is seen as an action, philosophy is seen as thinking, joy as a feeling and sweating as a physiological process. But each of these are behaviours and each has its other three components. Each is a total behaviour.

---

[16] Glasser uses the term "acting", a term that we in Ireland tend to reserve for what goes on in our theatres. Hence we often refer to this component as "doing".

Changing any one component will mean changing all four.

Consider what happens when I jump into a swimming pool. The physical jump is the "acting" component. My thoughts may be "It seems like a good idea" or "I need some exercise". The feeling could be exhilaration or even panic. Physiologically my pulse and my breathing are likely to change considerably. When I decided to jump I chose the other three components (maybe inadvertently).

The easiest components for me to change are acting and thinking.

For the average individual it is the acting and thinking that are most accessible to change and so these are the most useful gateways to changing the total behaviour. These become a major focus of therapeutic change.

Reviewing the overall thrust of Choice Theory it is clear that it emphasises that people are controlled from within. I am responsible

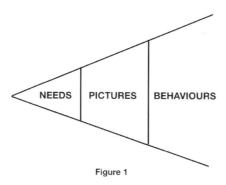

Figure 1

for my behaviour and my behaviour is my best attempt to make my pictures happen. They in turn are my personal formulae for satisfying my needs. The chart in Figure 1 attempts to summarise this chain of causality that underlies all human behaviour according to Glasser's Choice Theory.

At the root of all human behaviour are the NEEDS. We create a set of PICTURES as our ways to meet these needs and then choose BEHAVIOURS that make the pictures happen. So Glasser will not say, "The reason a person behaves is his past" or "That person behaves as she does because of external stimuli". The past and external influences have their roles but, in Choice Theory, they are not controlling roles.

Others or the past may indeed have an influence in the development of my pictures but, no matter how those pictures were formed, it is the pictures that govern my behaviours. As we shall see later, this explanation of human behaviour has a direct bearing on the processes of Reality Therapy.

Discussion of Choice Theory

One special characteristic of Reality Therapy is the belief in teaching clients the theory on which it is based since Choice Theory is not simply an explanation of therapy but has become a psychology of human behaviour. In practice, Glasser always taught the theory more by example than by a lecture or treatise.

Nevertheless, one way to teach this theory would be to give a copy of this chapter to a client (or, better still, encourage them to read Glasser's "Choice Theory")   and have some discussion of it at a later appointment. This approach might suit some clients more than others. Choice Theory has an immediate and personal relevance to life. Most people, on being introduced to these ideas, begin to see their own experience differently, especially the amount of personal control they have over their own lives.

Many forms of counselling do not include any theoretical discussion of this type with clients and so it could be useful to get some practice. For example, give a copy of the chapter to a friend who is willing to read it and discuss it with you later.

An Alternative Theory

If you do not accept Choice Theory it would still be a helpful exercise to write a summary of the theory of human behaviour that you do support. From your point of view, why do people behave as they do?

Incident Analysis

Take any particular incident from your own life, preferably from today or yesterday.

1. What needs were not being met?
2. How did you know?
3. What pictures did you have available for meeting those needs?
4. What did you choose to do?
5. Describe your total behaviour (your doing, thinking, feeling and physiology) just before and after your choice.

First Choice

What was the very first choice you made today? This question can give rise to quite an interesting discussion with friends. Some young people will say they did not choose to get out of bed, that their parents "forced" them to get up. Could they have chosen to stay (or go back) and accept the wrath of their elders?

A discussion of such issues with others can help focus on the many choices they make every day when they opt for what is reasonable in preference to what is most comfortable for them.

External Control Psychology

In this chapter you will learn about:

- The widespread use of external control psychology
- The underlying beliefs of external control
- The distinction between what we can and cannot control
- The seven "deadly" habits of external control
- Wider implications of the belief in external control
- The Choice Theory view of so-called "mental illness"
- The distinction between brain and mind
- The Choice Theory approach to dealing with the past
- Genetic influences

Unfortunately, Choice Theory is not what most of us practise in our daily lives. All of us, to differing degrees and circumstances, tend to use "external control psychology" in our day-to-day decisions.

We believe we can control other people or that they can control us and this set of beliefs often goes unchallenged by people in general, by our governments and by our schools. Unfortunately, using this psychology of external control drives wedges between ourselves and others and very often we fail to realise just how much harm it is doing. Believing in external control psychology or suffering from those who do generates many of the problems that bring people to the therapist's door.

```
┌─────────────────────────────────────────┐
│                                         │
│           The Serenity Prayer           │
│                                         │
│        God, grant me the serenity       │
│    To accept the things I cannot change,│
│    Courage to change the things I can   │
│      And the wisdom to know the         │
│              difference.                │
│                                         │
└─────────────────────────────────────────┘
```

At the core of Glasser's Choice Theory there are several fundamental ideas:

- I can only control myself.

- I cannot control others.

- To attempt to control others is not only ineffective, it is harmful to the relationship between us.

- Since relationships play a huge role in the ways we satisfy our Basic Needs, anything that harms relationships contributes to great unhappiness.

- Most human problems are relationship problems.

- Just as external control contributes to our unhappiness, internal control (in the form of making better choices) contributes to our happiness.

Until we become aware of the alternative internal control psychology ("Choice Theory") and its practical consequences for everyday life, we may wonder what it is that is not working in our lives. We may even ask ourselves why situations often seem to get worse instead of better in spite of our doing the "right thing".   Unfortunately, many people see external control as the "right thing".

It is a peculiar characteristic of external control psychology that, even when it is clear that it is failing, people tend to resort to even more external control. The child who breaks the school rules is given detention, an extra set of rules to be broken!   Parents even boast about their repeated failures, "If I have told you once to clean your room I have told you a thousand times!"

William Glasser returns again and again to the pitfalls of "External Control Psychology", the popular psychology of the world, and he regards it as the epitome of all that is wrong with modern civilisation apart from poverty and disease.

He claims that whereas technical progress and even political progress have advanced considerably in the last hundred years, basic human progress remains fairly static.   Drugs, crime, marital breakdowns and the like have not really changed. Most of this, he says, is due to people thinking they can change others by external force.   In other words, in spite of general medical, technical and socio-political advances, our basic day-to-day psychology has not improved.

External Control Psychology is as dangerous as it is widespread. We use it when we punish; we even use it when we reward. We sometimes use it in desperation when we do not know what else to do. Just as we believe we can control others we tend to believe that others can control us and this belief is just as dangerous. In fact, Glasser lists four aspects of this external control.

Aspects of External Control

1. **I try to make another person do something against their will.** Parents and teachers do this often with young people. Glasser, on the other hand, says the young people will change only if they want to change. "You can't control an adolescent's behavior when you're not with him and can control only very little when you are with him."[17] Unfortunately, our attempts to force others tend to make it less appealing for them to want what we want. What happens is that many people waste valuable time in their lives attempting to change others and, sadly, the main change they do achieve is unwelcome rejection.

2. **Someone else tries to get me to do something against my will.** We sometimes say "John makes me angry" or "My parents made me go to college" but in fact nobody made us do anything. When someone points a gun at me and tells me to hand over my money it certainly feels as if they are making me do something but ultimately I myself choose whether to hand over the money or to take the terrible consequences of choosing not to empty my wallet. If we erroneously believe in the power others seem to have over us

---

[17] Glasser, William. *Unhappy Teenagers: A way for parents and teachers to reach them.* New York: Harper Collins, 2002.

we can reach the conclusion that we ourselves have little power, that we are helpless in the face of life's problems.

3. **We attempt to make each other do things neither wants to do**. Many relationships that started out on a friendly and respectful basis often convert into an ongoing and ultimately destructive attempt to change each other. Glasser observed that "Many husbands or wives regard the marriage license as a license to criticize."[18]

4. **I try to make myself do something I find painful or impossible.** I may decide to embark on a career that is totally unsuited to me, forcing a square peg into a round hole. This may be due to my mistaken belief that I have no choice in the matter, that I "must" follow in my parents' footsteps or that I "must" do the "right thing". I internalise the external control. The other person is not trying to change me but I believe I "ought to", "must", "should" behave according to some pre-set formula. Many great therapists have rightly been critical of these "scripts" we tend to carry around in our heads. As often as not we choose them unconsciously simply because we have not paused to reflect on what choice means in our lives. We assume that we have no choice when in fact we do.

The Beliefs of External Control Psychology

Underlying all these aspects of control Glasser identifies what he calls the three beliefs of external control psychology:

1. I can be controlled by others.

2. I can control others.

3. I must control others as a moral obligation or right.

---

[18] Glasser, William. *Take Effective Control of Your Life*. New York: Harper & Row, 1984.

The first belief he regards as relatively innocuous but the second causes a lot of interpersonal problems. The last belief, in Glasser's view, is the most dangerous often leading to death and destruction. This third view very often masquerades as "justice". "My daughter stayed out too late and therefore she must be punished by grounding her for two weeks. My parents did the same to me and it was good for me. I am doing this for her own good." But Glasser's analysis of such an approach is that "even the kindest, most caring 'I know what's right for you' is still external control." [19]

He considered this righteousness as quite dangerous. "If everyone could learn that what is right for me does not make it right for anyone else, the world would be a much happier place."[20]

In Choice Theory the corresponding beliefs would be quite the opposite to the above:

1. I cannot be controlled by others. I control myself.

2. I cannot control others. They control themselves.

3. Attempts to control others are futile and even counter-productive. I can only take responsibility for my own life.

In a sense it is the adoption of these three beliefs that is at the heart of counselling. Becoming aware of what you can control and what you cannot control is very important for leading a happy life. Without this sense the individual engages in so much fruitless and even damaging behaviour.

---

[19] Glasser, William. *Warning: Psychiatry can be hazardous to your mental health.* Harper Collins, 2003.

[20] Glasser, William. *Choice Theory.* New York: Harper Collins, 1998.

What You Can and Cannot Control

Of course, the distinction between what a person can and cannot control has a well-established place in therapy. This is summed up admirably in the "Serenity Prayer"[21] that is popular with Alcoholics Anonymous and others.

These same ideas were also present in the philosophy of Ignatius of Loyola who advised people to work as if everything depended on them and pray as if everything depended on God.

Coming to terms with the great unchangeables of one's life is vitally important; otherwise we waste endless energy banging our heads against those stone walls of unchangeability. Even more important is the need to see what we can change, to realise just how much is within our control. Without this conviction we will not attempt to make changes in our lives. The Serenity Prayer sums up some great human wisdom and these ideas are a key part of Glasser's Choice Theory psychology.

When he distinguishes between true and false conflict[22], Glasser is targeting these same points. True conflict exists when the problem cannot be solved as in "I cannot be in Dublin and in Venice at exactly the same time". False conflict happens when the problem, though difficult, can be solved as when I want to lose weight but I keep eating lots of chocolate.

It is a curious aspect of human intelligence that we will spend ages trying to work out how to be in Dublin and Venice, an impossibility, and yet dismiss out of hand as a lost cause our little weakness for chocolate. We try to do something about the impossible and give up on the merely difficult. Glasser recommends we reverse these

---

[21] Attributed to Dr. Reinhold Niebuhr, of the Union Theological Seminary, NYC, who said he composed it in 1932 as the ending to a longer prayer.

[22] Glasser, William. *Take Effective Control of Your Life*. New York: Harper & Row, 1984.

using action to deal with false conflict and bidding time when faced with true conflict.[23]

TYPE OF CONFLICT	EXAMPLE	WHAT I TEND TO DO	WHAT GLASSER ADVISES
TRUE	I need to be in Dublin and Venice at the same moment in time.	I work hard trying to find a solution.	Do nothing about it. Wait. The situation might change.
FALSE	I want to lose weight by eating less chocolate.	I do nothing about it.	Work hard to find a solution. Options may be difficult but some choice is possible.

In fact, learning Choice Theory psychology is very much about becoming more aware of the choices we have in our own lives. We usually have more choices in areas we thought we had none and, conversely, we have fewer choices in areas we thought we had lots. We tend to live our lives far removed from the wisdom of the Serenity Prayer. Indeed, most of us adhere more closely to what I have called the "Anxiety Prayer".

Most of us live our lives according to External Control Psychology but without realising it. We use it so much that it pervades all our habits.

---

[23] Glasser, William. *Take Effective Control of Your Life*. New York: Harper & Row, 1984.

> # The Anxiety Prayer
>
> I hereby grant myself
> the pig-headedness
> to keep trying to change
> the things I cannot change,
> the excuses
> not to change the things I can
> and the short-sightedness
> never to spot the difference!

The Seven Deadly Habits

In a humorous comparison with the seven habits of success listed by Stephen Covey[24] Glasser lists the "seven deadly habits of miserable people"[25], a collection of the ineffective behaviours that External Control Psychology encourages:

1. Criticism

2. Blaming

3. Complaining

4. Nagging

5. Threatening

6. Punishing

7. Bribing

---

[24] Covey, Stephen R. *The 7 Habits of Highly Effective People*. New York: Simon & Schuster, 1989.

[25] Glasser, William. *Every Student Can Succeed.* Chula Vista: Black Forest Press, 2000.

Criticism, the first of these, is in his opinion almost always destructive to relationships, even when it is called "constructive criticism". Removing criticism from your life is one of the most helpful changes you can make.

What all of these habits have in common is their implicit belief in external control. Indeed, we could add an eighth, "aggression", the direct attempt to force another person to do what we want. "Bribing" includes the idea of "Rewards", a subtle form of bribery that relies on a philosophy of external control. Affirmation or recognition are quite different from reward and will be discussed later in the chapter on the language of therapy.

More External Control Beliefs

If in fact you examine Glasser's writings you find more than the three beliefs he explicitly links to an external control approach. At this point it may be useful to examine all these beliefs, including those already presented, and to understand just why they are so damaging.

Here is the longer list:

1. The belief that we can control others

2. The belief that others can control us

3. The belief that we can be controlled by a series of brain "disorders" or mental illnesses

4. The belief that we are controlled by the past

5. Belief that we are controlled by our genes

6. Belief in a whole range of external controls: destiny, fate, the stars, luck.

Before exploring each of these in detail it is important to recall one of Glasser's very important concepts, the idea that in any given situation we always choose the best behaviour we know at that time. If sometimes we do things that are at best ineffective and at worst harmful to ourselves or to others, we do so because we do not know of better alternatives. People in positions of authority often use punitive methods mainly because they do not know of any other way to manage their teams.

This applies just as much to the use of external control psychology in general as to any other beliefs. People believe in external control because it is the best they know. They will not choose a different theory until they see it as a better or more useful belief. This change may happen slowly over time or may happen in a sudden burst of awareness when "the penny drops".

Believing we can control others

Most of us invest a lot of energy in attempting to control others and this has several unfortunate effects. In the first place it does not work simply because people can only control themselves. Second, we alienate those we attempt to control. Given our genetic need for love and belonging and given the fact that we meet most of our needs through relationships, this distancing is very serious. Third, the combination of failure and alienation increases the overall need frustration in our own lives.

Sometimes of course external control appears to work. The official who threatens to clamp your car wheels if you park illegally usually gets results. But even in such circumstances you could choose to disobey and risk a fine. I do not recommend it but I do draw your attention to your freedom of choice in the matter. Ultimately it really is your choice. The best the official and the law he represents can achieve is temporary and possibly reluctant conformity. Just watch the speed cameras on the motorway. Drivers slow down as they approach them and then accelerate afterwards. Temporary conformity!

As parents we use rewards and punishments, bribes and threats in an attempt to "get" our offspring to behave. We do this out of genuine love and concern but then find that somehow we are jeopardising that very love. We also find that even if the child obeys in our presence, he or she is less likely to do so in our absence.

Even apart from the choice theory aspect, rewarding a behaviour somehow belittles it. Offering a toddler a reward if she takes her soup implies that the soup is a hardship. The experts agree that all you can do is make nourishing appealing food (and a positive mealtime atmosphere) available to children; you cannot make them eat the food and any attempt to do so can have a number of undesirable consequences. The child's relationship with food, mealtimes and maybe even with the force-feeder can suffer.

As spouses and partners we try to get the other to change or at least we criticise their resistance to change. The end result is the same. The main change achieved is a gradual deterioration in the relationship.

As teachers we apply the same approaches. We even invent complex reward and punishment schemes ("for their own good") and sometimes don't even notice that punishment schemes almost always escalate. Sean is put on detention for not having his homework done but what happens when he fails to turn up for detention? The problems increase and the distance between teacher and Sean increases as well. Martina did not complete her project and is given punishment work of four extra pages. Now she feels even less interested in her project, less confident in her ability in this area, less close to her teacher and whatever difficulty she originally had with the project goes unaddressed. On top of all of this, project work itself has been treated as a punishment. None of this is in line with the usual goals of education!

As citizens we clamour for punishment for those who interfere with the rights of others. Obviously in cases of serious interference we do well to restrain the offender. Society also wants to teach the offender a lesson but punishment tends to teach the delinquent to hate the punisher rather than the crime.

Another drawback of punishment is that while it attempts to teach what not to do, it has no way of teaching what to do instead. Traditional prisons that were meant to teach a lesson certainly did so but they tended to be lessons in crime and they helped distance the prisoner even further from the rest of society.

What Glasser lists as his third external control belief, "I must control others as a moral obligation or right.", I would see as an extension of this first belief. If I can control others then I "must" exercise that control. Control itself becomes an important end in itself. Teachers worry about having control in the classroom. Parents want to control their kids. Some societies want to control everybody.

There is often serious confusion between the idea of control and that of order. I am not doubting the virtue of some degree of order but such order is a natural ingredient of good relationships. Nobody ever worries about having control of their friends when we have them over for dinner but we do expect order. Indeed, it is probably safe to say that control and good relationships are mutually exclusive. Glasser writes that "Intimacy cannot coexist with external control."[26]

Believing others can control us

With an underlying belief that one person can control another, we often accuse others of "making" us do certain things or feel in a certain way. In relationships we blame our partners for problems in the relationship. As citizens we blame the government for practically everything that is wrong with society. Even our politicians join the blamers. They attribute our problems to the European Union, the

---

[26] Glasser, William. *Warning: Psychiatry can be hazardous to your mental health*. New York: Harper Collins, 2003.

Federal Government or whatever echelons of power are above them.

Of course, my life might be a lot more pleasant if my flatmate didn't throw all night parties, if the traffic at my door were not so loud, if the rain would stop! The fact is I cannot control these. I can decide to negotiate with my flatmate or campaign for better traffic regulation or use an umbrella ... but I cannot control my flatmate, the drivers outside or the weather!

There is, of course, a big difference between "controlling" and "influencing". It makes a lot of sense to try to influence, convince, negotiate with others. When we think we can actually control them, we then blame them for our misfortunes.

Blaming in itself is not an effective behaviour especially as it tends to distract us from what we ourselves can do in the situation. Hence it delays the finding of an effective solution. Just as serious, it can also alienate us from the one who is blamed.

A belief in the power of others to control us can sometimes take subtle forms. So many peace negotiations stall because each party is waiting for the other to make the first move, unwittingly placing control externally in the other's hands.

Believing we are controlled by "mental illness"

One of the most devious forms of external control is that which appears to come from within. If I believe that I have something inside me, some condition or affliction that "makes" me behave in certain ways then my attempts to change will naturally focus on removing that condition. If I am convinced that this condition is permanent then I either do nothing or exercise some maintenance behaviour.

Once we assign the "illness" or even "disorder" label to any human condition we are placing it in the category of things that "happen to" a person in much the same way as measles, chicken pox, diabetes or epilepsy. Obviously those who have a brain disease such as Parkinson's (properly identifiable by scientific tests) will have aspects of their behaviour altered beyond their control. In real diseases such as these, something invades us or harms us, makes us and our bodies or even our brains behave in specific ways. We turn to external agencies for a cure or at least to get a treatment for the condition.

Identification and treatment of all such invaders of our health is a worthy pursuit but what happens if someone classifies as "illness" a behaviour that is not a disease or disorder but rather is something that we have chosen, consciously or unconsciously? This may be illustrated by a simple example from everyday life.

If I go jogging and perspire a lot, should I accept pills offered by a well-meaning medical friend to stop my perspiration "disorder"? Here we have a clear example of a behaviour that is chosen and that has physiological characteristics that are not in the illness or disorder category. When I decide to jog I am automatically choosing to perspire. Not only is perspiration not a disorder but it is definitely not the "cause" of my jogging.

By the same logic, if I choose to overburden my working life I am choosing the stress that goes with it and I am choosing all the chemical changes in my body that accompany this. These changes are not a disorder! Quite the contrary, like perspiration in the jogger, the changes are part of an extremely healthy ongoing attempt to maintain balance ("homeostasis") and they certainly are not the "cause" of my stress.

What about behaviour that most people would identify as "mad"? To claim to be Julius Caesar, to repeat phrases to yourself all day long, to hear voices, to believe you are always being followed, to obsess about personal cleanliness to the point of washing the skin off your hands, to give up eating … surely all of this is caused by some serious internal disturbance, disorder, imbalance?

There are of course certain conditions that have well-documented evidence to show that they are produced by genuine internal disorders. Brain damage such as that caused by oxygen shortage at birth may result in involuntary muscle movements. The person with epilepsy or in diabetic shock may sometimes seem out of touch with reality. Any form of damage or interference that produces semi-conscious states may result in the person confusing inner and outer realities. (The same may be said about psychiatric drugs, many of which create semi-conscious states that in turn can cause phenomena such as confusion, hallucinations and hearing voices.)

Real "disorders" have certain characteristics not found in the so-called psychological disorders:

- They affect all people in similar ways regardless of race, nationality or upbringing.

- They are detectable by medical analysis. If they cannot be detected by scientific means then any suggestion that they are "disorders" or "illnesses" can at best be only a hypothesis.

- They don't mysteriously vanish in certain situations such as when playing computer games or watching television.

Is there a case then for distinguishing between "physical disorders" and "psychological" or "mental disorders"? The trouble with this distinction is that it is not enough. The words "disorder" and "illness" both suggest some tangible malfunction, something that can be measured accurately by scientific instrumentation. Such words are misleading when referring to the mind.[27]

I believe that many of the problems professionals and lay people experience in this whole area arise out of a confusion between "brain" and "mind". Obviously the two function together but they do have very different roles.

The mind is consciousness; it is where we think and feel and wonder. Modern technology can indeed detect mental activity but nobody can find out exactly what is going on in the mind unless we reveal it to them in some way.

The brain on the other hand is a tangible object, a soft substance in the skull that hosts the most important part of our central nervous system. We do very much need this complex electro-chemical system for our minds to function but brain and mind are two very different entities. The brain is like the hardware of a computer whereas the mind is similar to the software. They are interdependent but totally different in design and function.

Brain research has made great advances in recent years thanks to the development of non-invasive methods of exploring brain activity. Researchers such as Rebecca Saxe[28] have done exciting work in identifying specific locations in the brain for certain psychological processes.

I believe this can be extremely useful in a reverse diagnosis framework, where failures in psychological processes may help identify the location of brain damage. I am not so confident, however, that this research will point to ways of improving the psychological processes.

---

[27] Lynch, Dr. Terry. *Beyond Prozac: Healing Mental Suffering Without Drugs*. Dublin: Mercier Press, 2001.

[28] Saxe, R.; Kanwisher, N. (2003). "People thinking about thinking people. The role of the temporo-parietal junction in "Theory of Mind"". *NeuroImage* 19 (4): 1835–1842.

Hardware	Brain
• Provides storage and power.	• Provides memory cells and power.
• Maintains communication pathways.	• Nervous system is the body's internal communication network.
• Determines maximum speed of operations.	• Its speed and effectiveness can vary.
• Can be slowed down or even sped up ("over-clocking").	• It can be slowed down or sped up.
• Can break, wear out, be switched off.	• Can function badly due to injury or disease and can cease to function.
• Could have power surges.	• Could have a chemical imbalance.
• Can be "broken" or "fully functioning"	• Can be "ill" or "healthy".
• Can have planning errors or biases.	• Can have inherited problems.
• Can have fabrication faults.	• Can have congenital defects.

Hardware and software are different entities and I have no reason to believe that the parallel distinction between brain and mind should be any different. On my computer, my word-processor is a piece of software, a set of instructions with their own logic.

Obviously, this software would not work without having a hardware location for storage of the program and its files.

Software	Mind
• Controls sets of data, instructions and logic.	• Orders data, uses instructions and logic.
• Processes data.	• Processes thoughts and feelings.
• Evaluates and decides.	• Evaluates and decides.
• Can commit errors due to having erroneous or missing data, following flawed logic,	• Can make mistakes due to flawed perception, forgetfulness or faulty logic.
• Can operate inefficiently if input/output devices (hardware) are not matched properly.	• Can operate inefficiently if the brain is tampered with.
• Cannot break or have power surges.	• Cannot break or have chemical imbalances.
• Can be "bug-ridden" or "user-friendly".	• Can experience "distress" or "satisfaction".

If the software fails it may be due to a bug in the programming or it could be due to a defective hard disk, faulty wiring or memory. It is useful to have some idea where different parts of my software are stored and how to identify problems.

However, no amount of knowledge of the hardware will improve the quality of the program itself nor, unfortunately, of my writing style. Hardware and software are different, inter-dependent but different! The same may be said of brain and mind. They are different, inter-dependent but different!

There appears to be another type of confusion around brain research. Some commentators give the impression that it is more "scientific" than mind research. In fact science, insofar as it is a systematic study, is applied in different ways to different phenomena. Psychological research can be a lot more challenging than medical research but it is not any less scientific. After all, "psychology" is the science of the mind, of our internal "software".

Given this distinction between the brain and the mind, the term "mental illness" and even its counterpart of "mental health" send confusing messages. The mind cannot be sick or healthy but the brain can. The confusion is understandable due to the way brain and mind interact. In some cases the brain affects the mind. For example there are some brain illnesses that appear to have strong mental components as in the case of Alzheimer's Disease but it is more a case of physical decline causing a corresponding mental decline.

In other cases the mind affects the body. Mental problems can give rise to behaviours that could easily be mistaken for signs of physical illness as is the case with nervous tics, absent-mindedness, apathy and anorexia nervosa. These chosen behaviours are similar to other totally involuntary behaviours that arise out of real physical illness. "Similar" and "same" are different concepts. One person's absent-mindedness can arise from a reduction in brain cells; another person's absent-mindedness can be due to a mind that is struggling to deal with massive worries.

There are also genuine physical ailments that can be psychological in origin, where the brain or body becomes victim to the mind. These are the "psychosomatic" illnesses and can include rashes, paralysis and bowel disorders. Here we can also include any physical condition that arises from mental stress.

To complete the picture it is worth adding a mention of "hypochondria" where an individual does not have any physical illness but believes he has.

Why is it important to sort out the terms we use to describe states of the brain or mind? One reason is that in the case of problems the intervention will depend on the cause. If I blush a lot because of a very low self-esteem I have a very different problem from the person who is blushing because of a glandular or circulation problem. Usually low self-esteem will not be helped by glandular therapy any more than the glands will be helped by psychotherapy.

The search for a clarification of terms can be helped by some of Glasser's thinking[29] where he talks about a continuum between unhappiness and mental health, one that is similar to the continuum between physical illness and physical health. Just as many people are in the unfit couch-potato category, somewhere half-way along the physical health scale, so too there are many people who are only moderately happy, half-way along the mental health scale. Reality Therapy and an understanding of Choice Theory can help such people lead more fulfilling lives.In searching for words that parallel the physical conditions but make a clear distinction between physical and mental I would suggest the following terminology:

PHYSICAL ILLNESS	UNFIT	PHYSICAL HEALTH
MENTAL DISTRESS	UNHAPPY	MENTAL WELL-BEING

---

[29] Based on public talks given in Chicago and London, Ontario in the summer of 2004.

Thinking in terms of a continuum from mental well-being[30] to mental distress avoids all of the implications of "mental illness". But if the condition referred to by "mental distress" is not an illness, not a chemical imbalance, not some external intrusion in the body's health, what is it?[31]

Glasser points out that so-called "mental illness" is a behaviour and, although at first glance the suggestion may surprise or even shock, he explains that this behaviour is chosen. Not only that, but people choose these strange behaviours as their best attempts at the time to sort out a problem in their lives. This does not mean that their chosen behaviours are effective but they are the best they know at the time.

When I encounter a serious frustration in my life the first thing I do is what I do with any frustration: look for a solution. I check through all the behaviours I have accumulated in my Quality World for one that will solve the problem and restore my needs to a satisfied state. Glasser refers to these ready-made solutions as my organised behaviours. What happens if no useful options are to be found in this personal resource file? At such times Glasser believes that we use our creativity.

The more desperate our need frustration the more desperately we seek out creative solutions. For example, I urgently need to attend an important job interview. It has started to rain heavily and I cannot find a taxi anywhere (one of my organised behaviours for getting to interviews). I stamp my foot in anger. It is a creative attempt to do something but, although it gives some vent to my frustration, its helpfulness ends there. When I choose this behaviour suggested

---

[30] I have a preference for the term "personal well-being" over "mental health" or even "mental well-being" since, in Choice Theory thinking, we see behaviour as a totality. However, in this chapter I wish to compare and contrast physical problems with mental ones, hence the choice of terminology here.

[31] Lynch, Dr. Terry. *Depression Delusion: The Myth of the Brain Chemical Imbalance.* Limerick: Mental Health Publishing, 2015.

by my creativity I might even splash my shoes with the rain and create another problem or I could scare off a sympathetic driver who was about to offer me a lift. Creative solutions can sometimes be magical but they do have a tendency to backfire or at least be ineffective. It is in this realm of chosen creativity that Glasser locates psychotic behaviour.

It is a desperately creative attempt by a person to restore balance to his basic needs. It is not an illness but a creative choice and any attempts to help this person will examine the motivation behind such choices rather than the choices themselves.

But surely "clinical depression" is an illness! Is it not obvious that the depressed person has some serious chemical imbalance, an altered brain state and most definitely nobody would ever want to be depressed! I agree, nobody wants to be depressed but wanting and choosing are different psychological processes. Nobody wants to be cut open but we very sensibly choose medical operations that will save our lives. Few people enjoy the dentist's drill but choose it rather than lose teeth. In a totally different context I may not want a hang-over but I do choose it when I choose excessive drinking. In the same way I probably never want to depress but I may choose it and do so for very good reasons.

So what might these reasons be? One is that it is the best choice open to me at the time (from my own point of view). When my life is going seriously out of control and I do not know what to do there is a lot of sense in choosing to opt out or at least to slow down temporarily, to take a step back from the brink. A psychological pit-stop can make a lot of sense. It is also logical to send out distress signals, messages to those around me that I may need help or support. By depressing I am slowing down and seeking help at the same time.

Obviously this overall slowing down will show up in altered brain states and a body chemistry that differs from the norm. How could it be otherwise? Glasser prefers to describe behaviour as a verb rather than a noun and so he talks about "depressing" rather than "depression". So much of our language reflects the notion of external control that he recommends using active verbs more often.

Sadly, we are sometimes told that depression is chemical in origin because no cause can be found. There are a number of issues here:

1. Those who believe in a chemical origin of depression tend not to look for other causes.

2. In counselling as in medicine and other sciences it sometimes will happen that causes cannot be found. The fact that we do not know the origins of the amazing spirals at Newgrange does not mean we assume that chemical change in the stones themselves produced them. Sometimes no cause is identified because the person has so many potential "causes" in his life or is simply unaware of the causes.

3. The pro-clinical depression view is so widespread that people will often label themselves as depressed when, remembering total behaviour, more specific labels might be more accurate: tired, run-down, disappointed, worried, frustrated, apathetic. Depressing is usually characterised by a mental state of helplessness. Obviously a prolonged state of physical exhaustion or illness could lead a person to lose confidence in any recovery but the giving up is a mental process, not a physical one.

4. Believing himself to have an illness, the person may not look at things he could do for himself.

5. The use of medication tends to limit the brain's thinking capacity and so the individual is even less able to help himself.

6. Commercial interests in the sale of pharmaceuticals have more to gain from the illness model.[32]

Depressing does have one special characteristic, one that it shares with so-called "phobias". It can very easily escalate into a self-perpetuating state. It's a bit like switching off the car engine to check a problem only to find that the battery is so low it is hard to re-start the car. If I slow down too much I may not produce enough effort to make the necessary changes in my life. My attempts at seeking help from my friends by depressing may in fact backfire by scaring them away. My withdrawal from life may result in my interpersonal skills becoming so rusty that re-integration becomes daunting. The longer this goes on the harder re-entry to normal life becomes ... but "harder" does not mean "impossible".

Depression is indeed a very painful condition but it is one that is very wisely chosen by our amazing inner psychology. The role of the therapist is to help the client acknowledge that she has been doing her best but that, in the shared thinking of counselling, it may be possible to develop even better choices. Those who believe that body chemistry is the cause of depression fail to see the incredible power of the person to make choices in her life and therapists who adopt this chemical view often avoid helping the individual to seek the real causes of the depressing behaviour and to address them.

If others decide that I am "chemically imbalanced", something they usually do without any supportive test, and give me medication to counter this, my brain functioning may become very confused or be slowed down to almost total inactivity. Sadly, so called "anti-depressants" do not recharge weakened batteries but dull the mind so that it stops worrying about the battery it no longer detects.[33]

---

[32] Cf. Whitaker, Robert. *Anatomy of an Epidemic*. New York: Broadway Paperbacks, 2010.

[33] Kirsch, Irving. *The Emperor's New Drugs: Exploding the Antidepressant Myth*. London: The Bodley Head, 2009.

Meanwhile the difficult life-situation I attempted to deal with by depressing continues unattended and I may have added addiction to the medication to my list of problems.[34]

> WARNING: Psychiatric medications should not be stopped suddenly. It can be very dangerous to do so. All reduction should be under appropriately qualified and experienced medical supervision.

There are some who disagree with the chemical imbalance theories but at the same time believe that some medication may help temporarily. I have serious doubts about this and for a number of reasons.

- These medications dull or harm normal brain functioning, weakening one of the most important resources a person has for recovery, the mind.
- Many of these medications are addictive.
- It can be extremely dangerous to stop taking these medications suddenly or to reduce the dose too rapidly.
- They have many undesirable and usually predictable effects (sometimes called "side-effects" or "paradoxical effects" by the manufacturers in an attempt to minimise their importance).
- The research that "supports" their "effectiveness" is highly suspect in many cases.
- Anti-depressants work mainly by blocking or changing physiology; no medication can put new thoughts into a person's head but they can impede a person's thinking!
- Interactions with other medications are unpredictable.
- In older people all medications can have unpredictable effects.

---

[34] Cf. Glasser, William. *Warning: Psychiatry can be hazardous to your mental health.* New York, Harper Collins, 2003.

- It is extremely risky to provide potentially lethal drugs to people who may be suicidal.
- There is an implicit message that it is better to anaesthetise the pain rather than address the problem.
- A whole world of possible alternative "mood enhancers" is ignored. These are usually safer, healthier and cheaper. Examples: meeting friends, a massage, a walk on the beach, music, relaxation exercises and leisure activities …
- The argument in favour of how many of these drugs "help" could be applied equally to the use of alcohol yet few would encourage a "drinking therapy" as a way to deal with problems.
- The use of such external "remedies" can adversely affect the person's own sense of responsibility for her state.

Of course, there are situations where a person's anxiety or panic state threatens the individual's physical health (e.g., danger of cardiac arrest) and, in such circumstances, some form of sedation may be advised. The same reasoning applies to a situation where a person is a danger to self or others. The important thing to note is that sedation is not therapy.

Choice Theory holds that even apparently crazy behaviours are the best choice the individual can make at the time. Rather than being a "disorder" it is an attempt at "order". The person who has been stressed out for a long time due to financial and marital problems may suddenly experience a "nervous breakdown". Had the individual's creativity not chosen that option, the alternative could well have been death from a heart-attack. The person who has chosen depressing as the way to deal with serious marital problems could have chosen an even less desirable path such as violence.

Depressing can be one of the darkest, most painful of human experiences. Any form of mental distress or psychotic behaviour can be frightening to the person and to those around. I am always very aware, when explaining Glasser's view of this in the cold light of a theoretical discussion, that it may be a very personal issue for some readers and the whole idea of choice may be extremely difficult to accept.

What Choice Theory is saying to you is:

Don't let someone say you have a disorder or any form of weakness in your physiology without proof. You could have made much worse choices in dealing with your life but you chose this one. In the short term it can be an effective choice but any form of depressing or psychosis can become a big problem when it goes on too long. It creates other changes in your life that you probably do not want. Because these conditions arise from serious frustrations in your life, it may be necessary to look beyond yourself for ideas on how to deal with the problems. Just as you chose this way of dealing with problems you can choose alternatives. There is no guarantee that another person can identify or solve your problems but talking can increase the chances of finding solutions.

Let us suppose that you do not accept the idea of depression as a choice but instead you believe it is an illness. Can you still make choices about it? Almost always we can make choices that make a situation worse, choices that will not make it worse and sometimes choices that will actually make it better.

Believing we are controlled by our past

In the popular mind and to some extent in the professional mind there has been a confusion between cause, influence and correlation. The science of psychology has studied in considerable detail the influences on human behaviour with a particular emphasis on the early years. Such data is easier to obtain and lends itself to objective measurement. Research has probed child-rearing practices, social learning, cognitive development and many other aspects of childhood.

Glasser belongs to that group of psychological theorists who claim that we behave according to our perceptions and these perceptions are naturally influenced by our personal experience history. An important attribute of perception is that it works in the present. I behave now according to my perception now, no matter how or when it was formed. I never ever behave according to yesterday's perception!

In fact, if we return to the scene where a present perception was originally created, we will often find considerable differences.

Because my perception is in the present it is also within my power to choose to disregard my perception or even attempt to change it. This may not always be easy but it is possible. It is possible for me to choose to drive through the red traffic light even though my experience (and probably my better judgement) has taught me that I should come to a standstill. In the same way I can choose not to answer the telephone even though my perception of the constant ringing is that it tells me someone is calling me. I can even change my perception of the ringing from one of "a sound telling me I must pick up the receiver" to the more liberating perception of "a sound that simply gives me information that I can choose to act on or not".

If I have a problem with one of my perceptions it is a present problem. I cannot go back and change my experience. You will recall Glasser's comment that if you missed yesterday's dinner you cannot go back and eat it.

A situation that demonstrates this present nature of perceptions is the horror of sexual abuse. It is quite common for a child to appear relatively un-traumatised by earlier abuse for several years and then suddenly to display evidence of considerable distress. The child's original perception of the crime may be that it was just one more mystifying episode in her growing up. As she approaches puberty she learns the so-called "facts of life" for the first time and suddenly her perceptions of what was done to her change dramatically.

What may originally have appeared as no more than odd behaviour is now seen as evil; the perception of the perpetrator may change from friend to enemy; and sadly the abused person often changes their self-concept to view themselves as at least partly to blame and as "damaged" in some way.

The past trauma has not changed in any way but new learning in the present influences the person's perceptions considerably. The child with this terrible memory is behaving according to her present perceptions of a past experience. Reality Therapy in such cases will deal with the present perceptions rather than try to fix the unfixable past.

Believing we are controlled by our genes

One specific aspect of our past that we often blame for our present woes is our genetic inheritance. Naturally our genes explain many of our physical characteristics. We could speak of a direct bio-chemical link between child and parents. It is not difficult to understand how a child's innate intelligence (i.e., speed of processing) could be inherited from the parents. It is a totally different matter to expect genetic links in the content of thought. The literary daughter of literary parents usually has an abundance of non-genetic explanations for her similar interests (her parents' library, endless literary discussions, the high value placed on literature, and so on). I doubt very much if there is a literary gene!

Our voice, for example, is something that would appear to be totally physiological and some aspects of it must be purely genetic in origin. However, an Irish child brought up in France or in the United States will adopt the nasal sounds of his surroundings. The structure of our vocal chords may be genetic but not the way we use them.

We label ourselves as shy, weak, stupid, alcoholic, depressive, ... whatever! We see ourselves as trapped with a set of characteristics that we assume to be genetic. Implicit in this thought is the idea that there is little or nothing that we can do about it. As parents we may even use the genetic argument to blame our spouse for the misbehaviour of our children. ("Your son is fighting again!") As teachers we focus on the similarities between sibling students or we speak of "attention deficit disorder". As medics we classify almost all human behaviour as genetic and treat practically all the problems as illnesses.

Such an extreme faith in genetics becomes dangerous in the case of suicide in a family. Whereas death may be genetic in a manner of speaking, suicide is not. However, the social learning that goes on in a family is very powerful. A child learns a lot about how to cope with life, with frustration, with others from what she sees in her family. If a member of a family committed suicide, it is possible that other family members may have this behaviour in their repertoire. The crucial point is that they do not have to choose it, they do not carry some sort of suicide gene.

Believing in destiny, stars, fate, luck

Many people experience life as something that seems to be beyond their control. It is not surprising then that they come to believe in luck, destiny or even chaos.

If you have grown up in an environment where what you or others did led to very tangible effects you develop confidence in being able to change your environment. If there was no obvious link between what you and others did on the one hand and changes in the environment on the other then you are more likely to believe in randomness. In therapy such people will need to be introduced to the power of choice very gradually.

Choice Theory: A Psychology of Internal Control

Glasser's Choice Theory does not simply challenge the accepted wisdom of external control psychology but offers alternatives. The core belief of Choice Theory is that each individual is controlled from within. A corollary of this belief is that the individual cannot be controlled by others. Around these core beliefs Glasser constructs his approach to therapy and his recommendations about education, management, child rearing and relationships. If my life is not going the way I want it I start by looking at what I myself can do about it.

The irony of all of this is that even if we could be controlled by others, even if we did have some internal problem that affects our behaviour we would still have the option to decide to do something about it ourselves.

The hypothesis that I can do nothing is simply not as useful as the hypothesis that maybe I can do something, no matter what the situation, no matter what your beliefs are about human psychology.

The assumption that we can control others and that others can control us is one that is widely held. In the following exercises we explore several typical examples of such beliefs.

QUESTIONS FOCUSING ON CONTROL

Certain questions can help counselling clients become aware of the degrees of control they have in their lives.

- Who has any power to change this situation?
- Can you get others to change?
- Who can you change?
- What could you change (if you knew how)?
- Do you know how to make this situation worse? (An affirmative answer implies that the person would have a similar level of control to make the situation better or at least not to make it any worse.)

IMPROVING AWARENESS

The skilled counsellor will go beyond the more accessible logic of the client's thought by helping the person examine the pre-verbal area, sensitive to client attitudes that lie just below the surface of her full consciousness.

Glasser himself is not a great believer in the traditional psychological concept of the "unconscious" but it is obvious from his counselling role-plays that he helps clients elaborate their thinking processes beyond their initial levels of consciousness. There is of course a difference between "unconscious" meaning "unknown" and "unconscious" meaning "not fully conscious". Glasser implicitly acknowledges this semi-conscious state when he explains that we always choose although our choices are not always conscious.

One way we can help a person stretch beyond her fully conscious logic is to invite the individual to consider things from a slightly different view-point. For example, "Clare, you say you want to stop smoking but you seem unsure about your reasons for wanting this. Let's try this: imagine I meet you on the street at some time in the future and you tell me you have great news, that you have given up smoking. Can you picture that? Now talk to me about it. How does it feel? What is different? What has got better or worse?"

Take an example from your own life, one of your "good intentions" or "New Year Resolutions", one that you have not yet acted on. First of all, list all the pros and cons that you are aware of. For example, "tidying up the spare room". Advantages could include tidiness, extra space, sense of order. Disadvantages might be throwing out some items, creating new storage space, time and effort required.

As a second part of the exercise, imagine that you have completed this objective and now list the possible pros and cons. For our spare room example the advantages might include recovery of long lost items but the disadvantages could point to a new problem: what do we do with the ongoing clutter we feel is inevitable? What may be stopping my tackling the spare room is a belief that I can never really keep it tidy. Pausing for reflection can help awareness.

Our Perceptual System

In this chapter you will learn about:

- Phenomenological Psychology and the nature of perception
- The all-we-know world and the complexity of the perceptual processes
- The all-we-want world and the characteristics of its pictures
- Our inner logic
- The difference between common sense and science
- The role of perceptions in counselling

Glasser claims that we control our own lives. We are motivated by our own internal basic needs. In our Quality World we have pictures representing what we want, all our personal ways of meeting our basic needs. We then choose specific behaviours in order to achieve these. All the time we are monitoring the situation, checking whether we have got what we want or not and then choosing behaviours to reduce the discrepancy between what we have and what we want, all the time aiming to meet our basic needs.

This whole process depends heavily on our perceptual system. Psychologists talk about this as a phenomenological approach, one based on the "phenomena", on what appears to be rather than on what is. We put a picture in our Quality Worlds because we think it will be need-satisfying. We choose a behaviour that we believe will make that picture a reality and therefore make us happier (i.e., more need-fulfilled). Our personal perceptual processes stand between us and whatever the real world might be. Indeed, analysis of this process can spiral into whole galaxies of complexity. A phenomenological Descartes might have said, "I believe I think, therefore I believe I think I believe I am."

An astronomer, a physicist, a statistician and a phenomenologist were riding through Scotland. they passed a black sheep.. the astronomer said, 'Isn't that interesting, all sheep in Scotland are black.'

'No,' said the physicist. 'At least one sheep in Scotland is black.'

The statistician shook his head sadly, 'You are both wrong. At least one sheep in Scotland is black on at least one side.'

The phenomenologist began, 'My perception is that you, whoever you are, appear to be labelling an object in your phenomenal field as a "sheep" or at least as one "side" of a "sheep" and you are linking that to your previously stored perception of what you understand as "black" and ...'

Once we do accept the basic premise of Phenomenological Psychology, the idea that people behave according to their perceptions of reality and not according to reality itself, then it becomes important to understand just how this process works, how people manage their perceptions. Each of us lives his life not so much in terms of reality as of his perception of reality, what we might call his "personal reality".

What is equally important is to realise how delicate our interface with the world around us really is. When we are dealing with clients, a key-function is to help them clarify their personal realities: what is happening in their lives, what they want, the logic of their inner world, their own evaluations of how realistic their goals are and how effective their strategies seem to be. All of this depends heavily on the client's perceptual processes … and on our own.

In Glasser's Choice Theory there are two main sorting houses for perceptions, one focusing mainly on current perceptions and the other on stored perceptions. In his chart of how the brain works[35], he calls these two areas the "All-we-know-world" and the "Quality World". Ultimately it is any discrepancy between these that motivates the behaviour we choose so it is important to understand how they function.

The All-we-know World

The "All-we-know-world" holds the perceptions currently entering our consciousness from the external world. These are filtered through our senses, our knowledge system and our values and, as far as we are concerned, this is our "reality".

For example, I hear a sound that I identify as a car engine outside my house. My mind starts labelling it as soon as possible. (This is the function of what Glasser calls the "total knowledge filter". Somewhere in our evolution most of us learned that prompt labelling

---

[35] Included in Reality Therapy course documentation. Glasser often speaks of the "brain" when I believe he is talking about the "mind".

was generally a good idea; it helps us deal with "reality" more efficiently. The "total knowledge filter" is our very own internal ID checker.) I say to myself, "That sounds like Seán's car!" I haven't seen him for some time and I know that today is his birthday so my values system gives extra weight to seeing him now. But ... I could be wrong! In fact, there are several different ways I could be wrong.

- Sensory Input: The sound might not be coming from the outside at all. I may have developed a buzzing in my ear.
- Total Knowledge Filter: The sound might really exist but it may be a lawn-mower (no reflection on Seán's choice of cars) or a passing aircraft.
- My Inner Logic: I might not really know what day it is and so it may not be his birthday at all.

These components of our perceptual system can misinterpret the external reality and what follows in this chapter are examples of this. Whatever "reality" is, our grasp on it is a very flimsy one. Would-be counsellors do well to remember this.

The same external reality may be interpreted in many different ways.

Our fascination with optical illusions plays on this fact. What do you see in the graphic in Figure 2, a musician or a person's face?

Similar perceptual confusions[36] occur in our everyday lives. My boss transfers me to a rural area. I immediately decide that this is a demotion. The boss, however, has earmarked me for an important promotion and has decided that the rural experience will fill an important gap in my experience first. My American uncle sends me a birthday gift of €92.63 and what appears initially to be an odd

---

[36] I am indebted to those who created these graphics but unfortunately I have not been able to establish their identities to give them due credit.

Figure 2

amount suddenly makes sense when I realise that it left his account as $100!

Two people watch exactly the same activity for over an hour. At the end one is ecstatic but the other is totally miserable. Why? They were supporting different sides in the football game.

The classic BBC television comedy series "Fawlty Towers" (and many other comedy productions) have relied heavily on our enormous capacity for perceptual confusion. In real life such perceptual confusions can give rise to personal and interpersonal difficulties.

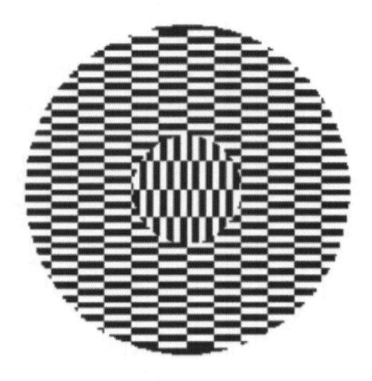

Figure 3

We sometimes perceive phenomena that are not really there.

Stare at the illustration shown in figure 3 for a little while and your eyes will begin to play tricks on you, leading you to believe that material in the central circle is moving. Try moving the figure in a circular motion. There is no real movement in the graphic but your senses perceive movement. Indeed, stare long enough and you may even see a three-dimensional depth that is not there either.

Similarly, when we are dreaming, we are perceiving a world that is not there at all. Most people have had the experience of hearing a noise just as they are dropping off to sleep. These experiences are of course due to that twilight zone between full alertness and sleep that is called rapid-eye-movement sleep (REM). It is probably due to this semi-awake state that certain psychiatric drugs provoke "hallucinations".

We sometimes fail to perceive phenomena that are really there.

Read the sentence shown in the panel below and count the number of occurrences of the letter "f".

> # Finished files are the result of years of scientific study combined with the experience of many years.

Most people fail to perceive everything in this simple example. Nothing is hidden and yet not everything is seen! Check your answer against that shown in the footnote.[37]

Sometimes a counselling client will claim, "nobody likes me". On helping such people list and then take a closer look at each of the other individuals in their lives they very often become aware of perceptions that had escaped them and that in fact there are indeed people who like them. If I believe nobody likes me even when that is not accurate, I still suffer the real psychological pain of loneliness.

---

[37] The correct number is six. This experiment in perception is quoted in Neave, Henry R. *The Deming Dimension.* Knoxville, Tennessee: SPC Press, 1990.

Previous perceptions influence current perceptions

The person who is asked to describe figure 5 after seeing figure 4 is likely to say that it depicts the second letter of the alphabet. However, if a person sees figure 6 first, figure 5 will be seen as the number thirteen.

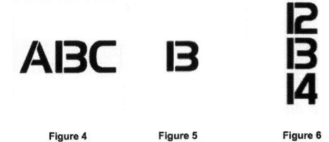

Figure 4   Figure 5   Figure 6

In a social context, each member of a family, for example, has his or her own personal interpretation of what is happening in the family based on previous experiences. Peter's drum practice is seen as welcome evidence of musical genius by his doting father but as spiteful annoyance by his sister in the next room!

Research into television debates has indicated that people tend to choose as winner the candidate who had been their favourite prior to the debate. Their previous experience colours their present perception. In fact, our values system, political or otherwise, is a very important part of our "previous experience".

A bad experience at the beginning of the day can cast gloom over the rest of the day. An unpleasant exchange with a person can bias our perception of that person and give rise to an escalation of negative exchanges.

One very important application of this principle in therapy is that a person's own self-concept will colour ongoing perceptions including expectations for that person.

Once a person becomes aware of the possibility of perceptual bias, she becomes more capable of choosing to ignore it. On my way to work I realise that my mood is low because there was no hot water for my morning shower. Once I become aware of this, I can decide that I will not let that negative experience cloud my day.

When people communicate with each other their shared perceptions are usually different.

Almost every word we use can be interpreted in a different way by another person. Take the simple word "man" for example. Its meaning is not clear unless we put it in context and even then others may misunderstand it. The founder of construct theory[38], George Kelly, claimed that all concepts have two poles and so he preferred the term "constructs" instead of "concepts". What someone means by "man" is clarified when we know what that person regards as the opposite of "man". It could be "woman", "boy", "animal", "mouse" or "god". Given the highly subjective nature of perceptions it is really quite remarkable that we ever achieve successful communication with others.

Perhaps the reader will begin to appreciate my assertion that it is impossible to understand another human being. We can only do our best. Indeed, relationships might be more successful if people were more often surprised at being understood than shocked at being misunderstood.

It becomes obvious that relating to other people, something that Glasser regards as fundamental for a happy life, is very much at the

---

[38] Kelly, George. *The Psychology of Personal Constructs* (2 vols). New York: Norton & Co., 1955.

mercy of our perceptual systems. Maybe the "all-we-know world" should be renamed as the "all-we-think-we-know world"!

The All-we-want World

In contrast to the all-we-know world, the all-we-want world (the "Quality World") is like a special internal photograph album of perceptions, all chosen for inclusion because we perceive them to be need-satisfying. This collection is our personal guide to need-satisfaction and we use it to direct our behaviour.

If the "All-we-know-world" is passive, receiving, then the "Quality World" is active, directing. It is a "wants list" and links easily to a "to do list". Anything I place in my Quality World will have a direct bearing on how I choose to behave. Indeed, this link is so strong that a review of a person's recent behaviour will tell us (and them) a lot about what is really in the person's Quality World[39]. But do not confuse the Quality World with a wish list or some sort of internal "ideal world". It is made up of the people, things, places and values that we really want to have or be close to and are prepared to work (behave) to achieve.

Getting back to Seán and the possibility that his car is in my drive-way … Past experiences have shown him to be a good friend and so I place him firmly in my Quality World. Ultimately what goes into my Quality World gains its place because I perceive it as need-satisfying. A Quality World picture is one of my personal ways of meeting my needs. Just as needs work in much the same way as hunger does, the wants in my Quality World have a function similar to a picture of my favourite food.

The fact that Seán is in my Quality World means I will choose behaviours that bring us together or that show him how much I

---

[39] In a later chapter we shall examine the Quality World in more detail.

value his friendship. His birthday will be important to me; I will have a present ready. Believing his car is in the drive I may rush to open the door, present in hand!

But something even more intricate may be happening! Because he is in my Quality World what I want may influence my perceptions. I am more likely to confuse the neighbour's lawn-mower for Seán's car because my perceptual system is watching out for him, wanting him to visit!

What then are some of the confusions that can happen in the Quality World?

A Quality World picture might not in fact be need-satisfying.

I put a picture in my Quality World because I believe it to be need-satisfying but the person, object, event or value that makes up my picture might never have been really need satisfying or may not be so any longer. Until I actually check its validity I will hold that picture in my Quality World and consequently may choose behaviour to achieve it.

Clients in counselling are often clinging to pictures that are past their use-by date, sometimes pictures acquired in early childhood and no longer really need-satisfying. Many people have drugs in their Quality World because these substances are deceptively need-satisfying especially in the short term.

Important Quality World pictures interact with my current perceptions of the real world.

This works in much the same way as hunger does. When my food need is high, hunger is the frustration signal that urges me to seek food. My Quality World provides pictures of appropriate edibles. My perceptual system (the part Glasser calls my "values filter") begins actively to watch out for these items. I may already initiate behaviour by moving in the direction of the nearest food supply. The greater my need-frustration, the more obsessional my whole system becomes which means I may misinterpret or might not even notice other phenomena around me.

The driving power of such priority pictures makes good sense for our overall well-being but can block or colour other perceptions. When my whole system is controlling for one particular picture or need frustration, it can become weaker at attending to other needs. My very strong wish for the team I support to do well in a competition may blind me to the unsportsmanlike behaviour of some players, may lead me to forget to eat ... or not notice my car being stolen! Similarly, my strong power needs at work may interfere with the smooth functioning of my love and belonging needs.

The brain-teaser quoted below is popular with children and illustrates this point. Read it carefully and then you will be presented with a question about it.

Imagine you are driving a bus with four people on board. At the first bus-stop two people get off and three get on. At the next stop four people get off, one person gets on. At the third stop, one person gets on, two people get off.

The question: What is the name of the bus-driver? Notice what area of your Quality World you used to control your perceptions as you processed this story prior to the final question[40]. What was your focus as you read through the story?

One of the reasons for the counsellor to create a relaxed atmosphere in the counselling session is to help clients stand back

---

[40] If you are unable to solve this, the answer lies in the second word!

from their current obsessions and re-evaluate them in a broader context.

Our Inner Logic

Whether we examine new incoming perceptions in the all-we-know world or the specially selected perceptions stored in our Quality World, of one thing we can be sure: none of these exist in a vacuum. They do not simply enter a brain, with its amazing and virtually infinite storage system. They enter a mind, a world with its own logic, its way of linking perceptions together. Ultimately the labels we apply to incoming perceptions and the meaning or linkages we apply to them are geared to improving our ability to satisfy our needs. This meaning or logic has special characteristics.

Everyone's inner logic is unique.

Two people look at a new red sports-car. Assuming equal levels of technical knowledge and interest, their perceptions of the vehicle are probably quite similar. However, the way these perceptions are processed can differ greatly from one person to another. One sees the car as too small for his family and too heavy on fuel for his regular commuting to work, and the car's storage space is a joke! The other person sees it as an ideal status symbol, as fast and powerful, as a way to attract admirers.

Consider then the even greater complexity in a family group or in a work-place where each participant can have his or her own logic about what is happening there.

In attempting to help a client the counsellor needs to be very aware of this complex world of inner logic and of its uniqueness to every individual. A very useful way of exploring this is to get lots of specific details.

For example, "When you say you fell in love with this car the moment you saw it what exactly did you like about it?" "When you spoke to your husband about you both going away for a quiet week-end, what did you mean by 'quiet week-end' and what do you think he meant by it?" "You said you didn't drink very much last night? What in fact did you drink and how many glasses did you have?"

By careful and precise questioning the counsellor can begin to unravel the complexity of the client's inner logic. But, a word of warning, it would be a mistake to assume that this inner logic is totally logical. Each person differs in the way they operate their logic.

A person's inner logic does not necessarily follow society's logic or the logic of science.

Our "central processor" or "inner logic" as the Adlerians call it, does not always appear to behave in a logical way. It certainly gives rise to disagreements between people otherwise there would be only one philosophy, only one religion, only one political party and only one accepted reality. Even within one individual this "logic" may not always appear to behave in a logical way.

For someone to say "Dublin is the most beautiful city in the world because I live there!" does have its own logic although it is not likely to fit neatly into the premises of rational philosophy.

The oddities of this personal logic can have more serious consequences. For example, medical science generally agrees that smoking causes a range of life-threatening conditions. In spite of this many people continue to smoke. Most of these know that their habit is bad for their health and yet they continue. People "know" it is dangerous to drive fast and yet they still break speed limits. People "know" that certain foods are bad for them and yet they continue to eat them. There would appear to be different types of "knowing" and different types of "logic". If I want to be healthy and I

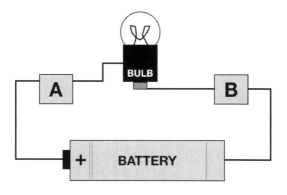

Figure 7

"know" that smoking threatens this want, why do I continue to choose smoking? It would be easy to attribute these illogical behaviours to careless thinking processes but research suggests there are other factors.

In one study of teaching methodology[41] a group of students were shown a simple circuit diagram (Figure 7) and were asked to compare the flow of electrical current at points A and B. Would the current be higher at A, higher at B or equal at both? Although the correct answer is that both would be equal, the majority of students chose point A as having more current. It seemed "logical" to them that the current diminished as it was used up by the light bulb.

Subsequent to this pen and paper test the students were given the opportunity to construct the actual circuits for themselves and to measure the real current at points A and B.

They were able to observe for themselves in a real-life situation that instruments showed the same reading at both points.

---

[41] Gauld, C. "Models, meters and memory". (Research in Science Education, 1986, Vol.16, pp.49-54)

Three months later, the same students were given the original pen-and-paper test again. And yet again a majority gave the wrong answer claiming A would have more current. This time the researcher asked them how they knew this and their answers were surprising. They said that they had done an experiment and were able to see for themselves that A had more current!

Somehow the "knowledge" they had at the outset indicating a stronger current at A was more convincing than the evidence of their senses. Their inner logic was even more powerful than perceptions of external reality. So much so that their memory of the external reality changed to fit the knowledge they had previously. Given the right circumstances these students could electrocute themselves and others with this erroneous knowledge.

Another example of this was presented in a television program where recent graduates of chemical engineering were asked whether trees grew because of the nourishment they got from the ground or from the air. In spite of the correct answer being the air, most of the graduates chose "the ground" as their answer. To the lay-person this would seem to be the logical answer but chemical graduates should know the correct answer.

Once again I surmise that somehow the "ground" theory seemed to have stronger support in the minds of these graduates. In other words there can be something stronger than scientific evidence. I do not mean that this is more correct or accurate than scientific evidence, simply stronger to the mind of the perceiver. Whatever it is, this is ultimately the control centre of the person's behaviour, right or wrong.

Society's logic does not always follow the logic of science.

Just as happens within the individual, society itself can at times follow a strange logic. In many of the dictatorial regimes of our history whole societies followed a logic we no longer accept. We admire those who stood against such regimes, often being labelled mad because they were out of step with the logic of their society. Even today, within the sciences of psychology and medicine there are major logical discrepancies between points of view. Where these variations lead to vastly different forms of treatment, it can happen that one approach will do as much harm as the other does good.

The following examples will illustrate just how widely different perceptions and judgements based on them can differ but hopefully this section will also serve to introduce some new views.

Does eating fat make you fat? It would appear logical that body-fat will be increased by eating fat. However, several medical experts, Eades & Eades[42] and Atkinson[43], claim that scientific evidence proves that it is how our metabolism processes what we eat that is the critical factor. If, they claim, we do not eat sufficient protein with every meal, our bodies cannot process properly any carbohydrate or fat that we eat and it goes into storage as excess fat. Relying on the public's confused logic around such issues a sugar company promoted its product by claiming, rightly but misleadingly, that it didn't contain any fat!

Is back-pain caused by spinal or muscular problems? Dr. Sarno[44] challenged current medical thinking on the treatment of back pain. His observations and research helped him conclude that most episodes of back-pain originated in the muscle system and that such problems were found in sufferers with certain personality characteristics. These included perfectionism, conscientiousness, and high levels of responsibility.

---

[42] Eades, Michael R. and Mary Dan Eades. *Protein Power.* New York: Bantam Books, 1996.

[43] Atkins, Robert C. *New Diet Revolution.* New York: Avon Books, (Revised Edition) 2001.

[44] Sarno M.D., John E. *Healing Back Pain.* New York: Warner: 1991.

Countering the belief that back-pain is always a product of structural problems in the spine he quoted studies that show that many spinal defects are to be found in people with no painful symptoms at all. Disc bulges were found in 81%, severe disc degeneration in 55% and disc protrusions in 33% of individuals with no pain whatsoever. Similar findings emerge for people with degenerative arthritis, scoliosis, and spondylolisthesis.

Although he called the back-pain phenomenon "Tension Myositis Syndrome", a medical-sounding term, Dr. Sarno did in fact use a psychotherapeutic approach to help people combat this extremely crippling pain. Dr. Sarno was Professor of Clinical Rehabilitation Medicine at the New York University School of Medicine and was also attending physician at the Rusk Institute of Rehabilitation Medicine, New York University Medical Center.

Is asthma due to lung pathology? The Ukranian Dr. Konstantin Pavlovich Buteyko believed that many asthmatics can be cured by learning new breathing techniques. Studies such as that carried out at the Mater Hospital, Brisbane, Australia show that even severe asthmatics who adopted the Buteyko treatment were able to reduce medication considerably, reduce steroids and have a greatly improved quality of life.[45] Many medical professionals dispute such claims.

Does acidity or stress cause ulcers? Stress or acidity were factors thought to cause or provoke peptic ulcers. However, in 1983 research by Dr. J. Robin Warren and Dr. Barry Marshall eventually led them to the hypothesis that peptic ulcers are generally caused, not by excess acidity or stress, but by a bacterial infection. It was ten years before their ideas met with approval and the

---

[45] http://buteyko.com/research/trials/index_trials.html

recommendation that special antibiotics be used in the treatment of peptic ulcers resulting in cures taking place in a matter of weeks.[46]

Does verbal reasoning ability indicate a flare for foreign-languages? There is a tendency for educators and school counsellors to interpret high scores in "verbal reasoning ability" as a sign of potential for language learning. However, as far back as 1966 Scottish psychologist Liam Hudson[47] showed the opposite to be true. Those with higher verbal reasoning ability tended to fare worse in learning foreign languages than those with lower verbal reasoning. Hudson reflected that competence in verbal reasoning in one's primary language may in fact interfere with learning any other language.

Is "mental illness" really an illness? The understanding of "mental illness" as proposed by William Glasser and others is diametrically opposite to that of traditional psychiatry. These differences have major implications for how people with mental difficulties are treated. Glasser wrote in 1965, "because we do not accept the concept of mental illness, the patient cannot become involved with us as a mentally ill person who has no responsibility for his behavior".[48] Writing almost half a century later Glasser holds the same views with even stronger conviction: "The 'mental illnesses' that establishment psychiatrists diagnose, treat, and list in the DSM-IV should not be labeled illnesses, because none of them is associated with any brain pathology."[49] Glasser does not doubt the existence of psychotic behaviour but he challenges the idea that this is an "illness".

---

[46] Marshall BJ, Armstrong JA, McGechie DB, Glancy RJ (1985). "*Attempt to fulfil Koch's postulates for pyloric Campylobacter*". Medical Journal of Australia. 142 (8): 436–9.

[47] Liam Hudson. *Contrary Imaginations*. London: Penguin 1966.

[48] Glasser, William. *Reality Therapy*. New York: Harper & Row, 1965.

[49] Glasser, William. *Warning: Psychiatry can be hazardous to your mental health*. New York: Harper Collins, 2003.

Are tranquillisers harmless? Traditional psychiatry also tends to support the wide-spread use of psychiatric medication although there is a growing body of scientific opinion[50] that is critical of this approach. A person who has been taking benzodiazepines (e.g., Valium) for a long time may have acquired one of the most dangerous of addictions. Those who stop taking the drug rather suddenly (an extremely dangerous thing to do) may very soon show all the symptoms of withdrawal and become highly agitated. Observers very easily jump to the conclusion that this is evidence of the person's "disorder" and of a need for a tranquilliser in the first place instead of seeing it as evidence of addiction, evidence of serious harm done to the individual.

Are rewards good for you? The educationalist Alfie Kohn writes that "Rewards work very well to get one thing and that thing is temporary compliance".[51] Not only that but he points to research that shows that rewards produce inferior work. Neither compliance nor inferior work tend to be the goals of education and yet reward systems abound in schools. It is a revealing exercise to ask young people themselves what they think of their school's reward system.

Sense and Science

If learned "experts" can differ so much in their perceptions of important issues, what steps can we take to reduce perceptual errors? I believe that the scientific method is the answer to this challenge. Of course it is imperfect and it can be abused but it does strive to achieve objectivity in the way we understand the "reality" of the world around us. This table is an attempt to summarise critical differences between the two approaches.

---

[50] Cf. Breggin, Peter. *Toxic Psychiatry.* New York: St. Martin's Press, 1991.

[51] Kohn, Alfie. *Beyond Discipline: From Compliance to Community*. Virginia: ASCD, 1996

Sense	Science
Gut feeling	Methodical research
Lack of thinking	Careful thought
Hazy thinking and measurement	Precise thought and measurement
Short-term view	Long-term view
Immediate context only	More global context
Over-acceptance of conventions	Distrust of conventions
Judgmental and closed	Flexible and open
Open to perceptual bias	Reduces bias by using double-blind techniques

Using a decision-making strategy is a simple example of using science rather than plain un-processed "sense". By carefully drawing up a list of all the options and then noting the advantages and disadvantages of each, we are more likely to get a happy decision than if we go for a quick conclusion based on guessing or gut feelings.

Perceptions in Counselling

The weaknesses inherent in our perceptual systems affect the counselling process in several ways:

- How the client perceives his own life
- How he interprets his Quality World
- How he sees his problem
- How he views the counsellor as a person
- How he understands the counsellor's role
- How the counsellor perceives her own role
- How she views the counselling process
- How she interprets what the client tells her

- How she understands the theories she uses to guide her counselling
- What outcomes both client and counsellor expect from the counselling process

This list could probably be expanded into several pages but a favourite saying of an old friend of mine sums it up in three words: "Nothing for sure!" I believe that counselling, and not only that based on Choice Theory, has always attempted to overcome the chasm of understanding that exists between counsellor and client. Processes such as "active listening" or "congruence" were always specifically aimed at increasing counsellor-client understanding.

The wise counsellor will always have some doubt about the "realities" presented in the counselling office. Although she will frequently have tentative assumptions about what is happening, she will be slow to jump to definite conclusions.

I believe that there are three core ingredients we can use in combatting the perceptual weaknesses of common sense.

1. Doubt – By constantly doubting what we hear and even how we interpret what we hear

2. Receptivity – By being open to new ideas and interpretations

3. Systematic Processing – By using ways of processing the information delivered by our perceptions.

Above all we need to acknowledge the absolute uniqueness of each client that enters our office. We can never fully understand other people. We can only do our best.

Strange Behaviours

AIMS:

- to show how our understanding of someone's behaviour depends on our perceptions
- to show the danger of making assumptions about understanding others
- to demonstrate that all behaviour is purposeful
- to emphasise need to work hard to understand our clients

This exercise may be done in small groups or one group up to 13 members.

Part One: Each person will get a card with instructions about how to behave and the following general directions can be offered to the group:

- Read your own card but keep it private until I give the word at the end of the exercise.
- Without saying anything, "perform" the activity on your card for the group. Simply do what is described on the card. Do not add any other actions or hints.

The rest of the group are asked to write:

      1. What they think you are trying to do

      2. How they would help you do it

The Cards

1. You have a nose bleed and have been recommended to stand with your head well back and arms by your sides.
2. You are a spy whose job it is to record a conversation secretly using your "wrist watch" (which is really a miniature sound recording device but does need to be held close to the sound source).
3. With your left hand you are blocking a serious water leak about seven foot up the wall while, with your right hand, you are trying to retrieve your mobile phone from the floor to call for help.
4. Your belt has caught on a hook on the wall and you are trying to raise your body enough to get free.
5. You have just spotted a very rare bird on the ground. If you make the slightest movement or sound you will scare it away but you do need to get past it.
6. It is dark and you are walking down a passage that is shoulder high. Don't bump your head.
7. You are about to have your right ear pierced and have been asked to sit and tilt your head to one side.
8. You have left your key-ring on one of the top shelves in the room. It bleeps in response to finger clicks. Your job is to search for it.
9. Your wig has come partially unstuck and it is windy. Be very discrete about how you hold it in place as you move around; you don't want anybody to know your hair is not your own.
10. The police are hunting you for a crime you did not commit. You need to move past everybody in the room but don't let the police (the people wearing glasses) see your face.
11. Your trousers or skirt has ripped at the back and you decide to move around the room without showing your "true colours" and without drawing attention to your plight.
12. You know that your long-lost cousin, who had a strong passion for garlic, is in the present company. You try to locate your relative using your sense of smell, discreetly of course.
13. Teach the group how to make the hand-movements necessary to play castanets. Use your right hand only.

Part Two: In full group, each person shares answers to questions 1 and 2. Then each "performer" can reveal their secrets and tell what he or she was really trying to do.

Part Three: Whole group discussion

What have you learned about:

- understanding the behaviour of others
- making assumptions
- learning how to help others

What was in each "performer's" Quality World?

What need(s) was each attempting to meet?

What alternative behaviours might each person have chosen to meet these needs?

This exercise can lead on to a discussion of the conditions, environment necessary for a counselling client to be prepared to reveal his or her internal perceptions and motives.

Activities and Your Quality World

Make a summary list of all the different activities that have filled the last three days for you.

What do these tell you about your own Quality World?

How Unique are You?

Answer these simple question with a YES or a NO.

- Do you have a good sense of humour?
- Will you be making a journey in the near future?
- Do you normally make better decisions when you are cool-headed?
- Have you ever told a lie?

You may recognise some of these comments as of the type that is frequently used in horoscopes.   Try a little scientific research yourself and find out just how many people say "yes" to these questions.

Exploring Inner Logic

Inherent in the process of probing a person's inner logic is the constant invitation to self-evaluation: "Is this a belief I want to follow in my life?"

- **Words**

Ask: "What exactly do you mean by ....?"

"When you called Jack 'mad', what exactly did you mean?"

Ask: "What is the opposite of ....?"

"You said Eileen was 'cool'. What would be the opposite of 'cool'?"

Ask: "If there was a .... here, what would it look like?"

"You said you had a row with your boss. What exactly happened; what did you say or do?"

Probe the connotations of words.

"You describe Ed as 'fussy'. What do you associate with 'fussy'?"

• **Beliefs**

Ask: "What are some of your favourite sayings, proverbs?"

Ask: "What rules do you follow in a situation like this?"

Ask: "What are the 'musts' and 'shoulds' in your life (or in this situation)?"

When a client gives an explanation for a decision or behaviour, be alert to the possibility of alternative explanations.

I don't eat in restaurants because I think they are too expensive.
[Real reason may be a fear of crowded places.]

Ask "If that happened, what would be the likely result?"
It may be necessary to ask this more than once.

Client: I don't want to study Art in the local college, although most of my family think it's the obvious choice.
Counsellor: If you did study there what might happen?
Client: I could have Rose in the same class.
Counsellor: And ...
Client: She used to poke fun at me.

- **Ask for evidence.**

    Client: I don't get on with people. Nobody in my class likes me.
    Counsellor: Does Seán like you?
    Client: Yes, he does!
    Counsellor: ... and Roisín?
    Client: Yes, but the others don't!
    Counsellor: What about Peter and Jason?
    Client: Yes, they like me too!

- **Ask about key people.**

    "Who are the really important people in your life? How do they influence you?"

- **Offer challenges to existing inner logic.**

    "If you were to leave out the last word in 'If a job's worth doing, it's worth doing well', how might it change your approach?"

    "If you were to stop trying to do this job perfectly, what is the worst that could happen?"

- **Do not take the client's story at its face value.**

    I know that you believe that you understand
    what you think I said
    but I'm not sure you realise
    that what you heard is not what I meant.

- **Take note of the underlying logic/assumptions of the client's story.**

Compare these two accounts of a similar situation:

"When I am debating holidays with my wife, she holds her ground and tends to argue in favour of faraway places and I fight for more familiar locations. Sometimes she wins; sometimes I win. It can be quite a struggle sometimes."

"When my wife and I have a bit of fun thinking about holidays, she plays around with the idea of faraway places and I content myself with more familiar locations. Sometimes she entices me to her way of thinking; sometimes I tempt her. It can be quite a giggle sometimes."

· **Use a spider diagram to map a person's inner logic.**

In Figure 8 we have a simple example where a person is considering the consequences of different options facing her.

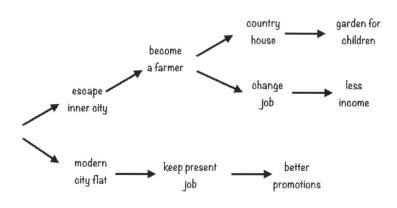

Figure 8

Total Behaviour

In this chapter you will learn about:

- The nature of Total Behaviour
- The four components of Total Behaviour: acting, thinking, feeling and physiology
- Special aspects of Feelings and their role as signals
- The link between Total Behaviour and personal responsibility

Glasser has said that his idea of total behaviour is one of the chief contributions he has made to therapy[52]. The importance of this concept arises from the way it redefines the extent of our control over our own behaviour and our capacity to change our lives. He describes the four components of total behaviour as acting (in the sense of "doing"), thinking, feeling and physiology. By "physiology" he refers to all the bodily processes that form part of our behaviour. No matter what behaviour we choose, we cannot help but choose to do something, think something, feel something and alter our physiology in some way. We cannot separate the components.

Although we tend to associate responsibility with our acting and thinking, in fact we are responsible for all four components and we can change all four by changing any one of them. This is a powerful concept. Glasser likes to compare these components to the four wheels of a car. If any one wheel tries to turn right all four wheels

---

[52] Address to the Institute for Reality Therapy Anniversary Convention by Dr. William Glasser, Cincinnati, July 1990

would change somehow. Of course, cars are designed so that the front two wheels are normally entrusted with steering. It's not so different with humans. The acting and thinking components in particular are, according to Glasser, the easiest to change. We normally make adjustments to our behaviour by altering our doing or thinking. Consequently these two elements tend to become the focus of planning in therapy. We do not try to change our feelings or physiology directly.

Although every single behaviour has all four components we normally label the behaviour itself according to its predominant component. So it is that dancing is regarded as an action whereas blushing might be identified as a physiological response. The way I dance, however, these two very definitely go together!

In any case, whether we are talking about dancing, planning, rejoicing or breathing, each of these behaviours has all four components. Glasser sees these as a real totality, all mingled together, hence the difficulty in representing the concept graphically. In a sense they are four layers of behaviour, doing being the most externally observable of all (Figure 9).

Some other therapies, for example, Rational Emotive Behaviour Therapy[53], come close to Glasser's position. A major difference between RETB and Reality Therapy is that Glasser sees the components as a concurrent totality rather than as part of a sequential chain where one component is seen as causing the next. Glasser says that they all function together.

His view does not rule out the sequential effect but goes beyond it saying that a change in any one component affects the totality. If I choose to do some physical exercise such as jogging I am choosing

---

[53] Ellis, Albert and R. Harper. *A Guide to Rational Living*. North Hollywood: Wilshire Books, 1961.

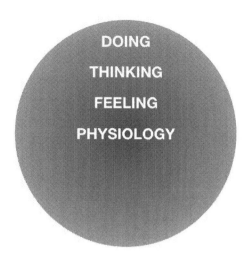

Figure 9

to increase my heart rate as well as choosing the thoughts and feelings that accompany my jogging.

At first glance it would appear that nobody would ever choose to be miserable but Glasser claims that what happens is that we choose the total behaviour of which misery is the feeling component. Similarly if I choose to work very long hours, not eating or resting well, I am choosing to put my physiology in danger and so heart problems may ensue. In that sense I am choosing my heart attack.

This does not mean that the Reality Therapy practitioner will say to her client, "I accuse you of choosing your ill health. You are to blame for it." Instead, she might say, "When you make constant decisions about working late at the office, could this have any bearing on your current ill health?" The underlying message is not a negative one of blame but a positive one of hope: "Is it possible that you have more control over your life than you may have thought?" If you can choose to do something, in all likelihood you can choose to undo it also.

The Totality

Several areas of research in psychology and in medicine support the concept of a close relationship between acting, thinking and physiology.

One early example is the innovative work of Edmund Jacobson who went on to develop his technique of "progressive relaxation".[54]   He set out to study the links between imagination and physiology.   He found that if a person were asked to imagine (thinking component) pressing a key but not to move a muscle, there were in fact measurable bursts of activity (physiology) in the muscles similar to those normally involved in physically pressing the key.

We can all experience this in our own lives when watching an active sport. As we urge our football stars on, we twitch our feet, striking at an imaginary ball. We stretch with the pole-vaulters and punch with the boxers. I recall, somewhere in one of my psychology text-books, a wonderful photograph of a pole-vaulter.   He was at the point of crossing the bar but what was really interesting was the line of spectators along the track. Most of them had a leg raised in the air, willing him over that bar with their own bodies!

The use of the polygraph[55] in lie detection is another area where total behaviour is well illustrated. Telling a lie (acting component) has corresponding changes in anxiety levels (feeling component) and in blood pressure, breathing and skin resistance (physiology).

The large body of research that has built up about "biofeedback"[56] testifies to the links between the four components of behaviour. Using the highly sensitive physiological measurements of biofeedback equipment it is possible to demonstrate how thinking

[54] Jacobson, E. *Progressive Relaxation.* Chicago: University of Chicago Press, 1958.

[55] Smith, Burke M. *The Polygraph*, Scientific American, January 1967.

[56] Brown, Barbara B. *Stress and the Art of Biofeedback*. New York: Harper and Row. 1977.

about something embarrassing, for example, is accompanied by changes in physiology.

In the brief discussion of each of the four components below I deliberately leave feelings to the last because I believe that Glasser gives a special role to this component.

Actions

Actions are the most tangible of all the components. We can observe an action and its consequences reasonably well. We can count how often a person sits down, eats an apple; we can measure how long somebody sleeps, how high they jump or how much they drink. Not only are outside observers more aware of an action but so too is the person whose action it is. This characteristic of actions means that this doing component is probably the easiest to change deliberately.

Thoughts

Thinking is also reasonably accessible since we can express it through speech or writing. We can summarise a person's thought or analyse the logic and complexity of that thought. In counselling it is mainly the thought component we use in our dialogue with the client and, like acting, it is a component that we have more direct control over than over feelings and physiology. Even in therapies that believe in dealing more directly with feelings it is through the person's actions and words that the feelings are accessed.

As George Kelly's Construct Theory illustrates very well, a person's thinking can be analysed in great detail and depth. Some constructs in particular seem to exert an extra-powerful influence on our behaviour. One of these is the self-concept and its evaluative dimension, self-esteem. This occupies such a central role in our lives that it becomes very important in counselling and will be the subject of a later chapter.

Control is another powerful construct from a Reality Therapy perspective. A person at one end of the scale thinks she has a very high level of personal control over her life. Someone else, who happens to be at the opposite extreme of this scale, believes she has very little control. Accordingly, this second person tends to think that her life is controlled from outside, by others or even by fate and so adopts external control psychology. "Locus of control"[57], as this construct is known, is a very powerful one that will impact on the way we run our lives.

Physiology

With modern instrumentation physiology has become much more observable than it once was. Nowadays it can be measured by heart and breathing monitors, EEG equipment and the like. It is not normally under our direct control but when awareness of it is amplified as through the use of biofeedback equipment, we can acquire direct control over the most subtle of physiological changes. People can learn to control their heart-beat and their skin conductivity. The amplification of minute electrical pulses in the muscles can in some cases help people recover from different forms of paralysis.[58]

Drug therapy is commonly used by medics to change a person's physiology. Indeed Glasser's assertion that a change to one component of behaviour will change the others could suggest that psychiatric drugs might help people overcome conditions such as depression and so-called "bi-polar disorder". Unfortunately it's a bit like taking alcohol when you feel cold. In the short term it does give the sensation of being warmer but it has the regrettable "side-effect"

[57] Crandall, V., Katkovsky, W. and Crandall, V. *Children's beliefs in their own control of reinforcements in intellectual-academic achievement situations.* Child Development, 1965,3691-109.

[58] Brudny, J., et al., *Sensory feedback therapy as a modality of treatment in central nervous system disorders of voluntary movement.* Neurology, 1974, 24: 925-932.

of actually creating a loss of body heat and ultimately it is not a substitute for fixing the real problem by lighting a fire or turning on a heater. Many psychiatric drugs have a similar pattern: short-term improvement and long-term dangers. Indeed, just as the alcohol may impair your ability to light a fire, the drugs may limit your ability to think of a solution.

Obviously one person might feel cold because the environment is cool and another person because of a cardiovascular circulation problem. The problem in psychiatric drug therapy is that there are no medical tests for the supposed chemical imbalances as there would be in the case of a circulation problem. The chemical imbalance theory is quite simply that, a theory.

Choice Theory sees chemical changes as part of the total behaviour. If I choose to take time out from a serious problem at work and I decide to stay in bed for most of the day, it would be reasonable to expect certain chemical changes in my physiology. It would be quite a jump in logic to suggest that the chemical changes "caused" the stay in bed.

Unfortunately, if I take drugs to alter my body chemistry, they also have other effects on the brain which seriously impair thinking capacity and so my power to make long-lasting positive changes in my life is blocked or inhibited.

But, whatever the cause, an altered physiology will have repercussions for the total behaviour of which it is a part. If I haven't slept for a few days the exhausted physiological state will be reflected in my actions, thoughts and feelings.

Feelings

Of all the four components the area of feeling is probably the most complex and at the same time possibly the most important of all.

Feelings are difficult to measure

It is certainly the hardest of the four components to measure, a feature that may be awkward for the psychological sciences but is a blessing for the artistic world. Indeed a life without feelings would be one devoid of wondrous riches. Nevertheless, in counselling we need to reach some understanding of feelings for all the reasons listed in the rest of this chapter.

We cannot really measure feelings except through a person's own expression of them. We can only take that person's word for it about what is going on in their inner space. Very often, however, the counsellor will help a client tease out more specific aspects of the feelings presented.

Eddie:	I am really miserable!
Counsellor:	Would you say you are miserable bored, miserable hungry, miserable lonely ....?
Eddie:	Lonely miserable, I suppose. Yes, lonely!
Counsellor:	And is there any particular person or even a thing or place you think about at such times?
Eddie:	Mmm ... yes, I suppose so, my home town springs to mind immediately.

Such a probe helps the counsellor to understand better the total behaviour of which the feeling is a part and ultimately to trace the possible cause of the pain experienced.

But even the terms used to label feelings have their complexity. For example, the name we give to a feeling seems to depend heavily on the thinking and physiology that we are experiencing at the time. If I am tired and a little sick (physiology) and I believe that I may not find a job in the foreseeable future (thinking), I may decide that I am "depressed" (feeling). On the other hand, if I am tired and a little sick but recall that I spent most of the previous night at a 21st birthday party I may label my feeling as "hangover" and may even boast about it. If I am running (acting), my heart is beating fast (physiology) and I am thinking about my health my feeling will probably be of the "joy of living" variety. On the other hand If I am running, my heart is beating fast and I am thinking about the bull that is chasing me I am more likely to call the feeling "fear".

I recall a person telling me that he always felt bad. He admitted that sometimes he felt better than at others but he always ended up feeling bad. In answer to my question about this he explained that when he felt better he believed it was due to his "manic-depression" and so he immediately felt bad. The label offered to him by a medical person had suggested this strange interpretation of his feelings. When I helped him reality-test this interpretation and acknowledged the normality of some of the bad feelings stemming carried over from earlier traumatic experiences he began to come out of the self-perpetuating diagnosis. Years later he told me that his psychiatrist was delighted at his progress.

The Choice Theory view of feelings has implications for therapy. It means that feeling labels are generally vaguer than the more detailed descriptions we can apply to acting, thinking and physiology. It suggests that although the feeling label may give useful clues about the nature of a problem it is only by investigating all the components of the total behaviour that an accurate picture can emerge.

It can be helpful to analyse each of the four components of a given total behaviour. However, it is vital in counselling that we do not lose sight of the totality, that we meet the client in a total way, fully open to all that he or she is.

Feelings have an important role in motivation

Glasser sees feelings as having a central role in the way we run our lives: "It is the hope of feeling good or better, immediately or later, that drives all of our behavior."[59] Personally I believe that in "total behaviour", it is the feeling component that is the totality, the binding agent, the summary of all that is happening in our lives. Feeling is the totality of doing, thinking and physiology as experienced by the individual. As such, no matter how difficult it may be to measure, it becomes vitally important to any supportive intervention in a person's life.

Although we behave ultimately in order to meet our basic needs, and all our efforts are directed more specifically at achieving a particular picture in our Quality Worlds, very often the subjective purpose of our behaviour appears to be to achieve a particular good feeling.

Feelings as signals

Glasser writes about how in early infancy it is the feeling component that helps the child know whether or not the needs are being satisfied. In Reality Therapy the feelings have always been seen as the barometer, the signal system of the needs. We feel "good" when the pictures in our Quality Worlds and the corresponding needs are being fulfilled and we feel "bad" when they are not. In

---

[59] Glasser, William. *Staying Together.* New York: Harper & Row, 1995.

fact, the physical feelings (e.g., pain) play a similar role. Without pain we would have no feedback about potentially harmful experiences.

NEED	LEVEL OF NEED SATISFACTION	
	LOW	HIGH
LOVE & BELONGING	Loneliness	Belonging
FUN	Boredom	Enjoyment
FREEDOM	Trapped	Free
POWER	Weak	Strong
SURVIVAL	Fear	Safe
GENERAL	Unhappy	happy

We can identify specific positive and negative feelings that relate to each of the needs and an awareness of these linkages can help the counsellor and client come to a better understanding of the client's life.

Glasser, seeing the signal role of feelings, has always treated them in a way that is quite distinct from other client-centred approaches. He avoids starting therapy by enquiring about the client's feelings since, he says, people come to therapy because they feel bad and asking about this at the beginning is neither informative nor helpful. It would be as superfluous as asking, "Are you here?" However, as his role-plays demonstrate, he does sometimes ask about the client's feelings later in the counselling session since they provide feedback about how the client is progressing.

I believe that it is the "signal" role of feelings that makes it so difficult for some people to express them overtly. Dogs have tails and people have feelings! Like the tails our feelings tell a lot about what is going on in our lives and this can be too much self-disclosure for some people.   Musicians, graphic artists, poets and dancers all know about this and practise their strange art of expressing the inexpressible.   The rest of us ordinary mortals are cautious about revealing our feelings to others.   One wonders what would happen if humans did indeed have tails.   Some would probably have them surgically removed, others would strap them neatly under their clothing and, hopefully, still others would decorate theirs with flags, bells and bunting!

Feelings are not changed directly

Another specific Glasserian view is that we do not change feelings directly[60] but through the other components of total behaviour, especially the "acting" and "thinking" which, he says, are the easiest to change.   If I am feeling bored I can choose to blame the government or the weather.   On the other hand I could choose to get ideas for new activities and I can decide to do something different, even if it is only going shopping (the infamous "retail" therapy).   The really important thing is that we can change total behaviour and even feelings come under our control ... and responsibility.

Total Behaviour and Responsibility

If I can choose my total behaviour then I am responsible for it. Unfortunately this word "responsible" has acquired overtones of blame and that is not the emphasis in Choice Theory.   The positive aspects of this responsibility could be summed up thus:

I choose my total behaviours.

We tend to think of choosing what we "do" as in the observable action but choice theory sees that as only one component of four. We choose all four components.   If, for example, I choose to drink

---

[60] Glasser, William. *Schools Without Failure*. New York: Harper & Row, 1969.

excessive alcohol, I am also choosing the impaired physiology that accompanies this choice. I might not be aware of this but I am choosing it nonetheless.

Therefore I can change my total behaviour.

This view of choice is very positive since it points to my ability to change not only my doing but also all of my total behavior.

I can even change my feelings or physiology.

Although we may seem to have little or no direct control over our feelings or physiology, choice theory teaches that we can control them by controlling our total behaviour. If, for example, I choose to go on a roller-coaster, I am choosing to alter my physiology considerably. It is highly likely that the feelings will also change considerably.

I change all components if I can change even one of them.

The inseparable connectivity of all four components means that any change in one component will result in change throughout the system, change in all four components. If I dive into a swimming pool it becomes difficult to continue to think about a list of chores for the day. If I ingest or inject some mood-altering substance into my system then it is likely to impact on my doing, thinking and feeling as well.

It is usually easiest to change my doing or my thinking.

Drugs may change my physiology and indirectly my feelings and thoughts. They may even influence my actions. However, by far the easiest way to alter the person's behaviour is through the individual's doing and thinking.

Changes in doing and thinking are more likely to impact on the real world.

Although drugs might alter my physiology or mood they are unlikely to have a positive effect on my interaction with the real world. Obviously in the case of an extremely dangerous individual, a tranquillising drug will render the person safer for those around. However, in the case of people whose lives have gone out of control or balance, they need their doing and thinking components to be extra effective, not less.

Aided and abetted by the chemical imbalance theorists and their pharmaceutical sponsors, "depression" can appear as a disorder, an affliction, something outside of a person's own sphere of control. Seen as mainly the feeling component of a chosen total behaviour completely reframes the depression and, more importantly, points to ways of dealing with this very painful condition.

Glasser's emphasis on the role of choice in behaviour is greatly enhanced by the concept of total behaviour and that is why it is so important.

Total Behaviour Exercise

Print and cut the following table into twelve cards.

Shuffle these and distribute them among the group.

Part One:

Ask them to examine each other's cards and see if they can reassemble the "total behaviour" for each of the three situations referred to.

Part Two:

Invite each person holding the "doing" card in their group to move to a different group.
Now examine the possibility that this new "total behaviour" could exist.

DOING	DOING	DOING
lying under a tree on a fine summer's day	playing tennis with a friend	sitting alone in a dark corner of my bed-room

THINKING	THINKING	THINKING
This is heaven	I'm getting more and more healthy	I can't do anything

FEELING	FEELING	FEELING
very comfortable, calm	full of energy	miserable, useless

PHYSIOLOGY	PHYSIOLOGY	PHYSIOLOGY
stable; gentle breathing; in harmony	fast heart-beat, plenty of adrenalin	heavy; breathing slowly

Feelings as Signals

1. The last time I was feeling stuck, trapped ...

   Where was I?
   Who else was there?
   What was happening?
   What was I doing?
   Which of my Basic Needs was not being satisfied?

2. The last time I was feeling lonely ...

   Where was I?
   Who else was there?
   What was happening?
   What was I doing?
   Which of my Basic Needs was not being satisfied?

3. The last time I was feeling afraid ...

   Where was I?
   Who else was there?
   What was happening?
   What was I doing?
   Which of my Basic Needs was not being satisfied?

4. The last time I was feeling helpless, useless ...

   Where was I?
   Who else was there?
   What was happening?
   What was I doing?
   Which of my Basic Needs was not being satisfied?

5. The last time I was feeling very bored …

Where was I?
Who else was there?
What was happening?
What was I doing?
Which of my Basic Needs was not being satisfied?

Total Behaviour Analysis

At any given moment all four components of our total behaviour can be "freeze-framed" to provide an interesting insight into current behaviour. On the other hand, it is possible to use this analysis to examine a period of time, the overall trends in a segment of our lives. This exercise explores both of these and are intended to help you become more aware of the nature of your total behaviour.

• Part One: Right now consider all four components of your total behaviour. What are you doing? What are you thinking? How are you feeling? What is going on in your physiology (pulse, breathing, etc.)?

• Part Two: Take a period of time in your recent past. It could be last week, a day at work. a week-end. Sum up your total behaviour over that period of time. What were you doing? What were you thinking about? How were you feeling? And what was your physiology doing?

• Part Three: Were there moments or periods of time when you recall your total behaviour changing quite a lot? Which of the components had changed between the earlier time and the later one?

Reality Therapy & Choice Theory

In this chapter you will learn about:

- The three fundamental questions to ask about any therapy
- How Reality Therapy defines human problems
- How Reality Therapy intervenes to help
- The nature of the counselling environment
- The processes of Reality Therapy especially involvement and self-evaluation
- A simple classification of problems using the Choice Theory framework
- Special characteristics of Reality Therapy
- The centrality of Choice in Reality Therapy

Reality Therapy has been in the public forum since 1965 when Glasser published his book of the same name.[61] The theoretical base of his approach has become "Choice Theory".

Any attempt to imitate Glasser's counselling demonstrations or to follow his advice without understanding his theory would result in a flawed version of Reality Therapy. Consequently, this chapter will attempt to explain the environment and the procedures of Reality Therapy with regular references to the theoretical approach on

---

[61] Glasser, William. *Reality Therapy*. New York: Harper & Row, 1965.

which it is based. Most of the ideas presented in this overview will be discussed in a more practical way in later chapters.

In the Introduction I recommended clarifying three questions about any approach to therapy:

1. What explanation of human behaviour does it use?
2. How does it define "problem behaviour", the type that people bring to counselling?
3. How does it intervene to help sort out such problems?

The answers to these questions will guide the counsellor in what she does, what she focuses on, how she processes it in her own mind and how she attempts to help the client.

We have already summarised Glasser's answer to the first question in earlier chapters about Choice Theory and specific aspects of it. Choice Theory psychology is Glasser's explanation of human behaviour.

What is a Problem?

So how does Choice Theory define a "problem" since problems are the subject matter of counselling? Why do people decide to seek counselling help? They don't normally do so when they can't find a taxi or because the weather is too hot so what is the special characteristic of problems that require counselling?

Obviously such problems tend to be "personal" and in Choice Theory terms this means they are problems where one or more of the person's needs are not being satisfied in a significant way. Because all of our needs rely so heavily on our relationships with others for their satisfaction, Glasser now believes that it makes sense to look for the relationship issues early in the counselling process.

It is worth noting that the client's "problem" will be something of personal importance no matter how trivial it might appear to others. People do not normally seek counselling for matters that they themselves regard as insignificant.

Another characteristic of the problem is that the client has not been able to solve it satisfactorily up to now. People simply do not come into counselling to say, "I have no problems" or "I have a problem but I have solved it".

In fact sometimes clients are not sure what the problem is at all and they may even talk about matters that are not really central to their difficulties. This is why it is so important for the counsellor to have some understanding of human behaviour. This enables him to see beyond the so-called "presenting problem" and help the client detect the real frustrations in her life.

Basically, Choice Theorists would define the problems as frustrations, situations where individuals are not meeting their needs. These frustrations would be important in the eyes of the client.

> I know that you believe that
> you understand
> what you think I said
>
> but I'm not sure you realise
> that what you heard
> is not
> what I meant.
>
> Anon

How Does Counselling Help?

Counselling is ultimately about helping a client eliminate or reduce the problems she has brought to counselling. In Choice Theory terms this means helping her plan whatever changes are necessary to have a more need-satisfying life.

Since Choice Theory explains that I cannot control another human being one consequence is that the Reality Therapy counsellor will not attempt to exert any control over the client.

Since Choice Theory holds that control is from within the person, it is the client's own control that is the focus. So, as Reality Therapy counsellors, we aim at helping the clients gain better control of their own lives through their own choices.

To do this we will need to know something about the client's Quality World and about what she sees as not working in her life. This will mean gaining access to the client's private world. Therefore an early concern of the counsellor is to do everything possible to make it easy for the client to talk openly about this private world.

This inner world of the client is usually in turmoil; it has been marked by a sense of personal "failure". It is not always easy to tell others about it. Some counselling clients have problems in the first place because of their poor communication skills. So one of the first goals of the counsellor is to create the atmosphere where clients can open up this private world.

The Counselling Environment

The special environment we need to create will depend on two vital ingredients: the atmosphere and the relationship and I hope to show how these components evolve from their Choice Theory foundation.

The Atmosphere

The actual place where counselling is offered must be safe and comfortable. The client will require privacy and a place free from interruptions. The client will want to be heard but not overheard. The location needs to have these characteristics and the client must know that she is safe.

The Relationship

The relationship between counsellor and client is extremely important. Indeed, for the client to engage in an effective interaction with the therapist, the client must be able to add the therapist to her Quality World. That very same attention to the details of the counselling environment, to the relationship and to communication with the client, will increase the therapist's chances of registering as a need-satisfying person in the client's life. If, on the other hand, the therapist is not seen as need-satisfying then the client is unlikely to take him or her into the Quality World. If this is the case then counselling becomes almost impossible.

Glasser describes this special caring relationship with the client as "involvement". The Reality Therapy practitioner deliberately aims at involvement with the client. This is not simply a version of courtesy nor is it based on a desire for warm human relationships. In counselling, involvement is a professional necessity for the reasons outlined earlier.

I like to refer to this quality as "professional friendship". The friendliness of a mechanic or solicitor is a welcome bonus when dealing with them but in the counsellor's case this special brand of friendship plays a central role in the job. It does differ from normal friendship. It has its own special limits and may be governed by ethical and legal considerations but a truly genuine friendliness is still required.

In one way counselling is even more demanding than normal friendship because the client is turning to the therapist for help in dealing with a problem. Ordinary friends are not always expected to help and sometimes we definitely do not want them even to attempt it! A close friend will often choose to be supportive rather than confrontational, mainly because it is the safer option and not everybody believes they have skills that will maintain the friendship through a confrontation.

The counsellor, on the other hand, has a primary task of helping the client even if that means being very straight with her. At the same time such an approach must be done in a way that is not critical of the client and that she can see as the work of a collaborator rather than of an adversary. It is a balancing act between challenge and friendliness, one that requires great sensitivity and skill.

Another important difference between the counselling relationship and friendship is that friends know each other and are tolerant of flaws in communication. We as counsellors on the other hand cannot give ourselves such lee-way; we need to do more than pay attention; we need to be seen by the client as really listening very carefully and thoughtfully.

Since many of our clients are having problems with relationships, the therapist needs to focus in detail on the quality of the relationship the client will find in therapy. Given that many clients have problems precisely because they have not experienced much safety or caring in their lives we as therapists will do well to communicate these particular qualities with extra clarity.

Many clients have experienced so many relationship difficulties that they are extra sensitive to anything that might appear to be "rejection" or criticism. Consequently the counsellor must create and communicate a very positive relationship.

The Process of Reality Therapy

No effective counselling can ever be presented as a series of techniques or procedures to be followed in a pre-set order. However, there are identifiable procedures that are used in Reality Therapy, procedures that link back to Choice Theory.

Exploration is one of these. It is an important procedure in almost any helping role but in Reality Therapy, the mind-map that guides this exploration comes from Choice Theory.

Recalling the earlier diagrammatic summary of key concepts of Choice Theory as NEEDS – PICTURES – BEHAVIOURS (see Fig. 10) it follows that a Reality Therapy counsellor will explore the

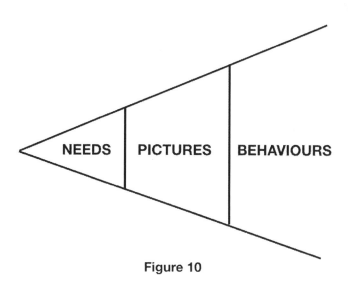

Figure 10

client's behaviours, pictures and needs, though not necessarily in that order. For a Reality Therapy practitioner, it is information about these key areas that forms the backdrop to the counselling and this information will only be forthcoming from the client provided the environment is satisfactory. In Reality Therapy case notes, the therapist is normally able to say which of these areas she is dealing with at any given moment.

On the client side there is a gradual process of awareness, one that happens at several different levels. In Choice Theory we know that the client will not change unless he himself wants to change. Therefore a very important "insight" in the process of Reality Therapy is that critical moment of awareness when the client fully realises that only he can change himself. Glasser never seemed too happy with the traditional interpretation of "insight" where the client realises just what is not working in his life.

Choice Theory's "insight" is forward-looking. Glasser prefers the emphasis where the client says something like: "I'm not sure how to fix this. I'm not even sure what's going wrong. I do know that I have tried different solutions and I realise they haven't worked. So now I know I need to look for new solutions."

> Talking about what's wrong is not going to change anything. It's like talking about a flat tire; you can talk forever, but unless you fix it, it stays flat.[62]

The moment in Reality Therapy that corresponds to "insight" is when the penny drops for the individual that she has responsibility for and control of her own life. This is not a moment of blame for the flawed use of control in the past but a moment of hope for the positive control of the future. Following on from this is the awareness that, however she got into her present predicament, she

---

[62] Glasser, William and Carleen Glasser. *Getting Together and Staying Together*. New York: Harper Collins, 2000.

herself may be able to choose a solution or at least an improvement.

Central to this special turning point is what Glasser calls "**self-evaluation**". Since the client controls her own life then it is she who must judge whether her recent and current attempts to solve her problem are working. A Choice Theory counsellor will encourage the client to make such an evaluation. After establishing a good relationship with the client the counsellor might say, "You say you have used all sorts of diplomatic ways to get your husband to stop drinking. Before that you claim you nagged him a lot. You love him with all your heart and can't bear to see him killing himself in this way. Have any of the things you tried so far worked?"

Involvement plays a critical role in the whole process of entry into the client's world and awareness of it by both counsellor and client. Then this second process, self-evaluation, becomes the vital turning point where the therapy moves to focus on solutions, on new choices and plans. A natural next step for the client is the personal decision whether to change or not. If she now sees that her behaviour up to now has not achieved her goals then she is in a position to make that decision.

Once a relationship of involvement facilitates clarification of the client's inner world, helping the client become aware of what he wants and what he is doing to get it, then and only then is a significant self-evaluation possible. Experienced Reality Therapy instructor Richard Pulk called "involvement" and "self-evaluation" the two pivots of Reality Therapy. They are the critical points in the process.

It is worth repeating that therapy is not a linear process. The counsellor may be intent on exploring specific themes in the client's Quality World one moment, then working hard on increasing involvement the next. Later he may revisit the Quality World, check out needs, talk about behaviours and he may do these many times.

The amount of attention paid to relationships will be an important thread running through all of this. Self-evaluative moments may also occur at many different points in the process.

In the information gathering stage of counselling different **themes** will emerge. The client may reveal problems at work, difficulty in paying a loan, and on-going arguments with his spouse. It is a function of counselling to identify the major themes, those that cause so much need frustration that the client decided he needed counselling. If there are more than one of these it may be necessary for the client to choose which one to address first. At some point the broad focus of exploration gives way to the narrower focus of planning new choices.

Effective planning is an important final outcome of therapy. This is a very important skill in any counselling process but vital planning cannot be done until the problem is identified and the client wants to change. Even before this point is reached it will always be necessary to do some planning at the end of one session in readiness for the next.

A Diagrammatic Summary

In a sense the therapist enters the client's world, helps her explore that world and then comes back with her to the real world of action plans. Figure 11 attempts to summarise that journey with arrows indicating the path followed. It shows therapy as a process of entering the client's inner world, exploring behaviours, pictures and needs. This creates the scene for self-evaluation, that most important of turning points, and the subsequent adjustment of pictures and/or behaviours that prepares the client for new choices.

The Reality Therapy practitioner creates an environment of involvement to make counselling possible. Without this there is no useful access to the client's inner world. She then listens to the client's story paying particular attention to the client's reason for

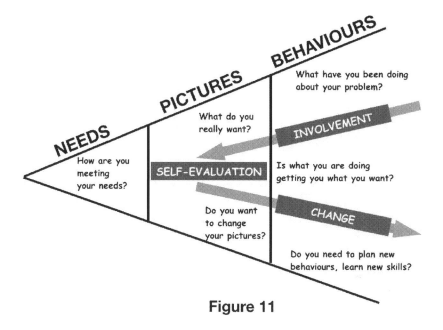

Figure 11

seeking counselling. Whatever the client may say, the RT counsellor is watching for specific themes in the client's life where there is major frustration. This will always concern one or more needs but normally will be expressed in terms of the client's Quality World.

The counsellor will be checking on what the client wants that he is not getting (or on what he does not want and is getting). By a very careful choice of language and approach the Reality Therapy counsellor gently helps the client become aware of his own choices. The Choice Theory assumption that everyone chooses the best behaviour they know at any given time helps the counsellor see the client's current behaviours in the most positive of lights.

Once atmosphere and process both combine to give the client a very safe context and sufficient awareness to evaluate his own behaviour the counsellor may encourage this self-evaluation by careful questioning. Here the client will decide whether current behaviours and/or Quality World pictures have been serving him well.

If the client decides that what he has been doing has not worked then it is time to consider a change, to examine new choices. The rest of the counselling will focus on new pictures or new behaviours. The counsellor will help the client examine and evaluate these. There may be new skills to learn or rehearse and the RT counsellor will engage in such processes if necessary.

Problem Types

Recalling that Choice Theory considers behaviour as an attempt to make pictures happen and the pictures are our personal catalogue of ways to meet our needs it becomes possible to identify three types of problems defined in terms of this process. I do not present these as "diagnoses" in the traditional sense but as aids to knowing where to look for the frustrations in a client's life. It is an analysis made from the viewpoint of Choice Theory psychology.

All three situations result in some form of need frustration but the specific origin of the satisfaction breakdown can be in one or more stages of the Needs-Pictures-Behaviours process. The numbered arrows in the Figure 12 represent each of these scenarios.

1. Activation of Behaviours: My problem is that I cannot meet my needs because I cannot make my picture happen; I cannot convert it into a behaviour. The picture may have huge potential for really satisfying my needs but I am unable to activate it. An example would be "joining the youth club". I know it would help some of my love and belonging needs but I personally do not have the social skills to carry it out; I am simply too shy. I know what I want but I cannot get it!

2. Efficacy of Pictures: I cannot meet my needs because, although I can make my picture happen easily enough, it is not really as

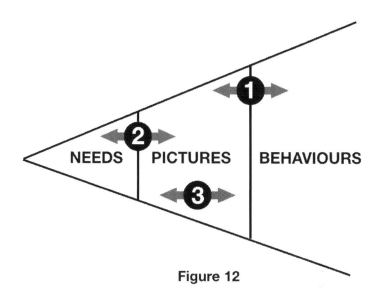

Figure 12

need-satisfying as I think. The picture of drugs is a good example. I think they will satisfy some of my needs and I can find them with relative ease (make the picture happen), but ultimately my needs are not satisfied or other needs suffer. In the long-term I can suffer bad health or imprisonment.

3. Logic of Pictures: I cannot meet my needs because of a problem within my Quality World itself. The personal logic I use to link my pictures together is not sound. For example, I believe that a certain qualification that is well within my reach would get me the job of my dreams but in fact it will not. If I don't detect this faulty logic in time I could well apply for the wrong course. Another example could be the logic I use to plan my life. In the picture I have for a "day's work", it is linked to ten sub-pictures of tasks to do. Each task is something I can do and each would be need-fulfilling. However, only eight of these will fit into my day. Because I don't spot this logical error I keep running out of time … and into frustration!

If a client has a problem of the first type, unable to make pictures happen, the counselling may eventually focus on the development of the necessary skills and resources. The counsellor might say: "Suzy, I suppose there are two routes we could take. One is to look at ways you could deal with the youth club. For example, would it help if you went along with one of your brothers? Another route I can think of is to look for something totally different from youth clubs, something that might be an easier first step. If you like singing, the local choir might be a possibility. What do you think?"

For those with the second type of problem, using pictures that are not as need-fulfilling as they appear, the counsellor might spend time helping the client do some reality-testing. "Al, you have been Margaret's boyfriend for nearly a year now but I hear you saying that by dating her you have even more problems in your life: you have missed more school; the police have questioned you about drugs; you have got more distant from your family. Would it help for us to spend some time examining your relationship with Margaret?"

With the third type of problem, the logic of the Quality World, there may also be reality-testing and some logical teasing out of the specific details of the pictures. "Marty, you have already saved a lot of money for the motorbike. You tell me your main reason for getting the bike is to have more freedom, to be able to get away. If you like, I'll be the devil's advocate for a moment or two. If you get the bike, will you have the money to maintain it? I'm thinking especially of insurance and fuel. Since none of your friends are into bikes is it possible you might end up with freedom but no money and no friends?"

Special Characteristics of Reality Therapy

Certain aspects of Reality Therapy make it very different from other therapies:

Dealing with the past: Reality Therapy does not investigate the past unless it is going to help clarify something in the present or identify a strength that the person could use again in the present.

> Choice theory explains that all problems are present problems because the needs must be satisfied now. You cannot eat a meal you missed any more than you can eat a future meal.[63]

Causality: Related to this is the fact that we do not believe the client always needs to understand his own psychological processes. In other words, "insight" in its conventional meaning is not one of our aims.

Reality Therapy analyses the current NEEDS – PICTURES – BEHAVIOURS dynamic to find out where the needs are being frustrated so that the client can be helped to satisfy the needs. There is one form of insight that is vital to Reality Therapy and that occurs when the clients realise that they are responsible for their own lives.

---

[63] Glasser, William. *Choice Theory*. New York: Harper Collins, 1998.

> If you have been starving for a long time, you need food, not an explanation why you weren't fed in the past.[64]

At the same time it is important to clarify that Glasser does not play down the importance of the counsellor understanding the "cause" of the client's problem in the sense of knowing the specific need and Quality World frustrations that are present. Where he differs from other approaches is that, one, he sees the cause in the present and, two, he does not believe in the therapeutic usefulness of discussing causality with the client.

If Sean has been "hearing voices" and it turns out that he leads a life devoid of friends then the counsellor will focus on helping him make new friends. It may be that he steers clear of people because he thinks he would be a bother to them. In this case the counsellor might help him tease out these pictures of relationship before exploring new behaviours. This is not the same as the traditional view of "insight".

Mental Illness: Since Glasser does not accept the medical interpretation of "mental illness", Reality Therapy deals with the client as a person who may be able to gain better control over his life. We do not set out to help the client feel better by helping him feel less pain; we aim at helping him feel better by removing the cause of the pain as much as possible and replacing it with greater satisfaction in his life.

Crazy behaviour will be, as the name suggests, crazy, that is, it will be irrational. We expect it to be so and in Reality Therapy it would

---

[64] Glasser, William. *Choice Theory*. New York: Harper Collins, 1998.

be rare to seek some profound logic in the psychotic behaviour of a client or to spend very long discussing psychotic behaviours. These we interpret as the client's best creative attempts to deal with some serious frustrations in his life and we believe it is better to spend time identifying and addressing these frustrations.

Feelings: Reality Therapy gives great importance to feelings but not in the same way as most other therapies. We see feelings as vital signals of how well a person's life is running. We also see them as part of total behaviour and we aim at helping the client change his total behaviour.

Teaching: Another striking characteristic of Reality Therapy is its belief in teaching during counselling. Glasser recommends teaching clients about Choice Theory where this is possible and appropriate. This can give a person the psychological tools to grow and to deal with further problems in his life.

Teaching can extend to helping a client learn new social skills, studying the details, rehearsing the approaches. Glasser goes beyond a view of therapy as helping people remedy the scars of the past; he aims to help clients achieve mental health and happiness. It is important to clarify that Glasser does not teach Choice Theory in some academic way to his clients. Rather he helps them see the control they have over their own lives. It is the application of Choice Theory that he teaches.

The Process: Because of its strong theoretical base Reality Therapy tends to be associated with a more pro-active involvement by the counsellor. The RT counsellor will ask more questions than some other therapies. Since Choice Theory emphasises the individual's ultimate control of his life, the therapist too can become more aware of just what part of the counselling he himself controls. The counsellor's role is to manage what goes on in counselling, facilitating the client's own self-awareness, self-evaluation and planning.

Reality Therapy is very much non-directive with regard to the client's life but the RT therapist has a strong sense of structure and direction within the counselling process. This is one feature of Reality Therapy that is very much appreciated by those who are new to it.

Pacing: Partly because time is not used up in exploring the past or in listening to excuses and partly due to the structure inherent in Reality Therapy it does tend to be quite swift. The focus on the client's responsibility plays a role too.

During a Reality Therapy counselling session, the counsellor should be able to tell you what he or she is doing at any given moment. At this point I want to delve deeper into this structure.

Choice: The Focus of Reality Therapy

The Basic Needs and the pictures we use to meet these may be like road-maps to our behaviours but all these important dynamics come together at one point, not unlike the steering wheel in our cars. This is the point of decision and action, the location of choice. I keep going straight because all is well or I adjust my steering to keep me going in the direction I want to go. It is similar with the way I control my behaviour. I choose to keep it the same or to adjust it as necessary in order to keep my needs satisfied.

I believe that it is this point of "steerage" that is the main focus of the practice of Reality Therapy. An exploration of the client's Quality World does help us understand the road-maps he is currently using. Knowing about the basic needs explains why he is making the journey at all. Ultimately, however, we want to help him steer in the direction he really wants to go.

Specifically, we help him fine-tune his steering (his choices) in relation to the major deviation in direction that has brought him to seek counselling. Glasser and control theorists before him likened this to the work of a thermostat or servo-mechanism that adjusts continuously to achieve a pre-determined goal. The person chooses pictures and their corresponding behaviours in an attempt to satisfy frustrated needs or to keep satisfied needs in that state. What the RT counsellor does is attempt to understand the client's present choices, to see what underlies these and then to help the client plan new choices.

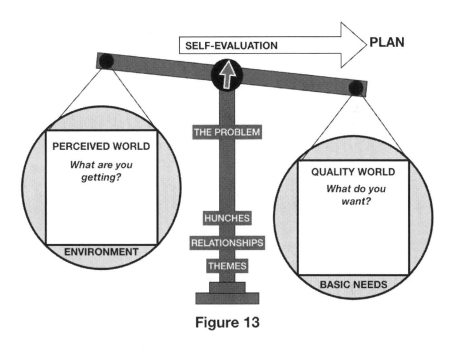

Figure 13

Figure 13 sums up this and is based directly on the "Chart of the Brain" that Glasser uses to explain how our minds work.

On the right-hand side of the balance is the client's Quality World made up of all his wants. On the left-hand side is what he observes himself to be getting. If there is no match between these two sets of perceptions, what he wants and what he gets, the scales are in imbalance and signals for action are sent to him.

As the counsellor works with a client, she will move through different sections of this diagram though not necessarily in any set sequence.

If I were to choose one special memory aid to guide me through the processes of Reality Therapy counselling, it would be this simple chart, the scale diagram (Figure 13) and it is for this reason that I repeat it many times throughout these pages.

Counselling is not a linear process that can be summed up in a series of steps. Rather it is a matter of moving around different areas of the client's inner world sometimes focusing on improving the involvement relationship, sometimes exploring the current perceptions and at other times probing the person's quality world pictures.

Guided by Choice Theory, the counsellor will explore different themes and often retrace steps to check on previously visited issues. When helping people train in Reality Therapy I like to ask them what they have explored on the scales chart, where they are currently working and where they might go to next. Indeed, Choice Theory provides a good sense of structure to the counselling process.

Dr. Robert Wubbolding, a leading exponent of Reality Therapy, uses the mnemonic WDEP to remind counsellors to explore Wants, Direction, Evaluation and Plan[65]. Counselling is a complex activity and memory aids can help greatly in the training process.

Although the counselling itself may appear just like a freely-flowing conversation to the client or to an observer, the experienced Reality Therapy counsellor is following a clear mental map. The main objective will be to seek out the major needs imbalance in the client's life and then help the client evaluate the situation. This imbalance will be found in some of the key relationships of the

---

[65] www.realitytherapywub.com/index.php/wdep-system

client's life. The counsellor's exploration of this will not normally be a simple series of steps but rather a journey around the components of the scales diagram (Figure 13), gradually building up a clearer picture of the client's life especially in the problem area.

Sometimes clients can identify their problems very well but more often than not the counsellor will need to sift through several themes in the client's life looking for the problem. At different points the counsellor will have hunches about what is going on in the client's life. On the one hand hunches are not to be seen as anything more than hunches and, on the other, they do tend to guide our exploration of the client's story.

In this book we will use counselling excerpts to illustrate different aspects of Reality Therapy. None of these dialogues are taken from real cases and similarities to any real persons are purely coincidental. At the same time the extracts are intended to reflect conversations that are typical of the counselling process.

Conor, in his early thirties and with a healthy even prosperous appearance, is not sure why he has come to counselling. Everything seems fine in his life and the recent birth of twins has brought a lot of joy to his family.

The counsellor checks out the themes that she would expect in his life: work (including ambitions), family, leisure time, health. Initially she is working with the behaviours that Conor presents as his problem story.

The counsellor notes that things seemed brighter for Conor before the birth of the twins and so she probes more deeply into the family theme.

1	Counsellor:	What changed with the birth of the twins?
2	Conor:	Well, you know, the usual upheavals in a family. I suppose you could say the babies' bodily functions take over our lives. It was a bit different with the twins of course. When one woke up she woke the other ... like a chain reaction! Brenda, my wife, has coped very well and we do share the chores as much as possible.
3	Counsellor:	In what other ways did this differ from the birth of your other child Thomas?
4	Conor:	Well, Thomas was the first and he wasn't a twin. Once we got over the initial few weeks we seemed to have more time to talk about him and how we were dealing with him ... and other things.
5	Counsellor:	... other things? (She had noticed a slight change in Conor's voice as he added this phrase, sometimes a sign that the client is touching a sensitive issue, an important theme.)
6	Conor:	Oh, I don't know, it's not important really. We can't expect to have things too easy with both the twins and Thomas to look after.

7	Counsellor:	That's true … but there was something you could do even when Thomas was younger, something that is not so easy now …
8	Conor:	Well, yes. We just shared more. We were a couple, a couple with a child but a couple. It doesn't seem like that now. It's as if we aren't a couple any more.

The counsellor probed further to find that Conor and Brenda had always shared a deep personal intimacy, something they have not had time to experience since the family got bigger. His love and belonging needs were not fully satisfied and it was this drifting apart that was at the heart of his unhappiness. The counsellor might explore several other themes before returning to focus on this one.

It becomes apparent to the counsellor that in Conor's Quality World Brenda and he would share more time together as a couple. Part of the counselling will be seeking clarification of just what that would look like to Conor.

The Quality World serves the needs and it is clear that the love and belonging need is running low for Conor. He and Brenda used to talk about each day's events, dwell on their joys and sorrows, discuss forthcoming events and generally share the whole process of living.

On the other side of the scales, in Conor's perceived world, there is a lot of family life but not the component he so badly misses, his greater intimacy with Brenda. Indeed, in recent times she had become increasingly irritable and it now dawns on Conor that the reason may be that she too misses this other aspect of their lives.

The counsellor also explores what is happening to Conor (the "environment" circle in the scales diagram) but pays particular attention to what Conor himself is actually doing. He had been criticising Brenda's irritable episodes and now sees that this was not helping.

Now both Conor and his counsellor have a clearer view of what is really going on in the scales (Figure 14), why they are out of balance. Because the counsellor has asked Conor about his own behaviour the client is beginning to see how much was and is in his own control.

Then the counsellor asks simply, "Is it time to look at other ways of dealing with this?" This is a central question in the process. This question is really asking "Is what you are doing getting you what you want?" Only the client can make this self-evaluation and can only do so when both sides of the scales are clear to him. The client clarifies what he wants and what he is currently doing about it before being able to answer the question, "Is what you are doing getting you what you want?" The counsellor in the example asks this in a different but equally valid way: "Is it time to look at other ways of dealing with this?"

Conor nodded slowly and repeatedly. Yes, it was time. Hopefully it was not too late. Yes, the deep anguish he had experienced went well beyond the words he had spoken so far. At this point the counsellor chose to be silent, to share with Conor these moments of new awareness.

Then the counselling session concluded with a surprisingly brief few moments of planning where Conor explained how he could avail of an offer of baby-sitting from his sister to allow himself and Brenda to go out for a short drive together on Saturday afternoon. Stopping at a local beauty spot for twenty minutes would be a luxury they had not shared for several months. It was where they had decided to marry and it would be very meaningful for both of them. Much as

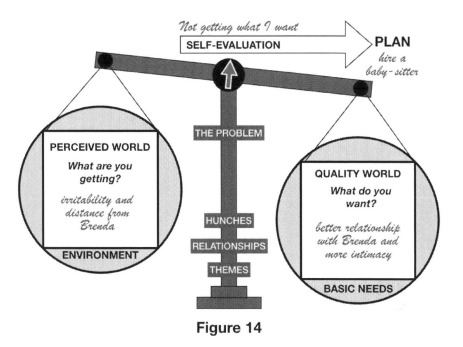

Figure 14

they loved their children it was time to charge their own dangerously low batteries and to trust a baby-sitter.

This single sample session contained most of the ingredients of Reality Therapy and in the following chapters we shall look at each of these in turn.

The Finger Tip Walk

This exercise for trainee counsellors aims to explore the fact that counselling is not about controlling the client. Indeed the client is the one who leads the way. The counsellor follows but, at the same time, does a certain amount of guiding. It is a very gentle process.

The participants divide into pairs and one person opts to be the first "client". She extends each one of the fingers of one hand and the "counsellor" does likewise touching the tips of the client's fingers with his own. On an agreed signal the "client" closes her eyes and the "counsellor" aims to guide her around obstacles (such as chairs, table, carpets) in the room. The important rule is that they must not lose contact and must not talk.

Later the pair may reverse roles and repeat the experience.

Finally they discuss:

- In what ways is this similar to counselling?
- What aspects of counselling correspond to the guiding behaviour of the "counsellor"?
- What other ideas about counselling are suggested by the exercise?

Counselling Friends

This raises the important issue of the advisability of counselling friends. Is it possible or advisable? There is not a simple answer to this but I do not think it should be an automatic negative. Where direct advice or criticism is concerned this is not counselling as we understand it in this book and any form of "telling" another person what to do or not to do is rarely part of counselling. Genuine counselling with a friend is possible but is somewhat more challenging than with a stranger. Here are some ideas but they are not hard and fast rules.

- Make a definite choice: I am now going to counsel my friend.

- Ask the friend's permission to deal with the issue in a counselling framework. For example, "Mary, if you like I can try and deal with what you are saying as I would in counselling rather than just have a conversation about it."

- Distinguish a counselling session clearly from the ordinary chat of everyday life.

- Define time limits, for the benefit of both counsellor and friend so that both know when normal conversation can resume.

- To communicate clearly the counselling intent it can be helpful though not essential to adopt a slightly more business-like context than usual. For example, the counsellor might say, "How about sitting down at the table and seeing if we can sort this out together?" With strangers involvement means being less formal but with friends an increase in formality may be important.

There are some situations where it would probably be counter-productive to attempt to counsel a friend:

- Where third-parties are involved who are also friends. A typical case would be talk of marital separation of two friends. It may be very difficult to counsel one of the partners without alienating the other.

- If the friend is already being counselled by another person it makes good sense for the other person to know about your involvement.

- If the friend's problem involves serious ethical issues it may be better for him or her to discuss it with someone who can be more objective.

- When the problem involves the counsellor it is very difficult to be player and referee in the same game.

Friends in Need

When working as a counsellor normally clients are self-referred or have made a clear agreement to see you perhaps on the advice of others. What can you do when you believe that a friend needs counselling but you suspect that he might not be very receptive of the idea? Obviously I am referring to apparent problems where your friend has not sought your help. For example, you believe your friend is seriously over-weight and is continuing to lead a very unhealthy life-style. How can you intervene ... or should you?

When problems are smaller, people generally find it easier to intervene and for their actions to be well-received by the friend. In other situations the friend may already have received a lot of unsolicited help or advice from others and may not be so receptive.

The existence of such unsolicited advice from other quarters may provide you with a way to bring up the topic: "Harry, you must be fed up with so many people telling you what to eat!" If he seems to be receptive to your remarks then a brief expression of concern and offer of help might be possible. "To be honest I am concerned about you but I don't want to add to the hassle. If you want to talk sometime, count on me." It is really important to judge your friend's receptivity well. We are not talking about techniques here but a way to express genuine friendship always respecting the other person's right to accept or refuse interventions.

From Choice Theory we know that we cannot force someone else to seek counselling or even to consider our advice. We need to be extremely respectful of the other person's ownership of his own life. Even in this context we can express concern and offer to do what we can. We really cannot do much more than that in most cases. There is some chance that such a friend will take up the offer now or at a later date. If attempts to offer help are too enthusiastic the friend may shy away from help and maybe even from your friendship.

Obviously if someone is harming themselves or others or is threatening to do so we may decide to take very definite action to save them no matter what they say. That is an ethical decision on our own part.

REALITY THERAPY

Learning How To Counsel

In this chapter you will learn about:

- The characteristics required in a counsellor
- The possibility that some are "born counsellors"
- The use of professional titles
- The learning process focusing on what, how and where
- The integration of Choice Theory into the counsellor's life in general
- The SESIR approach to learning based on Choice Theory
- The use of Role-Play in the learning process
- Ways to improve role-play
- How to use this book in the learning process

Before going into the practical aspects of Reality Therapy it is worth pausing to reflect on the process of learning how to counsel. Today it is a skill that is very much on demand. Based on the age-old wisdom of two heads being better than one, counselling seems a sensible and non-threatening way to sort out problems. It also appears relatively easy to learn and does not require any specialist equipment or even a specific location.

The interest shown by many lay-people in attending counselling courses is a positive step forward. Hopefully, more and more of the helping professionals will add counselling to their range of skills.

I have no doubt that almost anyone can learn to improve their helping skills by reading books on counselling. However, no book can provide all that is needed to practise as a counsellor. Just as no book on carpentry can show you how hard to hit a nail, counselling books cannot teach tone of voice, body language, the pacing of a counselling session and it cannot give personal feedback to the counselling trainee.

Understanding Choice Theory and its implications for real counselling is not enough to enable the reader to begin Reality Therapy counselling with confidence and success. Becoming a counsellor requires a considerable range of personal characteristics as well as specific knowledge and skills:

Genuine interest in helping others to help themselves	Obviously professional counsellors may need to make a living out of their work but one of their primary motives for being a counsellor must be to help others.
Interpersonal skills	A counsellor needs to be able to listen to others, to be sensitive to them, to be able to communicate with ease in their language.
Knowledge of theory	The counsellor will base her work on a solid foundation of theory.
Knowledge of the role	To work as a counsellor means knowing how the role is defined in that work environment as well as the legal and ethical norms that apply to it.

| Personal maturity | Counselling relies on having experience of living responsibly and of being familiar with human problems. |
| Acquisition of counselling skills and experience | A range of particular skills stem from the application of Choice Theory itself. |

In this book we are concerned mainly with the theory and skills components and how to acquire them. The complexity of these skills and the importance of them all working together in an integrated way means that training to be a counsellor needs its own special strategy.

The Natural Counsellor

The idea that some people are "born counsellors" is not one I fully support. However, I agree that some people do display an apparently natural ability to help others in a counselling way. I believe this to be the happy outcome of earlier life experiences and of the way that person has learned how to deal with them. A child who has seen her parents approach problems in a balanced way, using more choice than blame and being respectful of others, is more likely to learn these coping skills than someone who only saw blaming, arguments or chaos.[66]   But even for the "natural counsellor" to continue to choose and improve such an approach it is necessary for him or her to attempt to understand the underlying principles of effective counselling.

What is important, I believe, is that all individuals, whatever their current level of skill, can improve their counselling skills and,

---

[66] Interesting insights into Glasser's own early training in mental well-being are shown in the video interview, "Glasser in his own words" made in August 2004 and available from William Glasser Inc..

moreover, that these are skills that are useful to all people, not simply those who become professional counsellors, therapists, psychologists, social workers or psychiatrists.

Professional Titles

In some countries, the terms "counsellor", "therapist" or "psychotherapist" are controlled by legislation so that a person must acquire specific qualifications and experience before being granted permission to use these titles. In this book I speak of counselling, therapy and psychotherapy as a means of helping others and I leave it to the reader to seek information elsewhere on local accreditation schemes.

The advisability of such schemes to safeguard the quality and ethical standards of professional counselling does not detract from the usefulness of counselling skills for everyone. Accreditation schemes should in fact not only protect but encourage quality counsellor preparation. They can only do this if they base their recognition on real counselling skills that are effective in helping others manage their lives. Ideally accrediting bodies would engage actively in researching the effectiveness of different counselling approaches and techniques. The requirement to have a certain minimum number of training hours is no substitute for an evaluation of the effectiveness of the counselling.

The Learning Process

Many of the basic principles of different forms of counselling can be learned in a relatively short space of time but it usually takes several years to integrate the skills adequately. Some basic skills can be learned and practised almost in a drill format but the counselling apprentice will need to go over the same ground again and again using a spiral approach. This means covering the same material over and over, each time in more detail and gradually integrating the skills into the individual's own style. Frequent repetition is one of the most basic rules of any learning.

An important part of this learning process is training the mind to think in a Choice Theory way. For this reason it is important for the instructor or supervisor to pay a lot of attention to the processes of Reality Therapy. When the instructor openly attends to these, the trainee counsellor also learns to attend to them. Related to this is the need to use the terminology as much as possible. Trainees often focus more on the content of the counselling and in processing their work will tell the story of the content. It is more important for them to focus on the processes they have used.

As with any complex skill, the learner cannot expect to assimilate all the components in a short space of time. It is important to be patient and to have realistic expectations about one's own progress.

As in almost all learning situations there are three main ingredients:

- Learning what to do
- Learning how to do it (Practice)
- Knowing where to get help

Learning what to do

Theory: Having the skill of driving a car without knowing where you are heading is not be very sensible. The trainee counsellor in Reality Therapy needs to know Choice Theory very well. It is the compass and road-map for Glasserian counselling. Here are some approaches that people have found useful in learning the theory.

• Read about it over again and again. The chapter on Choice Theory in this book is intended to serve as a regular revision tool but the primary source is Dr. Glasser's "Choice Theory". Reading it several times is essential.

- Every day, examine applications of the theory in your own life. "This morning I was cursing the constant rain for making my life miserable and then I remembered that I could do something about it. My partner and I went off to the theatre for the evening ... and forgot about the rain!"

- Discuss the theory with others. The more views of the theory you get, the better you will assimilate it yourself.

Therapy: Know what specific approaches are used in Reality Therapy and how they relate to Choice Theory.

- Read books, chapters or articles about the strategies used in Reality Therapy. Particularly important is "Counseling with Choice Theory: The New Reality Therapy"[67] by William Glasser. Other good source texts are those by faculty members of the William Glasser Institute: Dr. Robert Wubbolding[68], Dr. Larry Palmatier[69] and John Brickell[70].

- Observe role-plays of Reality Therapy. Videos[71] of Dr Glasser are ideal for this since he has integrated the theory and practice so well. The advantage of a recording is that it can be played over and over again. The advantage of a live role-play, on the other hand, is that the counsellor can be questioned about what he is doing.

- Watch role-play videos with several other people and share your observations.

- Discuss how the theory guides the practice of Reality Therapy.

---

[67] This was released originally in hard-back as "Reality Therapy in Action" in 2000.

[68] Wubbolding, Robert. *Using Reality Therapy*. New York: Harper and Row, 1986.

[69] Palmatier, Larry L. *Crisis Counseling for a Quality School Community*. Washington D.C.: Accelerated Development. 1998

[70] Brickell, John and Robert E. Wubbolding. *Counselling With Reality Therapy*. Oxon: Winslow Press, 1999

[71] Video recordings are available from https://wglasserbooks.com/videos/

- Always try to use as much Choice Theory terminology as possible in your analyses of role-plays or cases. This is very important since ultimately you are trying to learn the "inner logic" of the Reality Therapy approach.

Learning how to do it (practice)

- Use role-play but start with a simple conversation with another counselling student.

- Progress to short role-play practice (5-10 minutes) of how to initiate counselling, focusing exclusively on "involvement".

- Repeat the same scenarios several times until you feel comfortable with them.

- Having a skilled tutor is important. Such a tutor should have the ability to counsel and the ability to teach counselling.

- Trainees love to ask "What was I doing wrong?" but time is probably spent more usefully by asking "What can I do differently or better?" It is more accurate to talk of effective and more effective interventions rather than right and wrong[72] interventions.

- The skilled trainer will know how to help you learn new skills and improve those you have already without any criticism or blame. A Reality Therapy tutor will use self-evaluation not only in counselling but also in tutoring trainees.

- Other chapters in this book will outline how to learn individual Reality Therapy skills in a modular format but the final goal is to integrate these.

---

[72] In the English language as used in Europe and North America we tend to use the word "wrong" with many shades of meaning and here it refers to what is ineffective or inappropriate and certainly not to any form of moral judgement.

- As in the learning of any skill, first attempts will feel strange, maybe even stilted and artificial. Be patient with yourself and eventually these skills can become second-nature to you.

- People do not all learn at the same speed. It can be counter-productive to compare your progress with other people in your training group.

Knowing where to get help

- There is really no substitute for official Reality Therapy training where instructors and supervisors are helping trainees through a carefully planned process.

- Consultation with and supervision by a Reality Therapy faculty member.

- Networking with others in your locality who use Reality Therapy.

- Attendance at Reality Therapy Branch meetings (for members).

- Attendance at Reality Therapy conferences.[73]

- Participation in Reality Therapy Professional Development workshops and seminars.[74]

- Subscribe to the "International Journal for Reality Therapy".[75]

- Reality Therapy web-sites and discussion forums.

---

[73] There is an international conference every two years and several countries have their own annual conventions. There is also a European Reality Therapy Convention every four years.

[74] In Ireland every spring we have the "Richard Pulk Seminar" for those certified in Reality Therapy.

[75] Details on the Journal web-site www.journalofrealitytherapy.com

Practising What You Preach

Many forms of counselling training require their students to engage in on-going therapy. In Reality Therapy the requirement really goes beyond this. It is not simply a question of processing our own life situations but of internalising the very theory that forms the basis of our counselling. As already mentioned, Choice Theory goes beyond being a theory of counselling intervention. It is better described as a theory of psychology, an explanation of behaviour. It would be unthinkable to use this psychology in helping clients sort out their lives without using this same psychology ourselves.

Consequently it becomes a priority to apply Choice Theory to our own lives, to initiate a process of self-evaluation using the tenets of this theory, to learn to become counsellors to ourselves. Formal Reality Therapy training requires journalling and similar ongoing processing of trainees' own lives using the Choice Theory model.

Choice Theory and Learning

Indeed, you can apply Choice Theory to the learning process itself, to the way you incorporate the ideas from this book into your life. In the first place Choice Theory teaches us that we only learn if and when we really want to. Nobody else can force us to learn something. All others can do is give us information. If then learning is my choice, it is also my responsibility.

Surrounding circumstances may make it harder for me to learn; I may not have a quiet place to study or I may not have a lot of available time. However, once I make the choice to learn something, my time is better spent in planning how to get around the obstacles rather than complaining and blaming.

Although Glasser's Choice Theory and Reality Therapy are both rich in ideas for everyday life, if you wish to become a counsellor then it is vital to work with other people. William Glasser International[76] provides formal training in Choice Theory and Reality Therapy and participation in this is certainly the best way to train in Reality Therapy.

Dr Glasser explains a procedure[77] that helps us to take responsibility for our own learning, and to evaluate our mastery of the material presented in a course. He uses the acronym "SESIR" to sum it up, the letters standing for Show, Explain, Self-evaluate, Improve and Repeat.

SESIR

Show — Show someone, who is interested, like a teacher, what we are doing. Do it carefully and completely so that this person can easily see that this is what we did.

Explain — If it is not obvious or there are questions, explain to that person how we achieved what we are showing him or her.

Self-evaluate — After we do this, we evaluate (self-evaluate) what we did to see if it could be improved.

Improve — Most of the time it is obvious that we could improve what we are doing so we continue working to try to improve it.

---

[76] See web-sites for information on courses: www.wglasserinternational.org, www.wgii.ie

[77] See Glasser, William. *The Quality School Teacher.* New View Publications, 1992.

Repeat We repeat the evaluation and improvement process, with or without help, until we believe that further attempts at improvement are not worth the effort. At this time, we believe we have done something that deserves to be called quality.

This provides a simple structure for working with a trainer or supervisor. Explaining what we are doing is quite an important part of the learning process. Many aspects of a counselling session could be interpreted by an outsider as a friendly or intimate chat. However, the deliberate process the counsellor is applying throughout makes it counselling. I believe it is very important for the trainee to explain his or her interventions in terms of the procedures used rather than to provide a verbatim or summary account of the client's story.

For example a trainee might comment on part of his counselling intervention: "When I asked the client to repeat what she had just said I was offering her a chance to reflect on her statement and perhaps make a self-evaluation at that point. That in fact is what she did but, had she not, I was planning to ask her directly about the effectiveness of her behaviour, was it helping her get what she wants. Now that she has said her chosen behaviours were not getting her what she wants I am going to ask her if she wants to consider alternatives."

Role-playing As An Aid To Learning

In Reality Therapy we use role-playing of counselling as a primary method of learning how to counsel. We do not regard it as ethically safe to use real counselling interventions (where clients play themselves) in front of a group and there are several reasons for this:

- The trainee may not be ready to deal with real clients even under supervision.

- Any client who is using her own life in a counselling situation is likely to reveal more about themselves than they originally expected.

- As role-plays often have observers a client may be disclosing personal details in a fairly public setting.

- If the counsellor detects an inappropriate level of self-disclosure in front of observers, she will probably want to end the session at that point or move the role-play away from the sensitive area. The end result is neither a good learning experience for the counsellor nor is it satisfactory counselling for the client.

As in any complex skill, components of the skill (e.g., self-evaluation) may be role-played separately but ultimately it is necessary to role-play the total counselling experience.

General Points about Role-Play

Clear Goals: The ultimate goal of counselling is to help clients improve the quality of their lives. The goal of your role-play is to practise the skills that help you achieve this ultimate goal.

Keep recalling the theory: This is what guides your practice and explains why you do what you do.

Observe quality: In the case of Reality Therapy it makes a lot of sense to watch and process as many role-plays by Dr. Glasser as possible. Watch other skilled counsellors also. Studying the recording of a role-play more than once can contribute greatly to a sense of the structure of the counselling. In formal learning schemes we tend to use a modular approach (as in this book). This is helpful but it can never convey the totality of the experience. Watching as many of Glasser's role-plays on video as possible and watching them as often as possible provides this vital "learning by osmosis" where we develop a sense for the overall dynamic of counselling. As I wrote earlier, frequent repetition is one of the most basic rules of any learning.

Have a Tutor: It is important to have someone who is skilled in Reality Therapy and who also has good teaching skills to watch your role-plays and process them with you. (In some counselling models this role is called a "supervisor" although the word does not fit comfortably into Choice Theory vocabulary.) In the later stages of your training (Advanced Practicum) it helps to have a supervisor who is familiar with your own specialist area of work.

Be ethical: Learning therapy through role-play avoids the ethical difficulties of practising on real clients but it is still important that the client stories you act out are well disguised by changing names and critical details. When you do eventually start to work with real clients, inform them of your trainee status and check that they accept you as a trainee.

Before the Role-play

Skill Focus: Before a particular role-play (or section of the role-play) it may help to target specific counselling skills to practise. For example: "I intend to find opportunities to explore the client's Quality World in the next five minutes".

Briefing: At the start of a real-life counselling session the counsellor would already know some facts about the client, for example, how the visit was arranged, approximate age and height of the client, apparent health. Before starting a role-play the "counsellor" should be told details like this and not simply details that relate to the problem. For example, "John, I'm going to role-play a girl of seventeen. You can call me Ann. This is my first time coming to

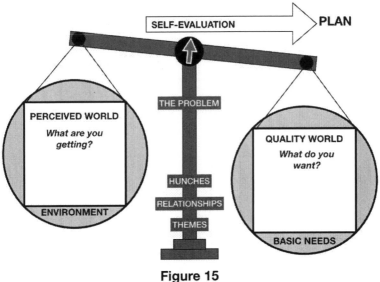

Figure 15

see you. As for my appearance, I look healthy but my clothing is a little conservative looking and I seem a little shy. That's all you would know about me. You are a counsellor in private practice and my father arranged the appointment."

Structure: Decide what names you will use and how you will sit. If there are observers the seating may be adjusted so that they can see the proceedings better.

During the Role-play

Stop and process: It is helpful to stop occasionally and take time-out to process the counselling. "What have I done so far?" "What is my strategy at this point?" If a role-play goes on too long the participants may forget important details. Even in real counselling pauses for reflection can be very important. I believe it is very beneficial for learning and for confidence levels for trainees to have and frequently to use this freedom to stop.

Constantly refer to the structures of Choice Theory Counselling: The scales diagram is useful in this context (Figure 15).

Self-evaluate: What have I done that is Reality Therapy? How is my level of involvement? Am I making progress in my counselling skills? Do I expect to display a high standard in everything all at once? Is what I am doing helping the client?

Getting "stuck": If a counsellor needs a constant reminder of his or her own human nature then getting stuck helps. Trainee counsellors very often see this as a sign of failure whereas it is a perfectly normal part of any counselling session. It may happen more often in training but, even with years of experience, there will always be pit-stops where the counsellor pauses and decides what to do next. Glasser himself recommends getting more information at such points. It is certainly not alien to the counselling process, whether practice or real, to say to the client "I need to think about this for a moment". In real counselling it may amount to making a professional consultation with someone else.

Consultation: Many counsellors are required by their employers to consult with others about their casework. Over and above such obligations the ethics of counselling would recommend consultation in dealing with sensitive issues. Furthermore, from a learning perspective, it makes sense to consult regularly with colleagues, superiors and instructors in a continual striving for improvement. It is important therefore to build consultation into role-play practice. When necessary in the role-play stop and consult with others.

Hunch evaluation: During the stops in role-play it is useful to make a one line summary of your current hunch about the client's situation. You do not necessarily share this with others. This is a guess because you only have a limited amount of information about the client. Indeed I believe it can never be more than a hunch since it is impossible to understand another human being fully.

Nevertheless, the hunch is important because it is a particular set of perceptions that guides what we do next in the counselling process.

Sometimes counselling authors warn against the dangers of making assumptions. But think about it; it is actually impossible not to make assumptions. We live our lives by them. (I assume the water I drink has not been poisoned, for example.) Rather than making a vane attempt to avoid all assumptions we need to learn how to use them wisely. When you have identified your current hunch, ask yourself, "What other hunches could I check out?"

Initially counselling is very much an open-ended process as the counsellor checks for the different themes in the client's story. To keep the counselling moving forward it is important to "tighten up" the process from time to time by using summary hunches.

In these pauses the trainee counsellor can ask "what am I going to do next?" In my experience these reflective pauses greatly enhance the training process and are very good for the trainee's confidence levels.

Multiple rehearsals, repetitions and fine tuning: Since the goal of role-play is to help the "counsellor" develop, then it makes sense sometimes to do all or part of a role-play again. This may have the aim of consolidating an approach you have used or of trying out a different approach. Sometimes trainees get so caught up in the role-play they forget it is a learning process. It can be very useful to say, "Hold on a minute. I would like to wind back to where you mentioned your in-laws and try a different approach with you!"

After the Role-play

Focus on the process: It is natural to be curious about the case content asking questions such as "And what happened with the real case? How did it end?" However, it is more helpful to stay with the therapy process that the trainee counsellor applied to the client's story. This means inviting the "counsellor" to explain what he did in terms of Reality Therapy and Choice Theory.

Feedback: If the goal of counselling is to help the client then it is useful to check on the client's observations of the counselling process itself. You as the counsellor trainee can ask "What do you see me doing?", "Are we talking about what is really important for you?", "How could I have improved my counselling?"

Alternatives: In role-play you can ask the "client" to step out of role and, as a fellow-trainee, suggest alternative strategies you could use in dealing with this case. These are not necessarily better but simply other ways of working. You are asking your colleague "Can you help me improve and expand my skills?"

Seek Affirmation: Ask your "client" what he or she as a fellow trainee has learned from your own work so far.

Check the evidence: Is the client really making progress? Ask the client directly about this with questions such as: "Are you making progress?", "How do you feel now?", "What changes have you noticed in your life since we started counselling?".

No criticism! Time spent in talking about what the counsellor "should have done" is generally better spent in acknowledging the person's strengths and talking about alternative ideas.

No praise! Affirmation is more important than praise. Frequently trainees confuse self-evaluation with self-praise making comments such as "I think I did the involvement very well". It is more helpful to make comments that affirm what happened and to give details, for example, "When I was chatting about the weather I was trying to build up involvement by helping the client relax." Observers sometimes show the same confusion praising the trainee instead of inviting self-evaluations as in "What process were you working on when you chatted to the client about the weather?" In training, focus on the process. That is what you are striving to learn.

Using This Book

The remaining chapters in this section of the book focus on specific components of Reality Therapy practice. I believe it is useful to take one at a time, to understand it more fully and to practise it more or less in isolation from other aspects of counselling. I emphasise that the division into modules is for explanation and training purposes only and a full counselling session should not be divided in this way. Neither is the chapter order to be taken as a reflection of the chronological order of counselling practice as this is simply not predictable. Counselling is not a linear process but a myriad of countless spirals and circles gradually narrowing in the direction of change in the client's life.

One way to use these chapters is to aim to gain confidence in each "module" so that its ideas and skills will be available to you when you start to do full session role-plays. If planning for success is a good idea, as we shall see later, then planning to learn one thing at a time makes a lot of sense. A final chapter in this section will propose ways to bring all the skills together.

How long should a role-play last? In the case of the modules, five to ten minutes is generally enough for any one situation. What is more important is to practise as many different examples as possible. In this way the trainee learns to distinguish process from content and gets better and better at using the process.

One learning technique that I would recommend is to go over the same thing again and again. That seems obvious but I would emphasise the word "same". We have all learnt the words of many songs simply because we have heard them in exactly the same format over and over. If I want to learn the process of Reality

Therapy then it makes sense to understand the process and then keep referring to that **same understanding** as you practise it in the early stages.

My way of facilitating this is to use the scales diagram (Figure 16) based on the key sections of Glasser's "chart of the brain". Throughout the book I keep referring to this same graphic and recommend the trainee counsellor to do likewise. For me this relatively simple illustration represents all the key ingredients that feed into an individual's moment of choice. By using this chart we are acknowledging the central position of choice in Reality Therapy.

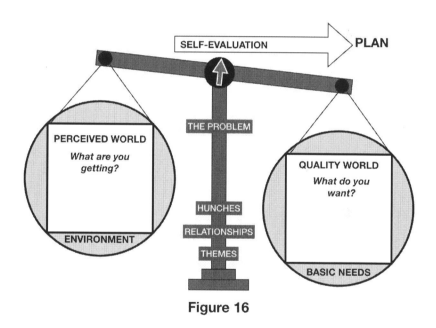

Figure 16

Keep asking yourself, "where am I working right now?", "what do I know about each section of this diagram?". In fact it can be a useful exercise in itself just after a role-play to pencil in your observations of the counselling process in the relevant sections of a clean copy of the diagram.

Choice of "Clients" for Role-play

Early role-play practice is best done with fellow-trainees. One person plays the part of the client while the other practises the skills of a Reality Therapy counsellor.

- The "client" should not play himself. This is important. Even when role-playing another person it is easy to lapse into self-disclosure. This can create problems for both the client and the trainee counsellor since it can move into material beyond the competency and experience of the trainee or observers.

- The role the "client" plays should be real, based on a real client or a composite of real clients whose story is known reasonably well to the role-player. Totally fictional "clients" can be useful for listening exercises but lack the themes and logic of real lives.

- In no way should anybody's confidentiality be jeopardised. Changing key facts, merging a few stories together and adding some fictional components can help improve this protection. Details taken from real life should be heavily disguised while retaining the core structure of at least one problem issue.

- The focus of the role-play is on helping the trainee counsellor improve his or her skills. The focus is not on solving a real problem. (Role-play can indeed be used very effectively for the purpose of exploring real cases by experienced counsellors but that is not its purpose here. It is easy for trainees to get distracted by discussions of what "really happened" and lose sight of the training emphasis.)

- Before beginning a role-play session, the "client" briefs the "counsellor" about information the "counsellor" would already know at the outset.

1. Is this a first session?

2. How did the referral take place?

3. What official capacity has the "counsellor" (e.g. a parole officer)?

4. What age and sex is the client and what name does he or she wish to use?

5. Are there observable details a counsellor might see sitting in front of the real client?

• No matter which format the role-play takes, the focus should be on the trainee counsellor. Hence the self-evaluation of the trainee is much more important than any external evaluation or feedback. Learning the skills of Reality Therapy means learning to think in a Reality Therapy way. Observers or even the "client" can invite the "counsellor" to describe what Reality Therapy procedures he or she was using.

• Describing the counsellor/client interaction in terms of Choice Theory is more important than simply repeating the dialogue.

Types of Role-play

A Reality Therapy instructor would normally progress from simple demonstration role-plays to short trainee involvement in a Round Robin or Fish Bowl mode. Later, as the trainees gain in knowledge and confidence, the practice would move to diads or triads and the sessions would gradually get longer and more complex.

All of the following formats can be enhanced through appropriate use of video-recording as this can facilitate more detailed self-evaluation and discussion.

DIADS

Two people are involved, one playing the counsellor and the other the client. Later they can reverse roles. After a pre-set period of role-play the "counsellor" self-evaluates her own work and can seek opinions and ideas from her colleague.

ADVANTAGES	DISADVANTAGES
Because only two are involved, each individual gets a lot more time to practise and to process what has been done.	The absence of a skilled trainer can be a drawback ... although it is possible for such a person to play the "client".
This can be a useful model when two trainees want to get extra practice.	
Each gets the chance to experience the client's view.	

TRIADS

Three people are involved and the third person acts as an observer. After the role-play, the "counsellor" self-evaluates and then may seek extra ideas from both observer and "client". Later the roles can rotate so that after three role-plays everyone has had "counsellor" practice.

ADVANTAGES

The observer has a useful external vantage point to study the role-play.

The observer is well-placed to act as facilitator, pausing the role-play where necessary to focus on a particular aspect of it.

Each can experience all three roles in turn.

DISADVANTAGES

The observer's role can very easily dominate the proceedings.

FISH BOWL

Two individuals role-play counsellor and client. Other members of the trainee group sit around, preferably in a circle or semi-circle, to observe the counselling and later discuss it.

ADVANTAGES

The observing trainees have a good opportunity to view an entire counselling role-play and share views on it with others.

The learning can be enhanced if each observer is asked to focus on a particular aspect of the process (e.g., involvement, self-evaluation, planning, body-language).

DISADVANTAGES

Fewer people get the chance to be the "counsellor".

The less active participation of observers makes this an unsuitable exercise when the trainees are tired.

ROUND ROBIN

One person plays the part of the client and all the others, sitting around in a semi-circle, take turns to act as counsellor. After the role-play the normal self-evaluations and discussions can take place.

ADVANTAGES	DISADVANTAGES
When the "client" is played by a skilled trainer, it becomes possible for the "client" to control and pace the role-play to everyone's advantage.	It can be difficult at times to know when one "counsellor" should hand over to another.
The "client's" statements can be selected to allow an individual "counsellor" to practice a specific skill.	
All the trainees are both observers and participants and this keeps the energy level quite high.	

Although the different formats are listed in order of approximate complexity, in the context of training it can be helpful to begin with a demonstration in fish bowl format followed by a round robin where each can get a little practice without taking on too much at first.

Training Evaluation

After a session practising Reality Therapy it is useful to evaluate the experience. Here are some questions that could be used at the end of a training day or session:

1. What I found particularly helpful or interesting today was:
2. What I would like to hear/learn more about would be:
3. My own evaluation of my own learning:
4. Skills I want to develop further are:
5. How I can improve the quality of my own learning:
6. Additional comments:

Counselling for All

The wish to help another human being is not limited to the caring professions and neither should the skill of counselling. Parents, managers, youth workers, shop-keepers, tour guides and practically everyone will find counselling useful in their dealings with other people. Outside of formal training courses the most accessible resources for people interested in counselling tend to be: reading, discussion, watching video recordings of Glasser and then practice using the diad model.

For example, a parent wants to be more helpful to her son who seems to be going through a bad time. She and her spouse could read "Unhappy Teenagers". (Other useful reading would be "Choice Theory", "Reality Therapy in Action" and "The Language of Choice

Theory".) Together they could discuss the contents of the book and self-evaluate their current ways of dealing with their son. What do they do to encourage a good relationship ("involvement") with him? Are there ways they can encourage their son to make self-evaluations instead of trying to tell him what he has done "wrong"? How many of the seven deadly habits do they use and what can they do that is different?

Rehearsing some of their new approaches together will help them gain confidence and check out possible weaknesses.

By the way, the son may get quite suspicious when their parents start behaving in "strange" ways! Counselling requires honesty and it can be a simple matter to tell the boy that yes, they care about him and have decided to try to relate to him in a better way.

The Client's Themes

In this chapter you will learn about:

- Explanations of why a client may not be able to talk about his or her problem
- The importance and frustrations of "fishing" in the early stages of information gathering
- The value of pausing in the counselling process to summarise hunches
- Techniques for identifying important themes
- The Choice Theory approach to psychosis ("crazy themes")

In an earlier chapter we saw that Reality Therapy defined clients' "problems" in terms of need-frustration. Identification of the specific frustration that is at the root of the client's unhappiness is a very important transition point in counselling but this is not always easy. Several factors can make things difficult for the counsellor:

- The client might not know what the problem is.

- Even when the client appears to know what the problem is, there may be aspects the client is not aware of.

- There may be so many apparent problems that it is hard to know where to begin.

- What appears to be an important problem may distract from what is the core problem.

- Rather than having just one or a small number of important problems the client's difficulty may be that almost everything is just a little out of control.

- Inexperienced counsellors sometimes focus so much on their method that they forget that counselling is about the client's problems.

The counsellor will seek out the discrepancies that exist in the client's life between what she ultimately needs and what in fact she is experiencing. The counsellor will explore this mainly through the client's wants ("Quality World") and how she perceives these wants to be fulfilled. In particular the Reality Therapy counsellor will focus on the main relationships in the client's world since it is here that most problems reside.

The Vitamin X Phenomenon

Often and especially with younger clients, they simply do not know what the problem is. I explain this by comparing the situation to that of vitamin deficiency. Let's suppose there is a newly identified vitamin called "X". Do you yourself get enough vitamin X everyday? How would you know if you had a vitamin X deficiency? You probably don't. But one day you go to the doctor and in a routine blood test the results show that you are seriously lacking in vitamin X. After a few weeks taking the prescribed dosage you notice certain very positive changes in your overall health. From this time on you now know what vitamin X does. From now on you will be more aware of any deficiency in your vitamin X intake. Before you had developed this awareness you could have felt unwell and not have known the cause nor how to remedy the situation. Now you have the awareness and the remedy!

Returning to psychology, there are people whose early life was almost totally devoid of love. They do not even know what it is like to be loved and so do not know why their life is not going well for them. They will not volunteer this love-deficiency information to you because they are not aware of what they have never had.

As Glasser says, the basic needs are genetic in origin and so this love-starved person will still have that need and will behave in ways that attempt to satisfy that need. This is not unlike the urges that mothers-to-be often get. The strange compulsion to chew a piece of chalk may surprise the lay-person and even the mother-to-be herself but the medic knows that the lady's physiology is transmitting calcium-shortage signals.

In all cases the counsellor needs to develop the "counsellor's eye", the ability to spot the important issues in the client's life and pinpoint the precise nature of the unhappiness. The counsellor needs to know about all the psychological equivalents of "vitamin X". In Reality Therapy we use our understanding of Choice Theory to guide our investigation of the client's life. More specifically the Basic Needs, the Quality World and the Perceived World give us a framework with which to examine the client's frustrations. For this reason Reality Therapy tends to be quite pro-active in its approach. We will help the client by asking questions based on the structures of Choice Theory.

Initial Information Gathering

For example, from the first moments of counselling we will be trying to form an idea of just how well the client is meeting each of the basic needs. We will be assembling an image of the client's Quality World, of its major pictures and, in particular, of those that are not turning out as planned. Based on the client's own details and on our observations we will be forming hunches about what the core problem is. We sift through the themes that emerge to find the central problem theme that has resulted in the client seeking counselling.

In the diagram (Figure 17) we first presented in the chapter on the dynamics of counselling, themes are represented at the bottom. When we begin to explore them we do not normally know very much about the other details represented in the diagram. In fact we cannot flesh them out very much until we have identified the critical themes in this person's life.

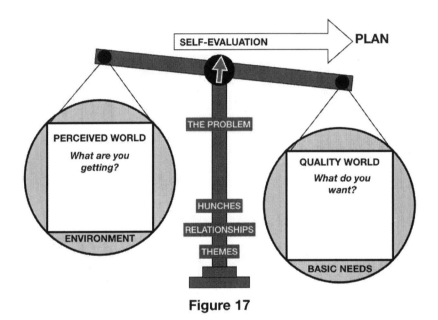

Figure 17

This will involve a certain amount of "fishing", exploring a selection of themes and gradually focusing on the critical issues. Some describe this as "hunting wide and fishing deep". Some themes will turn out to be cul-de-sacs, others may be important but not central to the client's current state. To check out a theme it will usually be necessary to probe some of the Quality World pictures associated with it and both the current experience and behaviour of the client regarding it. Eventually the counsellor's aim is to locate the critical theme (or themes) and then explore in greater detail the Quality World and behavioural aspects of it.

Each theme could be examined in terms of how the client wants it to be and how he perceives it at the moment. In other words, the scales diagram could be applied to each of them. (See Figure 18)

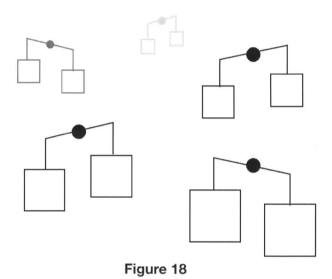

Figure 18

It would be easy for the counsellor to say, "Ah, I have found a problem theme here. Let's look at the Quality World pictures the client has for it" ... and so on. However, if this is not the central frustration that has urged the person to seek counselling, working on it may not be appreciated by the client. So the counsellor will pay particular attention to the major themes.

There may in fact be secondary issues that require attention before the central problems can be addressed. For example, a client who is seriously weakened by loss of sleep, poor nourishment or the effects of drugs may require this to be sorted out before becoming capable of dealing with the main problem.

The inexperienced counsellor will often find the initial stages of therapy quite frustrating and can very easily but mistakenly attribute this to his or her own inexperience. All counsellors, no matter how expert, begin from a zero point where they know practically nothing about the client. They then begin to collect information some of which may be relevant and some may not.

I like to demonstrate this important point by showing a video of Glasser in role-play. I stop the tape after about five minutes and ask the viewers what Glasser knows about the client at this stage. At best he may have one or two hunches but usually he is still fishing around looking for the central issues. More often than not the trainees are able to say, "At this point, Dr. Glasser knows nothing!" and suddenly knowing nothing doesn't seem so bad after all. In his book "Counseling with Choice Theory: The New Reality Therapy" where he comments on his own thinking during counselling sessions he shows how he often changes gear and direction when working with a client.

Counselling cannot be successful without this investigative phase. With experience the therapist frustrates less about this early searching and does indeed become more expert at it as he or she gets better at generating useful hunches.

Theme Processing

A favourite technique of mine is to pause frequently during counselling and ask myself "What is the problem?" A lot of the time my answer is, "I don't know … yet!" Liam Hudson writes about "divergent" and "convergent" thinking.[78] Divergent thinking is exploratory and open to new ideas whereas convergent thinking seeks to tie up things nicely and reach conclusions. Part of the counselling process is necessarily divergent, going out beyond the

---

[78] Liam Hudson. *Contrary Imaginations*. London: Penguin 1966.

present moment and the presenting problem, exploring the full canvas of the client's life. However, if the counselling cannot converge at some point, bringing all the information together to deal with the problem, it will be difficult to help the client choose constructive changes in his life.

George Kelly explains similar processes writing about his theory of Personal Constructs.[79] He talks about "loosening" constructs and "tightening" constructs (including a witty reference to people who suffer from "a hardening of the constructs"). Most learning experiences, and counselling is no exception, move from an initial "tight" position through a loosening process and then back to a tight conclusion. During the looser exploratory phases it is important to have periodic reviews of progress, moments of converging. This is the time to ask "What is the problem?" and to reflect on what I know as counsellor about the different areas of the chart. Crucial to success here is to identify the themes that we have found so far and to estimate their importance to the client.

The type of questions we use can help pinpoint important themes and here are some examples:

- General questions guided by the Basic Needs. Enquiring about how the person spends free time or week-ends may provide useful information about how well she meets fun, friendship and freedom needs, for example.
- Explore the meanings of words. If a client refers to several people as "fools" it can be important to seek clarification about what the word implies specifically for this client.
- Asking about when the person was last happy and then getting specifics about this. Comparing and contrasting that time with the present can point to the problem areas.

---

[79] Kelly, George. *The Psychology of Personal Constructs* (2 vols). New York: Norton, 1955.

- Asking about recent changes in the client's life especially around the time the client's unhappiness began.

- Use a third-party approach by asking "What do your friends (relatives) think the problem is?"

- Enquire about recurring dreams or nightmares and ask the client if these give any clues. Dreams have an uncanny way of illustrating a critical theme in an unfamiliar context.

- Ask how the situation could get worse. The answer can indicate the scale by which the person is currently evaluating his or her life.

- Guess what the problem might be given all you already know and observe about the client and ask him to comment. I might say to a client: "You keep saying that your main problem is your weight but from different things you have said I sense that, for you, "fat" means "no friends". What do you think?"

Good observation of the client's total behaviour during counselling can help us detect the themes. For example …

  - Changes in tone or volume of voice
  - Moments of silence
  - Tears
  - Signs of nervousness
  - Changes in eye-contact
  - Repetition of words, phrases, themes
  - Delays in answering a question
  - Strong denials

There are some more specific techniques that can be useful:

- Problem check-lists: The client reads through a list of problems that are typical for his age-group and ticks or rates these. An advantage of this is that a wide range of issues can be covered quickly. However, if the client is not aware of the problem area or finds it too big to deal with she might not rate it as a problem at all. Another disadvantage is that the client's difficulties may not be represented in the check-list. Sometimes too the problem is represented by only one item in the checklist and the significance of this can be overlooked by those more accustomed to other psychometric instruments. An extra angle, made possible by the computer, is to time the response-delay to each of the items as a way of detecting themes that are not apparent in the actual ratings.[80]

- Unfinished sentence exercises: Here clients are provided with a set of phrases, each representing the beginning of a sentence. They may complete the sentence in any way they wish. An example of such a ready-made instrument is The Rotter Incomplete Sentence Blank[81]. The opening phrases may be prepared by the counsellor herself, choosing the items to probe specific aspects of the client's world.

- Problem mapping: Invite the client to draw shapes on a piece of paper, each shape representing a problem in his life with the size of the shape in proportion to the size of the problem.

- Role-play: If, for example, a client has a problem with a colleague at work, asking the client to re-enact a recent flash-point situation with this colleague can be very helpful. The client acts as himself and as the colleague (using two chairs can help clarify the roles). From a Reality Therapy perspective such an activity helps clarify the all important details of the problem, the tone of voice, facial gestures, the totality of the interaction.

In Reality Therapy the counsellor can borrow ideas from many other therapies and all counsellors will have their own favourite styles. It is worth noting that the founder of Reality Therapy himself rarely uses anything other than straight conversation with the client. This

---

[80] See the author's "Problem Analysis Test", a computerised problem check-list.

[81] Published by The Psychological Corporation, USA.

does not exclude the use of a range of techniques and psychometric instruments in Reality Therapy counselling since most counsellors would not have the remarkable perception and experience of Dr Glasser.

Dealing With Crazy Themes

Glasser has always preferred the term "crazy" to the multitude of apparently technical terms generated by volumes such as the "DSM4" . Whether a person decides to stop eating, avoid all the cracks in the pavement, remain in the same posture all day, all of these are typical of what we call "crazy behaviour". Glasser teaches that people choose such behaviours from their creative system when their standard system of organised behaviours cannot solve whatever problem they find in their lives.

This is not unlike a person thumping the table in anger. It does not address the cause of the anger nor solve the problem although it might have some short-term effects such as getting attention or communicating the strength of the person's frustration. Thumping the table certainly does not restore bank balances or fix broken hearts. If I were this person's counsellor I would not spend time asking for further details about how he thumped the table, where he learned to thump, how he deals with the pain of the thump or the likes.

Instead, with my Choice Theory cap firmly in place, I would be interested in the real frustration that lay behind this crazy act. If he himself were not too clear about these I would be using the needs as my guide to exploring his life. In Reality Therapy that is how we deal with crazy themes; we search out the real themes behind them. There is no point in discussing the slimming intentions of the anorexic nervosa, the germ-threat for the compulsive hand-washer nor the theology of prayer with the obsessional church attender. These are creative crazy (=irrational) behaviours chosen in desperation by the person to solve a problem they simply don't know how to solve.

One obvious area of caution is where the person's behaviour poses a possible threat to someone, even the client himself.   In such a case it is essential to check out the level of danger and take whatever action is necessary to diminish it.

With the exception of this potential for danger, crazy themes are not normally regarded as the central themes in Reality Therapy.   To focus on the craziness would be like worrying only about the loudness of the fire alarm and ignoring the fire.   Studying the alarm does not extinguish the fire.   The alarm is important as a signal but the real problem is the fire.

Furthermore, taking some form of medication or other treatment that prevents us hearing the alarm is hardly an ideal solution.   In Reality Therapy the counsellor will see the crazy behaviour as a creative attempt to fix a major frustration and will then seek to identify the frustration itself so as to address it directly.

Theme Analysis

Choice Theory and Reality Therapy provide good structures for helping clients get information about a client's life, clarify his Quality Worlds, self-evaluate his current position and, where necessary, prepare successful plans for change. The purpose of this "Theme Analysis" tool is to provide a way for a trainee counsellor to self-evaluate their own counselling process or that of another counsellor demonstrating Reality Therapy.

Doing a theme analysis of a role-play can help highlight certain aspects of counselling:

- that there are in fact different themes
- that some are more important than others
- the counsellor does not know the client's themes in advance
- exploration means scanning the themes for signs of what is most important in the client's life
- analysis helps distinguish between "scanning" themes and "probing" themes
- some themes will be "dead-ends", areas of little significance to the client
- the analysis helps focus on the process used by a counsellor
- it can demonstrate that two observer's perceptions of the same session can be different
- the analysis presented here gives a useful structure for summarising a case for learning and discussion purposes

Procedure

Across the top of a page (at least A4 or Letter size and preferably A3 using the space in "landscape" form) write down each of the main themes as they emerge in the session.

- Horizontal movement: As each new theme emerges, a short descriptive title is placed at the top of the page, moving horizontally across the page for each new theme. In the example analysis below the first theme is "Feeling low". Each main point on a theme analysis chart can be numbered to help recall the sequence.

- Vertical movement: when the counsellor delves deeper into a particular theme this is represented by vertical (downward) movement on the page. The "Girl-friend" theme in the example has more details in its vertical column because the counsellor did more exploration of this topic.

In practice this means that if you hear a new theme in the counselling session you add it as *an extra column to the right of previous entries*. If the counsellor is delving deeper into a theme you write the corresponding notes as *an extra row below the last entry for that theme*. Each new theme or new connection with a previous theme is numbered.

Sample Theme Analysis

This short extract from a counselling session has been put together to illustrate how we might use theme analysis to sum it up and then discuss it. See what themes you can identify in the script.

1	Eamon:	I'm not sure what's happening ... I'm just feeling very, very low.
2	Counsellor:	Why did you decide to come and see me?
3	Eamon:	Well, I just felt so tired all the time. I'm not sleeping well at all.
4	Counsellor:	How much sleep did you get last night?
5	Eamon:	Oh, I went to bed at ten and got up at eight but I just didn't sleep well in between; it was a restless sleep.
6	Counsellor:	Can you recall your thoughts at these times you were awake during the night?
7	Eamon:	Thoughts? ... mmmm ... just that I can't go on like this, not in an exam year ... I just can't.
8	Counsellor:	Exams?
9	Eamon:	Yes, I have my final exams at the end of the year.
10	Counsellor:	How well are you doing at your studies?
11	Eamon:	Not bad actually. Well I wasn't doing bad, that is to say. I'm generally a good student and have been keeping fairly well. But this lack of sleep will wreck all that!
12	Counsellor:	Tell me, Eamon, do you have a girl-friend?
13	Eamon:	Yes ... but why do you ask?

14	Counsellor:	You just look like somebody who might have a girl-friend. It's not unusual. I like to check how things are going in a person's social life ... so how is it going for you?
15	Eamon:	Not great ... she says I'm moody.
16	Counsellor:	Moody?
17	Eamon:	Yes ... she says I have got very moody in recent times.
18	Counsellor:	Does that have anything to do with your exams?
19	Eamon:	No, not directly anyway. I only seem to get these moods when I'm with her.
20	Counsellor:	Is there a reason for that?
21	Eamon:	No, but she doesn't like it.
22	Counsellor:	When was the last time you were sullen with her?
23	Eamon:	Last night! we were having a quick drink on the way home and I just went all quiet all of a sudden.
24	Counsellor:	What were you thinking at the time?
25	Eamon:	Funny enough I was thinking how beautiful she looked. She's a wonderful person, kind and caring ... smart as well. She just looked great last night.
26	Counsellor:	So you decide to get sullen when you see how well she looks?

27	Eamon:	Decide? Who said anything about deciding. I didn't do it on purpose, if that's what you mean. I was just wondering what she was doing with me.
28	Counsellor:	You mean you think she's too good for you ... maybe, that you might lose her?
29	Eamon:	You've been reading my mind! Yes, I think a lot about that. I'm even afraid to say it to her.

There appears to be four main themes so far corresponding to entries 1, 3, 8 and 12 in the script. Notice that "feeling low" is not explored in itself. A Reality Therapy practitioner probes the frustration that is associated with the feeling. The counsellor explores several aspects of the client's life before paying special attention to the theme that seems to be the most significant.

Looking at the quick theme chart in Figure 19, the four main themes uncovered are: Feelings, Tiredness, Studies and Girl-friend.

While there is a logical progress between the first three, the girl-friend theme made a sudden appearance, a hunch on the part of the counsellor. He might explain that he was looking for relationships and one of the more obvious ones in the life of a student is the boy-friend or girl-friend. During the exploration of this theme the counsellor briefly re-visited the examination area but returned to the girl-friend.

As it stands, the theme chart does not cover everything that happened in this part of the counselling session but it is a useful summary. It could be helpful for a supervisor discussing the interventions with the counsellor or for the counsellor self-evaluation his approach. It can be reviewed in many different ways: Where did self-evaluations occur? What basic needs were predominant in each theme?   What hunches were in the counsellor's head at different stages?   Where did the counsellor seek specific details? What might the counsellor explore next?

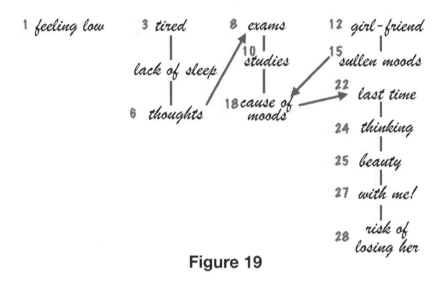

Figure 19

It could also be a helpful exercise to have several trainee counsellors deal separately with the same client, doing separate theme analysis charts and then come together to discuss their different approaches. Theme analysis is also useful in written case studies as it helps the trainee counsellor focus on the story behind the story, on what is really going on in the client's life.

Use of Recordings

One of the most useful things to do to develop a sense of theme analysis is to observe recordings of skilled therapists at work. A recording is better than a live role-play or real counselling since the viewer can rewind and replay sections.   Doing this with other trainees and a supervisor can be a very educational exercise. Mapping out the development of themes helps the trainee counsellor see just how complex the process can be at times. It also helps him or her observe the tell-tale signs of important themes.

Themes in Everyday Life

When talking to friends we can sometimes note that they are touching on themes that are particularly sensitive for them. In normal everyday conversation we tend to move away from sensitive topics not wishing to distress the other person or to appear inquisitive. With a friend, once we detect a sensitive issue, we may decide to leave it or to check if the friend wants to talk about it. The more sensitive we are to important themes the more freely we can make such a choice.

Involvement

In this chapter you will learn about:

- The importance of involvement in the counselling relationship
- The difference between involvement and friendship
- Characteristics of involvement
- Implications of involvement for seating, use of time, public relations
- Involvement and other aspects of the counsellor's professional role
- The use of a professional declaration
- Cultural aspects of involvement
- Dealing with involuntary clients
- Avoiding client dependency
- How to initiate a Reality Therapy session
- Listening

We have already described involvement as the Reality Therapy approach to creating an environment appropriate for effective counselling. This "professional friendship" is a very definite characteristic of Reality Therapy counselling. Empathy is an important ingredient of it but "involvement" goes beyond this to become an active working together with the client. More than listening to or feeling with the client, involvement is a friendly collaboration with him.

For the individual to feel safe to open up to someone a very special relationship is needed. Nothing about this should be left to chance.

The counsellor will work actively to create and communicate involvement to the client.

William Glasser describes involvement in the notes on his chart of how the brain works: "The counsellor should attempt to create a supportive environment within which clients can begin to make changes in their lives. To create this environment counsellors should consistently be friendly and listen to their client's stories. It is important that counsellors be perceived as people who have confidence that they can help their clients find more effective ways to fulfil their needs."

This supportive environment might begin even before counselling starts but must continue throughout. In schools, for example, an important advantage for the Guidance Counsellor and one that makes this role so valuable is that involvement can be built up with many students long before they visit the counsellor's office.

The actual "support" offered in the counselling environment is specifically directed at therapeutic change and not at prolonging the misery. In Reality Therapy there is more emphasis on empowerment than on facilitation. Helping clients take responsibility for their choices does not necessarily make things easier for them but we do offer our support in the process using the language of collaboration.[82] "It might not be easy but I will help you."

Several years ago, looking for an alternative to the term "facilitator" I decided to invent a new word: "possibilitator". Somebody has to invent new words! The Reality Therapy counsellor will communicate a belief that maybe something better is possible and will work to create an environment where change is possible. He will not say, "It will be easy" or "I will do it for you". Helping another human being without debilitating that person in the process is a special and highly sensitive skill.

---

[82] A later chapter focuses on the use of language in RealityTherapy.

Involvement And Friendship

As "professional friendship", the involvement of Reality Therapy Counselling differs from normal friendship in several respects.

- it is structured, has time limits
- it may involve a fee
- it has a specifically helping purpose
- it is aimed at change and not simply support
- it respects and encourages client responsibility, never diminishing it
- it may involve taking notes
- it may require outside consultation or referral
- it has a specified level of confidentiality
- the counsellor may not be a typical friend of the client
- the counsellor may challenge the client more than most friends would
- the counsellor will adhere to a specific code of conduct or ethics

Characteristics of Involvement

Here are some possible characteristics of involvement:

- being pleasant, patient, kind and good humoured
- being strictly honest
- listening with attention and seeking clarification where necessary
- helping the client build confidence in you and in counselling process
- affirming the client's strong points, present and past
- being supportive to the client who is experiencing pain

- using vocabulary and language appropriate to the client
- using appropriate levels of physical contact or distance
- using appropriate levels of eye-contact
- pacing the counselling process for client growth
- respecting the client's rights
- clarifying the limits of your professional role
- explaining the precise nature of the confidentiality you offer
- informing clearly about when you may need to refer them to others
- giving clients control over any notes you take about them
- respecting clients' rights to see notes written about them
- choosing an appropriate setting for counselling
- ensuring that the counselling location is undisturbed
- providing a comfortable temperature in the room
- sharing your own experiences insofar as it may help the client
- displaying your own doubts and weaknesses honestly
- stating your own needs and wants honestly and clearly
- using any research or consultations which might help the client
- preparing adequately for client visits
- writing to or telephoning client when this is helpful
- sharing some non-counselling activities with your client
- ensuring that counselling does not go on longer than is necessary

Learning to be a counsellor does not mean swotting up on all of these and certainly not in a few hours! Sometimes with a particular client, a smile, a handshake or even a look may be enough to establish involvement. It has more to do with the quality of the relationship than the details of the relationship.

It is not a technique that somehow works independently of human beings. Neither is it something that can be role-played except in a token way. Sincerity, for example, cannot be rehearsed! Involvement must be tuned to the counsellor and client. The way the counsellor welcomes the client, the first impressions of the counselling office, the type of furniture, the temperature, levels of background noise ... all of these can play a big part in getting the atmosphere right.

> Some years ago when I was explaining the confidential aspect of my job as Guidance Counsellor to a group of twelve-year old students one apparently distracted boy interrupted the proceedings several times to ask if I "drank" (as in "consume alcohol"). Taken aback a little, I enquired if that had anything to do with the current topic and he said it did. "If you drink, you might get drunk and tell everybody what we tell you in counselling". Yes, he was listening after all!

Generally it is a good idea to offer a client a variety of seating options. Low softly upholstered arm-chairs are not to everyone's taste and indeed some counselling clients may have back-pain and prefer firm seating. The position of the client's seating should be such that he is not facing any major distractions. A typical example of a far-from-ideal situation is when the counsellor opts to sit near a bright window obliging the client to look into the light.

Since the primary purpose of counselling is to help another person, furniture should not get in the way. It is very easy to fall into the trap of thinking of counselling as a formal session in an office as we tend to borrow too readily from the conventions of other professions. An equally common trap is to see counselling as requiring lots of soft furnishings and a face-to-face arrangement. Sometimes an excellent counselling session can take place with a teenager when both counsellor and young person are half-sitting half-leaning casually on the edge of a table. Indeed it can be quite threatening for a young person to sit face-to-face with an adult. In Ireland a lot of communication is indirect and so an indirect seating arrangement can be a perfectly appropriate format in many situations.

Normally a counsellor will need to maintain some sense of time and yet it can be harmful to the counselling process to keep looking at a watch. In fact a client who has experienced a lot of rejection may feel a little unwelcome if the counsellor keeps checking his wrist-watch. A simple solution is to have a clock on the wall the counsellor faces. Another is to make a very clear reference to your need to keep track of time and consult your watch openly.

In those counselling positions where there is an opportunity to work on the relationship even before the client comes for the first counselling session it is possibly the easiest involvement to create. A school Guidance Counsellor for example has several ways to communicate her role to students: talks to groups, word-of-mouth reputation from other student-clients, being seen chatting to students in the corridors, participation in school events, notices, through what other teachers say and a host of other informal contacts with students.

Such a counsellor can use public contacts with clients to demonstrate just how she will deal with them in private. Consider, for example, phrases such as "If someone comes to me and says they might be pregnant ... ", "Sometimes the person who comes to see me just doesn't know what to say". By mentioning such issues before a whole class group, for example, the counsellor is communicating the message, "I deal with matters such as these, they will not shock me, I will not ridicule the person, I will do my best to understand".

Role Clarification and Professional Declaration

In most employment and voluntary situations the counsellor is bound by regulations about information sharing and referral. For example, if what we discuss in counselling will be shared with a team of psychologists, psychiatrists, social workers and parole officers, then it is part of our relationship with the client to communicate this information clearly to him. It is especially important to clarify the limits of confidentiality before the counselling begins. A highly recommended way to do this is to provide a "Professional Declaration" to your client in advance of the first counselling session. This will contain details such as the following:

- Your name
- Your contact address
- Your office hours
- Your telephone, e-mail address
- Details on how to make an appointment
- Your qualifications as a counsellor
- Summary of your basic approach to counselling (e.g. Reality Therapy)
- Details about areas of special expertise or interest
- Membership of professional organisations
- The degree of confidentiality you apply to the counselling session
- Exceptions to this confidentiality
- Your fees and payment arrangements
- The Code of Ethics you adhere to

Ideally a copy of such a declaration will be given to the client and it may also be displayed clearly on a waiting room wall. These are facts that form part of the working relationship and some of them, if not clarified in advance, could destroy the involvement created between counsellor and client.

Cultural Factors

A vital dimension to consider in creating the right counselling atmosphere is the culture and even sub-culture of the client. There are some key issues that are almost always heavily influenced by a person's cultural background. Answering the following questions can give you many insights into some of these issues for a given cultural group:

- How do you greet a person at first encounter? (Handshaking is not universal!)
- How close do you stand to a person?
- How much eye-contact is normal?
- What types of physical contact are expected, tolerated, rejected?
- How does gender, age or other factors influence the previous topics?
- How are names used in this culture and what different levels of familiarity are recognised?
- How does the culture define family and family ties?
- If using a language other than English, what is the appropriate use of familiar forms of personal pronouns (for example, "tú" and "usted" in Spanish)?
- How does this culture view relationships including a professional relationship?
- How does the culture view the adolescent years, dating, gender identity issues?
- What are the major belief systems in the culture?
- What are the strongest values?
- What taboos do they have?

- What is regarded as the biggest "crimes" in this culture?
- How does the culture deal with death?
- How does it deal with the future?
- What are the most popular sayings and proverbs?
- What are their most important legends and what values do they represent?
- What is a normal conversational style in this culture?

In Ireland, for example, people often approach strangers with a certain reserve but very quickly move from there into a chatty friendship mode. At the same time, when there is something important to be discussed, we will approach the topic gradually, even in a roundabout way. A counsellor who is too friendly too soon or not friendly enough soon enough could be trampling on cultural toes!

There can be interesting contrasts between the perceptions of involvement when counselling is free and when it is fee-paying. A client who is paying an hourly fee for counselling may not be very impressed if a lot of time is spent in what he regards as "small talk" but at the same time this client still needs to experience the counsellor's involvement. The client's decision to see a counsellor on a fee-paying basis is to some extent a vote of confidence in the counsellor and so, for involvement to be complete, the client only needs to have that confidence ratified. Where counselling is free, more involvement work may be needed.

All of the counsellor's work should be contributing to involvement but sometimes it has to become a priority in itself. This could mean 30 minutes out of a 40-minute session or could even extend to a series of sessions where building involvement is the priority.
There is one type of client whose presence in the counselling office seems to render involvement unattainable and that is the so-called "resistant client".

Involuntary Clients

Just how do we deal with the involuntary client, the person sent by a parent, a teacher or a judge to see the counsellor? Is involvement impossible in these situations? In Choice Theory terms we know that we cannot "make" this person participate in counselling. We also know that she will only commit to counselling if she takes both it and the counsellor into her Quality World. Although she may appear to be "blocking" or "resisting" the process all she is doing is protecting herself.

My personal approach to this is to clarify as soon as possible that the client is free to leave. I may say something like this: "Jennifer, I understand you were sent to see me by your parents and, by coming here, you have done what they asked. I get the impression that you do not really want to be here and so you are free to go. I cannot and will not keep you here against your will. If you wish, I can explain what I do in counselling and you are very welcome to stay if you want to." It is important that what I say is what I mean. I really do believe that I can achieve very little with a "captive client".

When I make this clarification, there is usually an immediate change in the client. She relaxes her posture, facial tensions ease and a half-smile may even appear. The defiance ceases. In a sense it is easier to communicate the fully voluntary nature of counselling to such a client.

Dependency

If a caveat is needed on the topic of involvement it concerns dependency. By the nature of counselling we will come across people whose friendship needs have long been starved, a condition arising in many cases out of inadequate social skills. When we share our professional friendship with such people it is easy to understand why they may wish to see us more frequently and may even confuse boundaries by inviting us to share in other aspects of their lives. The easy friendship we offer is extremely welcome to such clients.

These situations do not require us to withdraw our friendship but do require us to be aware of what is happening and to help the client develop the social skills and friendships which diminish his or her dependency on the relationship with us.

A dependent relationship of this type is related to the Freudian concept of "transference". Not only will we be friendly to our clients but with some we may temporarily fill a role of parent, brother or sister. The real danger does not lie in in filling such roles but in doing so in a way that encourages the client (or ourselves) to depend on them. Naturally it is important that the counsellor is not using any aspect of the counselling role to meet major deficiencies in his or her own life.

Starting a Reality Therapy Counselling Session

It is useful to examine how a Reality Therapy practitioner will open the counselling dialogue with the client.

Glasser has always claimed that talking about the past is not generally helpful since people behave in terms of their present perceptions. These he readily admits may have come from the past but going back over their origins does not change them. So Reality Therapy will not normally start by inviting the client to recount his or her past.

It would be equally rare to begin with some form of case-history form-filling exercise. The focus will normally be on the present. The past will only be explored insofar as it clarifies or strengthens the present. Asking about a person's earlier life can very easily become a way of avoiding the present, of seeking some external factors to blame instead of looking at what we can do about the situation now.

Some counselling theorists speak of the need to "re-live" or "re-visit" a past experience. This is impossible. All a client can do is visit her current set of perceptions. These may of course include perceptions based on a past experience. It may indeed be helpful to unravel faulty logic in such perceptions or to check them against present reality. To an outside observer this might look like working with a past situation but an experienced Reality Therapy practitioner will be very aware that he is working with present perceptions.

The Reality Therapy approach to feelings is another of its distinguishing marks. Glasser sees feelings and physiology as the two components of Total Behaviour that are hardest to change but, and this is an important addition, we can change them by altering the total behaviour of which they are a part. Glasser does not see much value in asking a client about his or her feelings at the start of therapy. He surmises that most clients will feel quite miserable at the outset since that is the chief reason they come to counselling. He does sometimes ask about the client's feelings during a counselling session to gauge the effectiveness of the therapy.

It is of course perfectly possible to use feelings to explore a client's story. If Jason says he is feeling bored, it gives me an idea that he has not been choosing much in the way of fun or excitement and I would probably explore these areas with him. In other words, the feelings can be used as part of the exploration process but they themselves are not the end-goal of that process. In Reality Therapy we will always see them as part of a total behaviour.

So how might a Reality Therapy counsellor begin? After the initial salutations and helping the client feel more at ease the counsellor could ask questions such as:

> What would you like to talk about?
>
> What is your story?
>
> What do you hope to achieve by coming to counselling?

What is the problem?

Do you want to begin?

As is apparent from this list another notable characteristic of Reality Therapy is its use of questions. RT practitioners tend to be quite pro-active in their counselling rather than sitting back and hoping that the client will eventually describe all the relevant details. It is very important not to confuse this pro-active emphasis with directive counselling. The RT person may structure and guide the counselling **process** but does not direct the content. The counselling must remain fully client-centred at its heart. Reality Therapy is based on the idea that we cannot control another human being and this must be apparent throughout the counselling.

In a later chapter we shall see that the Reality Therapy counsellor will introduce the "language of choice" into the therapy to help focus on the degree of choice and control that the client has in particular circumstances. However it makes sense to gather some background information about what is going on in the client's life, to seek some awareness of the environment in which the client lives. With young clients I almost always ask about their families. I find out how many members there are and their own position in the family. In fact gathering this information fits well into the small-talk that we often use the first time we meet a person. Exploration of relationships is a key-component of Reality Therapy and so we will often ask about friendships and also about family and work relationships.

From the very first contact with the client and almost without thinking we will be forming preliminary hunches about him or her based on the evidence of our senses. One client looks wealthy, well-fed, another appears exhausted maybe even drugged. Yet another client looks like he could be the life and soul of a party, extremely sociable and apparently very relaxed. Our senses take in information and our own previous life-experience almost automatically classifies and labels it. As counsellors we will make the effort to become more and more sensitive to these hunches, to their strengths and limitations.

Similarly our clients are sizing us up from the very first moment of contact. If they do not perceive us as a person they can talk to with some hope of improving their situation it will be very difficult to have a good counselling relationship.

So many clients seek counselling because relationships have gone wrong for them. They may have experienced a lot of rejection and their perceptual system is finely tuned to detect the first signs of rejection from new people in their lives. As counsellors we do not simply listen but communicate very clearly that we are listening. It's like the driving-test candidate who does not simply look in the mirror but makes it very obvious to the examiner that he is looking in the mirror! This very special form of heightened communication is essential to involvement.

I have already indicated that this cannot be artificial. Indeed, involvement is a good example of total behaviour. We must be fully present to the other person, alert to their doing, thinking, feeling and physiology. We engage in the process as counsellors with our own doing, thinking, feeling and physiology. Martin Buber's concept of "I-Thou"[83] is highly relevant to the counselling relationship. As trainees our communication may feel stilted and even formula-like but with practice we integrate all the components of therapy into our person, the whole person that attends to the whole client.

Listening

One of the most essential skills in counselling is that of listening. I have already mentioned the importance of making this listening very obvious to the client. Another aspect of this professional skill is that

---

[83] Buber, Martin. *I and Thou*, Edinburgh: T. & T. Clark, 1958 (revised edition)

it is "active listening"; we are striving to understand what we hear and reflect back our understanding to the client. We are dipping into the unique and very different inner world of another human being and we need to remember constantly that every word and nuance can have a totally different meaning for that person compared to our own assumed meanings.

Accepting: We accept the other person's story without criticism or advice and with minimal interruption. This means we allow for silence, moments when the client does not talk for whatever reason. We accept the client's feelings and tears. It would not normally be very accepting to say, "How could you do something like that?", "It could have been worse!", "Don't cry!", "You're young. You can always get another boy-friend!"

Attending: We show that we are listening attentively by our posture, our eye-contact, non-verbal cues such as nods, verbal cues such as "yes", "I see", "Uh-huh". Staring, excessive physical closeness or distance, over-use of verbal or non-verbal cues could all get in the way of our attention to the client.

Understanding: We emphasise the importance of our clear understanding of the client's story by seeking clarification from time to time, by paraphrasing what we have heard to find if it is accurate. I believe it does not show great understanding to say "I know exactly how you feel", "I fully understand". A more helpful message to communicate is "Although I can never understand what it's like to be you, I'm doing my best to put myself in your shoes!"

Supporting: We indicate our support by using the language of alliance ("we can talk about it"), by reframing what we hear ("you say you argue a lot; does this mean you have some very firm convictions?"), by affirming the client ("were you doing the best you could at the time?"), by normalising the client's behaviour ("most people would feel very low after losing their job"). Although we help the clients take greater control of their own lives we would not normally say, "It's all up to you!"

Involvement in all its dimensions is something that must pervade every session and so the counsellor will be constantly assessing how it is faring. Sometimes it can be important to stand back temporarily from the main business of the session to chat for a few moments about leisure interests or current events. Humour, where it is possible, is a wonderful component of involvement and can create welcome respite for both counsellor and client.

> ## Start where your clients are.
> ## They cannot grow
> ## from anywhere else.

Involvement Worksheet

Identify anything that the Counsellor below is doing that is contributing to his involvement with Niall on his first visit

1 Counsellor: Come on in. I must say you are very punctual. That is not a bad day we're having.

2 Niall: Indeed it's not too bad at all! How are you?

3 Counsellor: Grand. Have a seat.
4   You're obviously not a big football fan or you'd be away to the match.

5 Niall: Well, normally I would go but I thought it would be better to see you. Are you sure you can spare me the time?

6 Counsellor: That is why I am here although I do have to see someone else in forty minutes time. If we need more time than that there is no problem in arranging another appointment.

7 Niall: Thanks a million, I appreciate that.

8 Counsellor: It must be important for you if you have decided to give up the match for it.

9 Niall: To tell you the truth I am not really sure what the problem is ... or if there is a problem at all ... sometimes I think I am only imagining things and then there are times I get funny feelings in the pit of my stomach, feelings that tell me something terrible is wrong.

10 Counsellor: Whatever it is it sounds as if you have done the right thing in setting time aside to discuss it.

11 Niall: I have a fairly good job ... indeed any job is good nowadays ... and it is one I can do fairly well. I work in quality control and my bosses have been very happy with me. Of late 'though, I keep getting the urge to pack it all in. Last week I even wrote a letter of resignation but at the last minute I decided not to hand it in.

12 Counsellor: That would be a big step to take and I see you realise that. Somehow or other, things have gone off the rails so much that you sometimes think the only thing to do is to resign. Is that it?

13 Niall: Exactly ... and then I worry that this might be a rash step I would regret all my life. I really do not know what to do.

14 Counsellor: Niall, you have decided to face up to this problem. You made sacrifices in coming here today. You are obviously willing to put effort and time into this matter and I would be hopeful that together we can find some way you can improve your situation.

Comment on the use of small-talk, affirmation, active listening, mention of choice, references to collaboration, hope.

Nightmare Counselling

Work with a partner and take turns at playing the counsellor. The client will tell a simple story, not necessarily a problem as this exercise concerns itself mainly with the listening process.

Pick any one or more of the situations listed below to role-play. If working with a group different pairs could use separate role-plays. Give each person this role on a card and ask them not to share the cards with their partners.

It is important to brief the "clients" in advance, letting them know that they will be experiencing less than effective counselling! I forgot to do this once and the results were interesting to say the least

CLIENT'S STORY	COUNSELLOR'S APPROACH
Talk about your school-days. (Use fictitious details.)	Whatever the client tells you, pick something in your own life it reminds you of and tell the client about this (enthusiastically).
Explain what you regard to be very important in a child's education.	Do not say very much but use body language to communicate to the client that you are not really interested in what he or she is saying.

Explain to the counsellor how you would do a three-point-turn with a car.	Sit back-to-back with the client but otherwise do your best to show you are listening attentively to the client's story.
Tell the counsellor why your five (imaginary) brothers were fighting over an inheritance. Give details.	Incorporate distractions into the session: answer phone, adjust window, surf the web, check door, drop your book, etc. but otherwise show you are listening!
Explain your terrible fear of lifts and escalators.	Give good psychological analyses of what you are hearing and communicate your expertise by using technical language.
Tell the story of your childhood. (Use fictitious details.)	Periodically reflect back what the client is saying by quoting verbatim from what you have heard.

After the role-play discuss what happened from the view-point of both client and counsellor. Use the ideas to generate positive guidelines about what would help the counselling process.

Positive Involvement Practice

Work with a partner and take turns at playing the counsellor. The client will tell a simple story, not necessarily a problem as this exercise concerns itself mainly with the listening process. For example, pick any one or more of the "client's stories" in the previous exercise to role-play. If working with a group different pairs could use separate role-plays.   The counsellor should try to incorporate as many of the following into the role-play, or may choose to practise only two or three of the suggestions.   Good involvement certainly does not need 100% of the following:

Body Language
- Use appropriate greeting
- Facing the client (not necessarily directly).
- Adequate eye-contact.
- Calm relaxed posture.
- Slight positive lean towards client.
- Occasional head nods to show attention.

Language
- Allow client to speak.
- Use same type of language as client.

Interactions
- Ask for clarifications where necessary.
- Occasionally summarise to check for understanding.
- Rephrase the summary to offer client alternative view.
- Use appropriate humour.
- Open questions are generally more useful than closed ones.

Physical distance
- Be close enough to show interest.
- Respect cultural and individual mores about personal space.

Environment (this may be difficult to role-play but you could discuss what you would change in the present environment to improve it).	• Comfortable temperature. • Appropriate level of light. • Avoid noise, drafts, bright back-lights. • Reduce distractions (telephone, door). • Relaxing colour scheme. • Nearby toilet facilities.
Furniture (again not easy to change in role-play but discuss what changes you would make to the present furniture arrangements.)	• Have several types of seating to offer. • Sit at an angle to the client rather than head-on. • Desk should not intrude in the counselling. • Availability of tea or coffee making facilities. • Drinking water. • Tissues.

Involvement on Show

As it is difficult to "practise" involvement, a humorous exercise can help trainees recall the different components that contribute to it. This role-play requires a "counsellor" and a "client". They will role-play in front of the other trainees but should have a few minutes to plan their production. The idea is that the "counsellor" will exaggerate as many different components of involvement as possible. This could include excessively friendly hand-shakes, many references to the comfort of the chairs, countless offers of refreshments and so on.

Those not planning this role-play could prepare another to demonstrate the "counsellor-from-hell", one who breaks every possible rule in the involvement book.

Involvement in Everyday Life

In practically all our interactions with others we have some very important choices. We can behave in a way that will draw us closer or a way that can separate us. If we wish to work well with a person then it makes sense to choose in the direction of involvement. Wanting to work with a person and choosing to be distant from them at the same time is not a very effective recipe.

The employer who is having problems because a particular employee is often late, the parent who is concerned about the friendships of his teenager, the teacher who finds that a student is not doing very much work, all have a similar challenge: how to help the individual and maintain their good relationship with the person.

Parents often assume that when their child has a problem they will turn to Mum or Dad for help. Even in the happiest of family relationships this does not necessarily happen. What is important is that the parents create the environment where the children are free to talk about issues that are important for them. This normally requires the parents to establish a good relationship with the children by first having spent time talking about the small things of their lives.

In this context the "vibes" we give out to those around us become very important.

Tips for Parents

Parents are ultimately responsible for their children but this does not mean that every aspect of the relationship should be of a supervisory or authoritarian nature. Involvement is very much about trying to understand the other and about collaborating. This type of relationship becomes extra important when children become teenagers.

1. Be able to talk to your teenager about small every-day things and they are more likely to be able to confide in you about the bigger things in their lives.

2. Teenagers are not children. Child-rearing strategies that worked in their first twelve years must give way to a new relationship between parent and teenager.

3. Their bodies, minds and nearly everything else in their lives are temporarily "out of sync". You can't fight this so learn to live with it.

4. Yes, teenagers are indeed from another planet! They are from the earth of the future. Their world and the future they will create is not like our past. The parent who is open to this will share in an exciting voyage of discovery.

5. Teenagers' friends also come from that same other planet! To move into their new world it is inevitable that teenagers will appear to be moving away from you and your world. Don't confuse "discovery" with "rebellion"!

6. Nagging destroys relationships.

7. Most students prefer not to talk about school just after returning from it.

8. Telling teenagers about how things were when you were their age tends to be counter-productive (and convinces them that you are much older than you really are).

9. For reasons I do not understand, most teenagers are "allergic" to cabbage. It is not in their Quality Worlds! The way to a teenager's heart is not through cabbage! All forms of real and metaphorical cabbage are to be used with extreme caution.

10. Work "with" your teenager, rather than "at" or "over" them.

11. Remind yourself frequently (1) that they are no longer children and (2) that they are not perfect yet!

12. You are not the only ones who do not understand teenagers. They don't either!

13. Grounding doesn't work! (If in a moment of angry weakness you issue such a sentence later ask your victim to suggest alternatives. That gets everybody off the hook.)

14. Dealing with problems: In summary form one approach is: "We have a problem. Here is how I see it. How do you see it? Let's discuss our ways of dealing with it." This tends to be better than the "audio-visual" method ("You can hear my voice and see my fist".)

15. Their music is OK but it may be hard for you to understand. Your inability to understand it or to listen to it does not make it bad.

16. Learn how to deal with stress in your own life.

17. Know how to look after your own health and development.

18. Be in regular contact with other parents of teenagers. Your shared experience is a very rich resource.

19. Don't hesitate to use the experience of your child's teachers. They spend every day with very large "families"!

20. However you interact with your teenage son or daughter, whether in everyday situations or when problems arise, you can choose an approach that damages the relationship or one that safeguards and even improves the relationship.

The Basic Needs

In this chapter you will learn about:

- The important background role of the Basic Needs in life and in counselling
- How Glasser developed his needs theory
- How the theory of the needs guides the counsellor's information gathering
- Possible interactions between the basic needs
- Glasser's theory of Basic Needs Intensities

According to Glasser our Basic Needs are Survival, Love and Belonging, Power, Freedom and Fun. Although they are the ultimate internal motivators of all we do they often behave like the vitamin X phenomenon I mentioned in a previous chapter. We do not go around thinking consciously of our needs, evaluating how well each is being met. However, they are at the very heart of our mental and physical health. Fortunately, we have in-built sensors to detect when any given need is somewhat neglected and although these do not always work at a conscious level, they have their ways of telling us that remedial action is needed.

Our feelings play a primary role in this feedback mechanism. We feel good when needs are being met and feel poorly when they are not. Physical feelings of hunger, pain and discomfort can accompany deficits in the survival need. Psychological feelings of loneliness, helplessness, entrapment and boredom are examples of warning signals about the other needs. Happiness and depression tend to be more comprehensive measures of our overall level of need satisfaction. This table gives examples of feelings relating to needs.

NEED	NEEDS NOT MET	NEEDS MET
Survival	fear, discomfort	safety
Love and Belonging	loneliness	warmth
Power	helplessness	strength
Freedom	trapped	free
Fun	bored	joy
Overall	Unhappy, depressed	happy

Although we may not be fully aware of our needs we do tend to be a lot more conscious of our Quality World pictures. These are our personal sets of "need-fulfillers". In a Choice Theory context we refer to them as "pictures" and sometimes as "wants". We may want a new car, some time to ourselves, a course in interior design. We can want to get on better with our partner, to be less impulsive, to be more relaxed. As our consumer society knows only too well the list of human wants is endless.

I explained earlier that it is normally the discrepancy between what we want and what we have that drives our behaviour and I summed this up in the balancing scales diagram (Figure 20) based on Glasser's own charts. So, rather than think to myself, "my love and belonging need is running rather low" I am more likely to express it in terms of my Quality World pictures: "I miss Laura". On the wants side of the balance I want her to be present. On the "What I am getting" side, I detect that she is not.

In Reality Therapy interventions a lot of the exploratory work will focus on these two areas: the perceived and the Quality Worlds.

However, in the background guiding the counsellor's information-gathering are the Basic Needs. He might not ever mention them but they give him clues about what to check out in the client's life.

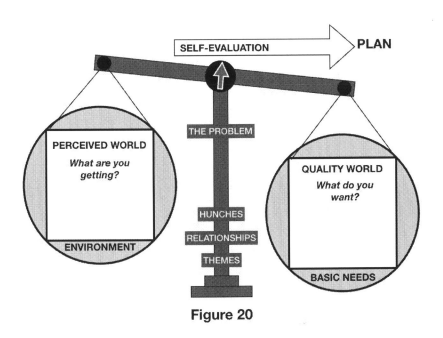

Figure 20

Glasser sees the needs as five main "purposes" in our lives. The need for survival is one we share with the animal kingdom but, as humanity evolved away from animal origins, the newer part of the brain grew to accommodate blueprints for a quality survival. One of the more colourful explanations of this growth is the so-called "radiator theory"[84] which holds that early humanoids started walking on two legs to avoid the heat of the African ground, the brain was then able to cool more efficiently due to gravity and consequently it began to grow. Whatever its origins, the human brain has a psychological potential that the animal kingdom does not share. It would appear that for a relatively modest increase in the hardware

---

[84] Falk, D. (1990). *Brain evolution in Homo: the "radiator theory"*. Behavioural and Brain Sciences, 13: 333 - 381.

we evolved an amazing amount of extra software: our thinking and feeling abilities.

The greater complexity of the human brain meant that the basic need for survival could evolve into a need for quality of life. Relating to others safeguarded our survival better than by being alone. By increasing our personal power, protecting our freedom and through the fun of learning we moved further and further from the edge of mere survival. Even today ask someone how they are doing and the answer "Surviving!" suggests a less than happy state of affairs.

Evolution of Glasser's Needs Theory

In 1960 Glasser published his first book, "Mental Health or Mental Illness?" and the importance of needs in his theory was evident as the very first chapter was titled, "The person and his needs". He wrote about:

- Physiologic needs – food, air, water, warmth, (sex).
- Psychologic needs - love, social needs, achievement.

Still using the vocabulary of his psychiatric training the young Dr. Glasser wrote: "To develop an effective ego a person must have a meaningful, two-way relationship with someone who has an effective ego – a relationship in which the ego of the giving person is available for use by the receiving person in a consistent atmosphere of some love and a minimum of hostility or anger." The many themes in this one quote were to be repeated by him throughout his publications and to receive even greater emphasis with time.

In 1965 Dr. Glasser's first statement of the basic needs in the context of "Reality Therapy" referred to "the need to love and be loved and the need to feel that we are worthwhile to ourselves and others". By 1984[85] he was talking about five needs: Love and

---

[85] Glasser, William. *Take Effective Control of Your Life*. New York: Harper & Row: 1984.

belonging, Power, Freedom, Fun and Survival. In 1995 he had added the concept of the intensities of the needs, something he believes to be genetic, and he was beginning to see all the needs in the context of relationship.

By the time "Choice Theory" was published in 1998 there was a new emphasis with an old familiar ring: "I believe that humans have additional genetic instructions, as strong as survival, that drive us to be closely involved with each other all our lives." "Choice Theory" was barely released when Dr. Glasser was already developing this emphasis further. In his address to the International Convention of his institute in Orlando, Florida in 1998 he claimed that all human problems are relationship problems and that in therapy we should seek out this relationship as soon as possible. In the word "connectedness" he had found an excellent description of the key to human happiness.

Essentially what he is saying is that, although Love and Belonging is listed as one of five needs, there is something extra special about relationship. It is mainly through our links to other people that all our needs are met.

We meet our power needs through working with others, learning from others. Fun is almost always achieved in the company of others. Freedom is rarely a solitary freedom. Love and belonging requires other people by its very nature. Survival (shelter, warmth, health, food) also depends heavily on our co-operation with others.

Even the inner logic we use to size up our world relies heavily on relationships. The meaning of the construct "tall-short", for example, depends fully on our experiences so far of the heights of others. The day I meet a seven-foot tall individual I will readjust the meaning of "tall". If this experiential influence is happening with our constructs it is also happening with our meta-constructs: our values. My life experiences so far may convince me that "tall" is good and "short" is bad. Taking all of this one step further it becomes clear that how I evaluate myself and how I judge my own life has a lot to do with the constructs I have developed in my relationships to others.

Needs Exploration in Counselling

So the main focus of Reality Therapy exploration tends to be the client's Quality World, the set of pictures that steer the person's behaviour more directly and more specifically than the basic needs. Whether referred to or not, the needs are very much present to the practitioner's mind serving as a guide to exploration of the client's psychological life. Just as the medical doctor will watch out for certain basic indices of the patient's health (blood pressure, eating and sleeping habits, for example), the Reality Therapy practitioner will always attempt to estimate the condition of the client's basic needs.

Sometimes the counsellor might seek out very definite information about a specific need but, with experience, will rely to some extent on hunches derived from the client's appearance and general story. Time spent checking on such assumptions will never be wasted. Even if a client presents with a problem that seems to be causing a major power deficit, the counsellor will want to know something about the overall state of the other needs too.

For example, a client does not always know just where the frustration is occurring in his or her perceptual world. If I don't eat today I get hungry fairly soon and rather than dwelling too much on my hunger I start looking around for food to "fix" the hunger. Such is not the case for the psychological needs. If I have never experienced much love and affection or never had very much fun I might not even know I am short of these fundamental necessities. One of the counsellor's tasks is to help the client check out different areas of her life and, in Reality Therapy, will use the basic needs as a guide.

This pro-active approach extends to helping the client come up with new choices in her life. Even if a the individual is helped by a skilled counsellor to see that she is leading a social life that is quite dissimilar from her peers she still may not know how to make the necessary changes in her life. Simply to ask the socially inadequate client, "What do you think you could do to increase your number of friends?" may be useless. The client may have no idea how to deal with this. Glasser's recommendation that we share our expertise and experience with the client is useful here. The therapist might ask, "Would it help you get to know more people if you were to enrol for one of those evening classes in furniture restoration?"

The rest of this chapter will focus on how the therapist might assess a client's needs in different ways. Obviously the age, culture and life circumstances of the client will be important considerations in the selection of ways to probe the needs. Checking on a teenager's fun needs, for example, you might ask him how he spends Friday night whereas the corresponding question for his parents might enquire about the full week-end or the holidays. The following table gives examples of the ways need-related topics might differ for three clients.

	TEENAGER	BUSINESS EXECUTIVE	PENSIONER
LOVE & BELONGING	Pals, parents	Family and associates	Children, grand-children, cronies
FUN	Football, music	Golf	Bowls
FREEDOM	Sport, camping	Bahamas	Mobility
POWER	Sports trophies, part-time jobs	Business deals	Family achievements
SURVIVAL	Family home	Stocks & Shares	Health care

Obviously there are no hard and fast rules and it would be inappropriate to stereotype people but we do work on hunches when exploring the needs and these vary from client to client.

Here is an example of part of a counselling session with a teenage boy. He's not sure why he has been so miserable in recent times. The counsellor has a hunch this might be a "vitamin X" phenomenon where the boy simply does not know what he is lacking because he never had it in the first place.

When counselling with Choice Theory, the structure of the Basic Needs is in the counsellor's head and rarely on her lips. The counsellor tends to focus on the activities and pictures the client might have for different needs.

REF		DIALOGUE	COMMENTS
1	Counsellor:	So, Anthony, you have been feeling miserable of late and you don't know why. You have told me that school is going well and your story about your sister's birthday party last Saturday suggests that you are fairly happy at home.	At this point the counsellor may believe that Survival, Power, Love and Belonging are in a healthy state … but this is only her assumption.
2	Anthony:	That's right. I don't seem to have the usual problems others have, you know, like not getting enough pocket money or having to come in too early.	Freedom seems satisfied too.

3	Counsellor:	Who's your best friend at the moment?	Moving in to focus on the intimacy aspect of Love and Belonging.
4	Anthony:	Jack. We have been in the same class for about three years.	
5	Counsellor:	Tell me about him. What football team does he support?	Fishing for details to see just how Anthony perceives what "best friend" means.
6	Anthony:	I'm not sure. I don't know if he even likes football.	Strange!
7	Counsellor:	What sort of things do you like to do when you're together?	Checking for further details.
8	Anthony:	Maybe go to the shops ... yeah ... just go to the shops.	
9	Counsellor:	When was the last time you did that?	This could be a fun activity they do every day ...
10	Anthony:	Eh ... em ... I think it was the day before my birthday ... yes, it was. I remember now!	... but it's not ...

11	Counsellor:	And when was your birthday, Anthony?	
12	Anthony:	The twentieth of April. I was fourteen!	April is two months ago! At this point the counsellor suspects that Anthony might not have a lot of peer friendship!
13	Counsellor:	I see .. and do you see Jack between classes at school, maybe during the lunch-break?	
14	Anthony:	No, he plays basketball and I don't.	

This boy may have had quite a happy early childhood. Family life seemed very pleasant and at primary school he may have got along well with the kids he grew up with. Now at second-level school[86] friendships are not so automatic and Anthony's lack of friendship-making skills may have had its first real test.

Following on from the above intervention the counsellor would probably check for more details of Anthony's friendship patterns at school. She would still be open to the possibility that Anthony has other need deficits that may be even more important.

---

[86] In the Republic of Ireland this spans the ages 12 to 17 years. Children almost always change schools around age 12 moving from the Primary School to a Second-level school. At this point friends might go to different schools.

The counsellor uses her knowledge of the Basic Needs as a guide to her probing of Anthony's story. By enquiring into specific details she is able to estimate the state of Anthony's needs. At no point did the counsellor say, "Tell me about your friendship need, Anthony" … though she might if she was counselling a Choice Theorist!

Some Choice Theory authors have developed different ways of evaluating a person's needs including a psychometric approach (see the panel below). While these may be useful in counselling I believe it is of primary importance that the counsellor has a solid understanding of the basic needs and how they might be satisfied in a particular client's life. An understanding of the basic needs provides a very useful background structure for identifying what is missing or what is awry in a person's life.

Brown, Timothy & Stuart Swenson. Identifying Basic Needs: The Contextual Needs Assessment. *International Journal of Reality Therapy*, Vol 24, No. 2, Pp 7-10.

Geronilla, Linda. Helping clients assess and evaluate their needs. *Journal of Reality Therapy*, 1985, Vol.5, No.1, Pp 31-35.

Huffstetler, V.C., Mims, S.H., & Thompson, C.L. (2004) Getting Together and Staying Together: Testing the Compatibility fo the Need-Strength Profile and the Basic Needs Inventory. *International Journal of Reality Therapy*, 23(1).

Peterson, Arlin V. and James Truscott. Pete's Pathogram: Quantifying the Genetic Needs. *Journal of Reality Therapy*, 1988, Vol 8, No 1, Pp 22-32.

Smith Harvey, Virginia and Kristen Retter. The Development of the Basic Needs Survey. *Journal of Reality Therapy*, 1995, Vol 15, No 1, Pp 76-80.

The Interaction of the Needs

We cannot classify our life experiences into five neat groups each corresponding to one of the basic needs. Going to a football match, for example, can be an occasion for fun, friendship, freedom and even power.

Some of the heated debates about sexual issues owe much of their energy to opposing sides classifying sexual behaviour under different needs. Most of our Quality World pictures are intended to satisfy more than one need and there are certain very important multi-need satisfiers in our modern world: money, telephones, cars, computers. When something has the potential to satisfy many of our needs it achieves a high value in our world.

The inverse of all of this is that when we change any one activity in our lives we may be creating a new set of need frustrations. For example, the student who finally decides to get down to some hard work (satisfying the power need), may find that the extra hours of study have removed almost all his friendship, fun and freedom. Very often we are not aware of just how need-fulfilling something ... or somebody ... is until that thing or person goes from our world. Since counselling usually means making changes in the client's life, it is vital that these changes are introduced gradually and with an eye to the overall effect on the person's need satisfaction.

To quote a simple example, giving up smoking cigarettes might seem a very positive step for a person. For one individual, however, this may have unexpected negative consequences. He now no longer calls at the shop near the bus-stop where he used to buy his cigarettes. His regular looking for a cigarette lighter from work colleagues has ceased. Without intending it or maybe even being fully aware of it he has reduced his social interactions. Safeguarding his survival need may be causing frustrations in his belonging needs. The wise counsellor will watch for secondary effects such as these and help the client deal with them.

Basic Needs and Their Intensities

In the first edition of "Staying Together"[87] published in 1995 Glasser introduced the idea of needs intensities. Over and above the daily fluctuations in our need strengths he holds that there appear to be genetic strengths or "intensities". At a given point in time my need for friendship and belonging may be running low but, for some people, this need always behaves as if it were running low. They seem to need to have people around them all the time. Glasser would describe these as having a high need intensity for love and belonging.

If our five basic needs could be compared to five fuel tanks, then the needs intensity theory would claim that there is no fixed standard size for the tanks and that each of our own personal needs tanks can be of different size too. This gives rise to interesting situations when two people enter into a relationship.

Where they both have high power or freedom needs their shared existence will require more effort. Even if one of these two needs intensities is high in one partner things can be difficult. The person with high power needs may spend endless hours at the office at the expense of love and belonging while the freedom seeker may make similar sacrifices on the golf-course.

---

87 William Glasser. *Staying Together*. New York: Harper & Rowe, 1995.

Questions about Needs

The questions below are not meant to be used in checklist fashion nor to be used at all necessarily, but the Counsellor will have the spirit of these questions in her mind as she listens to the client and asks about his life. In some cases overt use of some of these questions could even be seen as threatening. Asking someone if they have many friends or any close friends is not quite as helpful or non-threatening as asking what they do with their friends or how they spend their free time.

Belonging, Friendship, Love:

- Who are your friends? .. in your class/neighbourhood/ at work?
- Who is your best friend right now?
- What do you like to do together? (Check nature of friendship)
- What do they like about you? (strength building)
- Tell me about your family.
- Who would miss you most if you went to a foreign country for a year?
- What clubs, sports, community activities are you involved in?
- Who would you take to a desert island? Who would take you?
- Which would you rather be - funny, rich, friendly, clever ...?
- How would you describe yourself - in five lines?
- Have you had a boy/girl friend in recent times?
- Do you have a mobile phone and what do you use it for mainly?

- How many numbers do you store on your mobile phone?
- Are you an avid e-mailer, internet chatter?

Power, Esteem, Worth:

- Do you ever feel bossed around?
- Are you ever asked to look after something/ somebody?
- Tell me about the work you do.
- If you were boss for a month what would you change?
- If you won a prize for achievement what would it be for?
- Do you run your life or does life run you?
- When do you feel important?
- Who really listens to you?
- What situations do you find embarrassing?
- When did you last feel "on top of the world"?
- Who is your "idol"? Why?

Freedom:

- If you could dress any way you liked what would you wear?
- Do you feel pressurised by anybody at the moment?
- What sort of things do you find you ask permission for?
- What permission is hardest to get?
- When/where do you feel most at ease, most relaxed?
- If you could really do what you want tomorrow, what would you do?
- What would you like to do but, for some reason, cannot?
- Have you ever joined a public protest about anything?

- Have you ever written to the newspapers about anything?
- Tell me what freedom means to you.
- Are there people who try to control you? Who?
- If you won the Lottery, what would you do?

Fun:

- What is your idea of fun? What do you do for a bit of "craic"?[88]
- What is the craziest thing you ever did?
- What do you think of people who "let their hair down"?
- What type of books or magazines do you like?
- Tell me about something you really enjoyed doing recently.
- What is your favourite comedy?
- Tell me what you like to do in your free time.
- What are your favourite television programmes?
- What sports or games do you like?
- When is the last time you had a really good laugh … and what was happening at the time?
- What do you think of discos, latest fashion …?

Survival:

- What do you generally eat each day? … yesterday?
- How well are you sleeping?
- How is your health?
- Do you ever feel very cold?
- How frequently have you visited the doctor in recent times?
- Are you involved in any sports or other forms of exercise?

---

[88] In Ireland "craic" (pronounced "crack") is more meaningful than plain "fun". It's an old Anglo-Saxon word but at this stage it has well-nigh honorary Irish citizenship.

- Do you always stay at home or do you sometimes stay elsewhere?
- Have you ever been in hospital?
- Financially are things going OK for you?

General:

- If you could be any age you liked, what would it be? What would be different?
- You hear news that makes you very happy. What?
- When did you last feel very happy? What is different now?
- What are you looking forward to at present?

No Questions about Needs

With a partner and using all that you know about creating involvement, have as normal a conversation as you can. This is not counselling. There is no specific problem, no counsellor and no client. You are simply having a conversation. Your task is to find out as much as you can about the other person's needs and how that person normally satisfies them BUT you may not use the names of the needs. After fifteen minutes, tell each other what you learned about each other's needs.

Your Own Needs

The needs that often stay in the background in counselling sessions can very usefully come to the foreground as a helpful tool to evaluate one's own life. Just how well are you meeting your needs? Is there one need that you have neglected for some time? This first exercise is simple but provides a structure for taking stock of your needs.

1. Take a clean page.

2. Across the centre write the following words evenly spaced.

LOVE   POWER   FUN   FREEDOM

3. Think of things, behaviours, persons, places, etc. that in some important way contribute to each need. Draw a box representing each of these with its name inside and locate it above the corresponding need to form a bar chart. You can vary the size of the boxes. (Figure 21.)

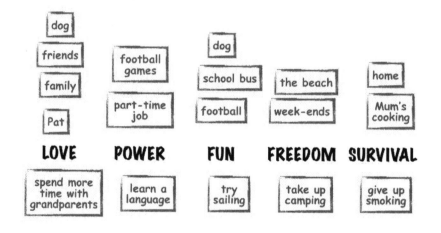

Figure 21

4. Think of other "boxes" which you are not using at present to build particular needs but which are reasonably possible for you. Draw and label these placing them just below the corresponding need.

5. Find a partner and compare each other's bar charts.

DISCUSSION: Would swapping boxes with your partner satisfy him or her? How much control do you have over these boxes? How have you met each of these needs today?

Needs Intensities Questionnaire

If Glasser's theory about needs intensities is accurate then it means that each of us will have certain need "hungers" that predominate. Some people are very clingy with an apparently hyper-active need for love and belonging. Others avoid at all costs any attempt to hem them in or tie them down to time and this can indicate a strong need for freedom. And so it is with each of the needs. The questionnaire on the following pages could be used to examine your needs at this moment in time but, for the purpose of needs intensities, I suggest that you complete it in terms of how you usually behave rather than right now.

When finished, total the scores in each column and you will have five scores corresponding to the needs Love and Belonging, Freedom, Fun, Power and Survival in that order. The points for each need relative to the others will give an approximation of your needs intensities profile. It is important not to treat the results as highly precise mathematics but the questionnaire does contribute to discussion of the needs intensities.

Your Needs Intensities

Read each phrase and then decide how well it describes you. Then put a number from 0 to 4 in the box alongside the phrase showing how true it is for you most of the time.	4 = always 3 = often 2 = sometimes 1 = not often 0 = never

1	I want to be liked by people.	☐
2	I like to do things my own way.	☐
3	I often try to see the funny side of life.	☐
4	I like to do a job well.	☐
5	I give a lot of importance to being careful with money.	☐
6	I often say I'll help people even when time is short.	☐
7	I tend to side with the underdog.	☐
8	I am usually positive about things.	☐
9	I try to get things done, organising others if necessary.	☐
10	Sometimes I feel nervous for no particular reason.	☐

11	I go out of my way to be with people.	☐
12	I don't feel I need do things the same way as everybody else.	☐
13	My friends would regard me as playful.	☐
14	I have strong convictions.	☐
15	I think it is important to plan well for the future.	☐
16	I find it hard to deal with people who put me down.	☐
17	I do not like to feel tied down, controlled, hemmed in.	☐
18	I find it hard to cope with people who are very serious.	☐
19	Making a fool of myself would be very serious.	☐
20	I believe there is a lot of evil in the world.	☐

	L&B	FREE	FUN	POW	SUB
Add up the scores in each column and put their totals here:					

Here are some ways of using the questionnaire:

- Do it with someone you are very close to and then compare scores.
- How do differences in your needs intensities reflect in your behaviour in the relationship?
- Do you agree with the results of the questionnaire regarding your own profile and regarding that of your friend?
- What could you do so that differences in needs intensities could contribute to your relationship rather than cause problems?
- Make a needs profile for each of your parents, guessing as best you can what scores each might get for each of their needs. Then compare the two profiles. Have the differences you noted in the profiles reflected in their behaviour as a couple? Has your own needs profile been more or less the same since your childhood? How did differences with your parents reflect in you daily life with them?

Parents could do a similar exercise with their own children.

(This exercise can also be used as a preparation for the "Blind Date" exercise by dividing the final scores by a factor of four.)

Blind Date Exercise

AIM: To explore the needs intensities in relationships

BACKGROUND: You are participating in a new type of Dating Game and the outcome is that you will spend one week with each of the five people listed in the table below. Code names have been given to protect their real identities. The organisers of the competition hope that you will get on really well with at least one of the candidates. Before you meet any of them you are provided with their needs intensities profiles (in the table).

	LOVE & BELONGING	FREEDOM	FUN	POWER	SURVIVAL
HEARTBEAT	5	2	1	4	3
JUGGERNAUT	2	3	4	5	1
FOURWINDS	3	5	2	1	4
LAFALOT	1	4	5	3	2
CENTRALBANK	4	1	3	2	5
YOU					

- Work out your own personal needs intensities profile and insert it in the last row of the table. Remember that 1 = LOW, 3 = AVERAGE and 5 = HIGH.

- Which of these candidates do you think you would get on best with?

- Which might you have most difficulties with in a relationship?

- Discuss how you think your interaction or relationship with each of the candidates might be. Does the gender of the candidate have a bearing? What could work really well in your relationship with each?   Where could there be problems?   Give examples of specific situations and what might happen.

- Next work out your individual strategy for dealing with each of the candidates in such a way as to improve the chance of a good relationship basing this approach on a comparison of your needs intensities.

- Finally, in your group, compare your own profiles and discuss what part they have played in the group activity, if any.

An alternative to this exercise would be to ask participants to name a number of famous people. These could be their personal heroes or simply well-known personalities. In small groups they discuss and estimate the Needs Intensities of each of the individuals. An article by Robin Clark[89] suggests needs intensity profiles for a wide range of legendary figures.

Although we can only guess at other people's needs intensities, the concept has value in the context of counselling. We can watch out for patterns that reveal the client's needs intensities and even those of the people in his environment. The frustrations that a person brings to counselling can arise out of need deficiency but also from a conflict of needs intensities with a colleague, a friend or a family member.

[89] Clark, Robin. *Legends of the 20th Century.* International Journal of Reality Therapy, Vol 24, No.2, pp. 23-26.

248

The Quality World

In this chapter you will learn about:

- How pictures from our Quality Worlds drive our behaviour
- The important role of the Quality World in counselling
- Characteristics of the Quality World pictures
- Positive and negative aspects of the power of the Quality World
- How to classify problems according to needs, pictures and behaviours
- Different ways to explore a person's Quality World
- Layers of meaning and logic in the Quality World
- The link between the Quality World and interests and obsessions
- The difference between a fantasy world and the Quality World
- The Quality World of Groups
- The role of Education with regard to the Quality Worlds of students
- How to get what we want

A big part of our day is taken up with getting what we want. Try to spend even part of a day without wanting anything and you will understand what I mean. In Choice Theory terms, our wants are our Quality World pictures in action and the pictures are our personal collection of ways of meeting our basic needs. We accumulate these from our experience or from observation and although they may come from the past, when they are called into service it is their present form that is used.

According to Glasser we behave in order to achieve our pictures, to make them happen. So our behaviour is our attempt to reduce the discrepancy between the picture in our head and whatever we perceive to be happening in reality. This difference is felt as a frustration and the resulting urge to behave is expressed as a "want". We behave to eliminate the frustration just as we seek food to reduce the discomfort or pain of hunger.

For example, I am killing time waiting for a train. After looking in vain for a familiar face in the station and after counting all the pigeons pecking around the platform and reading all the billboards I am bored. This feeling is the frustration signal associated with a shortage of fun, one of my basic needs. A picture I have in my head for dealing with this need, especially in a railway station, is to read a magazine about my favourite sport. The reality is that I don't have a magazine. There is a discrepancy between what I would like to have and what I do have. (Figure 22.) Now my frustration is becoming more specific and I want a magazine. My next step is to behave in order to achieve this want. I go to the station shop and buy the magazine. I want a magazine and now I have the magazine; I have what I want; the frustration is gone; my scales are now in balance.

Another example: a young man sits alone studying while the rest of the family are enjoying a film on television. From time to time he pauses and daydreams picturing himself getting the good news of examination success. A good result will mean he can take up the job he has dreamed of for the last few years. The brief visit to his dreams reminds him that the lonely study is worthwhile and he turns back to his books. He chooses a behaviour that will help make his Quality World picture a reality, gradually shortening the psychological distance between where he is now on the one hand and career success on the other.

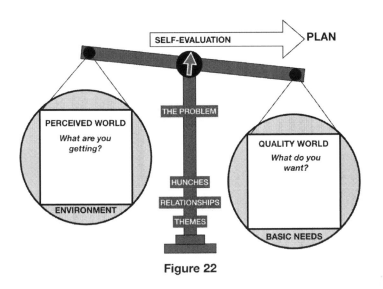

Figure 22

The Role of The Quality World in Counselling

People seek counselling when things are not turning out well for them. They are not achieving their Quality World pictures and consequently their needs are not being satisfied. For a counsellor to help a client, the person's Quality World becomes an important component of the counselling process. We help our clients (and ourselves) become more aware of their Quality Worlds and then we may help them choose new pictures and/or new behaviours to lead more need-satisfying lives.

As the counsellor sets out to uncover or clarify the nature of the client's problem, an examination of the client's wants is very often the first step. "Want" is a perfect word to explain what is going on since it indicates both the lack of something and the desire for that something, the urge to get it. The wants are Quality World pictures that are currently activated.

Even if the counsellor does not ask about wants it is common for clients to describe how things are not the way they want them to be. Ultimately the counsellor will focus on the pictures that relate to the client's most important problem. By sifting through the themes that the client presents the counsellor is almost always exploring his Quality World.

Obviously such a search is not done separately from the client's perception of his current reality. When a mother says, "I want my son to give up drugs", we know that a drug-free son is in this woman's Quality World and we know that a drug-taking son is what she is currently perceiving. The difference between the two perceptions is the reason the parent is seeking counselling. Making a counselling appointment is one of the behaviours she has chosen in an attempt to reduce the distance between "drug-free son" and "drug-taking son".

The counsellor and client may have talked about several different issues before settling on this as the core problem. However, the exploration must go further. What exactly does the mother mean when she says her son is taking drugs? In her perceptual world vitamin capsules or any type of pill may be seen as a "drug". She may mean he takes one pint of beer per week. At the other end of the scale she may be describing someone who is injecting heroin on a daily basis. Finding out such details is all part of the exploration of her current perceptual world.

As the counsellor explores her Quality World in detail, he may ask what she means by "drug free". It is always dangerous to assume that we understand another person! She might mean giving up caffeine, drinking "only" five pints of beer per night, abandoning heroin but keeping the marijuana …. Anything is possible!

In Reality Therapy the counsellor is targeting the major theme and then eliciting details about both sides of the scales diagram (Figure 1), the Quality World aspects and the current perceptions.

Characteristics of Quality World Pictures

The pictures that make up the Quality World have certain commonly found features:

- they are usually very specific
- a picture may serve one or more needs at the same time
- pictures come from our own experiences, from our families and friends, from our culture
- pictures are always good in the person's view
- pictures can be very hard to change
- everyone has different pictures
- individuals differ in the number and complexity of their pictures
- flexible pictures are easier to make happen
- pictures can be in conflict with one another
- a person may lack the skills or opportunity to realise pictures
- the pictures might not in fact be need satisfying
- the pictures could be very destructive to myself or to others
- the pictures could be seen by others as immoral, illegal or even as evil
- pictures may be very satisfying but only for a short time
- pictures link to other pictures by our own inner logic

A straightforward example of a Quality World picture is your picture of a "good restaurant". One of mine is in Malahide, County Dublin. It has a long room packed with tables. There is moderate noise level. The food has a strong but not exclusive Italian influence and I can only describe it as exquisite, a feast for the palate. The staff are genuinely friendly but discreet. The cost is a little above average but not too expensive for a good meal with wine. For me it is quite a specific picture.

If one or more of those characteristics were to change a lot I might reduce the picture's status in my Quality World and at a certain point remove it altogether. Some changes would not really matter: background music, oriental food, moderate price increase. On the other hand, if I wanted a "good restaurant" for a wild birthday party with 20 friends, this one would not be suitable in my view of the world. Neither would it meet my needs if I wanted a quick lunch at an economical price.

As you will appreciate even more if you look at your own Quality World, the details of any one picture are very specific and ultimately are unique to each person. Your view of a "good restaurant" may be totally different from the above or you may love the same restaurant as I do but for completely different reasons. And the same applies to everything: a good breakfast, how to talk to officials, what constitutes "great fun", healthy living, family life … everything. Whatever the picture, if (1) it does not in fact satisfy the person's needs or (2) the person's behaviours do not or cannot realise his pictures, then the overall effect is continued need-frustration, unhappiness.

The Constructive Power of The Quality World

The importance of people's awareness of their own Quality World is demonstrated by the emphasis on mission statements, vision statements, policies, goals and the like. The link between the pictures in my head and the behaviour I choose to make them happen is greatly enhanced the more aware I become of the pictures in all their specific detail. By constantly recalling and visualising a Quality World picture I can boost my motivation to behave in order to achieve it. Sports competitors do exactly this when they imagine the moment of glory, crossing the finishing line ahead of the opposition, seeing their national flag raised in their honour, a trophy in their hands. We all do it. A father buying a camera as a birthday present for his daughter may have in his mind's eye the image of his daughter opening the present and using it. Looking at a particular camera in the shop he may even comment to the assistant, "I can't see her using this one." There is a definite link between the picture in his Quality World and his purchase and he uses the picture as a reference to guide his behaviour.

When people want to work together it is important for them to clarify the shared Quality World pictures that will guide their efforts. Discussing what they want as a group and constantly recalling their goal will help motivate the group members to work harder towards that end. Almost as important is the streamlining of their efforts that results from a clearly shared goal.

In a similar way, when a counsellor chooses to work with a client, detailing the main pictures in the Quality World is important. Of one thing we can be certain: when a person comes seeking counselling there is at least one Quality World picture that is not working well and, according to Glasser, it usually has to do with a relationship.

The Destructive Power of The Quality World

Glasser has a solid belief in the goodness of the human being. A person accumulates pictures that appear to be need-satisfying and the behavioural expression of these pictures is always the person's best choice at the time. Unfortunately this does not mean that an individual's pictures or behaviours are all positive in any absolute way. There are teachers who believe that shouting and threatening their students will make them work harder. They choose this picture because they think it is good educational practice and they firmly believe that ultimately it is good for their students.

There are political leaders who believe that all those who voice dissent should be imprisoned or even killed. There are individuals who believe that they should carry out horrific deeds in the name of their cause. In all these cases we are referring to pictures in people's Quality Worlds but they are pictures that others, myself included, would abhor completely.

Even in these cases Choice Theory teaches that these people opt for these behaviours because they really believe they are the best options available to them at the time. It may be difficult to accept this analysis when thinking about a person who is prepared to bypass all the norms of civilised society but it is nonetheless accurate.

In no way does such a Choice Theory analysis diminish the legal imperative to imprison dangerous people and safeguard the lives of citizens. One of the purposes of prisons is to protect citizens from those who would do harm. At the same time it is worth recalling that punitive methods do not normally convince people to change their Quality World pictures although they may adjust their behaviour in the short term. The educational value of imprisonment is not guaranteed! If we hope to see long term changes in individuals we need to help them find new pictures for their Quality Worlds.

At another level we must work to create situations where wide-spread need frustration is diminished, a society where people can learn more effective ways to express their worries and even their anger in an atmosphere of understanding and justice. One of the main purposes of general education is to help people enrich their Quality Worlds as they learn a big variety of ways to meet all of their basic needs.

As citizens, counsellors, educators, managers or parents we may sometimes find ourselves in situations where our own pictures conflict strongly with those around us. In some cases the conflict may be so great as to require ethical or even legal decisions on our part.

When Pictures Don't Meet Needs

In an earlier chapter we mentioned the different types of problems a person can have and we revisit these with a little more detail here as they all involve the Quality World. We saw that the link between

NEEDS, PICTURES and BEHAVIOURS does not always work smoothly to guarantee satisfaction of our needs. There were three main ways this could break down. See figure 23.

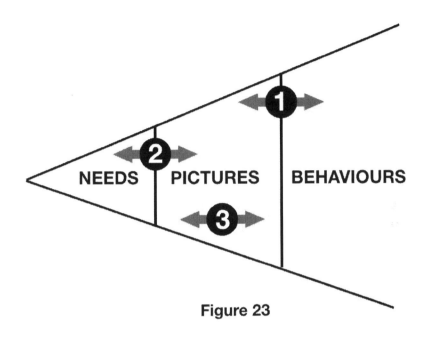

Figure 23

❶ Activation of Behaviours: My picture would probably meet my needs quite well but I am unable to make it happen.

- I want to take my wife to our favourite restaurant (mentioned earlier) for her birthday but it is closed (or my bank balance is recommending something more economical).
- I want to be a professional basketballer (but am not very good at basketball).
- I want to marry some day (but have never learned how to talk to other people).
- I want to emigrate to another country (but cannot afford it).

❷ Efficacy: The picture is attainable but would not really meet my needs in the longer term.

- My favourite restaurant opens a branch in the city centre and I go there expecting more of same only to find that they play loud rap music all the time (not big in my Quality World when I think of restaurants).
- I want to take drugs because I need FUN.
- I want to work long hours because I need FREEDOM from problems at home.
- I want to pay for everybody's drinks because I need FRIENDSHIP.

❸ Logic: The linkages between my picture and other pictures are not as I take them to be.

- I assume that my favourite restaurant will be ideal for my friend from school days (but I do not know that he is vegetarian and that the restaurant does not have a good vegetarian selection).
- I want a paint brush (but if I use a brush to paint my car I will not like the result).
- I want to drop French as a school subject (but this would close the door to my favourite university courses).
- I want to keep my job in spite of my current stress (but I am a brain surgeon).
- I want to continue my extra-marital affair (but I want to keep my spouse and kids).
- I want to give up my job and sail around the world (but I want to keep my pension rights).

One of our primary concerns in counselling will be to access the client's Quality World particularly in the area relevant to the problem he is bringing to the session. It would be wasteful to discuss at length the client's Quality World pictures about something that was not central to the current problem. The client himself may be totally unaware of the problem or of the relevant aspects of his wants and so the counsellor's job will be to help tease this out. On the other hand, the client may be only too aware of every aspect of his frustration and talking about his frustrated wants may be very painful for him. This is why involvement is so important.

Behind the teases about hair-styles that a young man mentions to the counsellor may be nagging doubts about his own sexual identity. A very high level of involvement is almost always required before probing a person's Quality World in a counselling situation. That Quality World hurts most in the area that led the person to seek counselling.

Ways To Explore The Quality World

Here are some ways we can use to explore this inner world:

Listen.

- (Let the client tell you.)

Observe.

- Preferred topics of conversation
- Choices the person makes (behaviour reflects Quality World)
- Badges, scarves, colours, emblems, tattoos

Ask.

- What do you want?
- What is missing in your life now?
- What is not right for you?
- What is the problem you want to discuss with me?

Ask about wishes, hopes and dreams.

- What would you do with €1000?
- Who is your hero?
- What is your favourite dream?
- What would you like to change in your life right now?
- What is missing in your life now?

Use metaphors or similes.

- What film title comes closest to the story of your life now?
- If you were a car, which part would need servicing?

Get specific details.

- You want people to be "nice" to you. Tell me what "nice" would mean in practice.
- Tell me how you would like tomorrow to be.
- You want a "better" office. What would a better office look like?

Compare before/after.

- What was different when you last felt happy?
- What would be your ideal age ... and how would it differ from now?

Compare with other, hero, model.

- How do you differ from Mary who never has these problems?
- Which of your friends would handle this well? How?

Asking about "not wants".

- What do you really want not to happen?
- What is the worst that could happen?
- How do you not want this situation to be?

Hypothetical.

- If you got this new job, what difference would it make in your life?
- If you phone me in a week to tell me that you are now very happy, what would be the reason?

Imagination.

- Use of coloured stones or similar objects. (E.g., move these around to show me how your family members relate to one another and then show me how you would like them to relate.)
- If an evil wizard had cast a spell on you, what would it say?
- What do you day-dream about? Does this tell you anything about yourself?

Artwork.

- Design a family shield representing all that is important to you.
- Draw your family and tell me about it.

Role-play

- Act out conversations, confrontations.

- Stump, Cabin and Stream fantasies (Gestalt exercise[90])
- Identification with clay model.
- Use of puppets.

In the following sample extract from a counselling interaction we see a straightforward opening up of the client's Quality World. The counsellor is asking how the client would like the situation to be.

1	Counsellor:	You say you are not getting on very well with Liam, your boyfriend ...
2	Orla:	That's putting it mildly. He just doesn't seem to care; it's not like it used to be. I don't know what's happening. (sobs a little)
3	Counsellor:	Whatever is happening you are hurting a lot from it. If he showed clear signs of caring for you, what would he be doing that is different from what he is doing now?
4	Orla:	Well, he would listen to me for a start. At the moment he keeps talking about his new motorcycle and the chat at the pub.

---

[90] Passona, William R. *Gestalt Approaches in Counselling*. New York: Holt, Rinehart and Winston, 1975.

5	Counsellor:	Anything else …?

6	Orla:	Lots … on Sundays we would always have lunch together either at his parents' house or mine. Now they have motorbike trials on Sunday mornings and our lunch together just doesn't happen.

The pictures in a person's Quality World are always very specific and so the counsellor looks for detail. "What would he be doing that is different?"

Somewhere in Orla's Quality World she has a picture for "caring boyfriend" but, when she looks at what she has got, Liam's behaviour is not measuring up to the Quality World picture. What Orla wants and what she is getting are quite different and so the counsellor teases out the details of "caring boyfriend".

Her picture might have included details such as "he will walk me to the bus-stop every morning", "he will telephone me three times a day to see how I am", "he will be warm and affectionate to me even in front of his mates".

There are many possibilities but Orla's specific picture has to do with listening to her and being with her for Sunday lunch. These are the specific details of her Quality World around the problem with her boyfriend and further counselling will seek even more clarification here.

Later this counsellor will probably work with Orla on what she can do to get the type of boyfriend she wants. It may be a question of her dealing differently with Liam or even of dealing with a different boyfriend. But before any planning work can be discussed it is necessary that the client's wants are clear in the counselling session.

This next extract from a counselling session demonstrates how the counsellor gradually homes in on the key frustration in the client's life by exploring his Quality World but in this case the client himself is not clear initially about where the problem lies. The counsellor picks on what John, his client, wants or does not want. Comparing a before/after (happy/unhappy) scenario is the technique the counsellor draws on to help in this process.

1	Counsellor:	John, you tell me that you are very unhappy at work but you find it hard to pinpoint what is wrong.
2	John:	That's right. The pay is good, my colleagues are excellent, the boss is a very nice lady. I just don't understand it.
3	Counsellor:	Have you always been unhappy there?
4	John:	No, everything was great until ... (pauses)
5	Counsellor:	... until ... (the counsellor has spotted an opportunity to compare before/after)

6 John:		... until Liz's retirement party!

7 Counsellor: Tell me more about it.

8 John: But that has nothing to do with my problem. I never even knew Liz very well and it was a great party!

9 Counsellor: Was there any particular incident that stood out for you that night? It might not have included Liz at all. (The counsellor suspects there was some important perceptual shift that happened that evening.)

10 John: Well, Paddy – that's the bloke I share an office with – Paddy asked me if I was looking forward to my own retirement. Don't get me wrong. He's a nice guy and there was no malice in his question. There was something about it that didn't go down well with me. It annoyed me. Maybe talk of retirement annoys most people.

11 Counsellor: Can you put your finger on what it is about it that disturbs you? (Note the use of the present tense.)

12 John: I'm not sure ...

13 Counsellor: What were you thinking just after he spoke to you? (The specific moment can help recall the specific thought.)

14 John: I was thinking that Paddy and I would probably retire around the same time. Then I remember wondering who would staff our office if we went together ... and then ... now I remember ... it's only hitting me now!

15 Counsellor: What?

16 John: The thought flashed through my head that in twenty years time I would probably still be in the same office. The firm is very nice but there's no room for movement in it at all. That's the bit that really annoys me. (John's voice begins to sound angry.) It really cheeses me off!

17 Counsellor: So it would seem that the job is very good for you right now but you don't want to be in the same position for the rest of your working life. (After saying this the Counsellor was silent for a while since John had become much more solemn.) ... John, if a good change did come up what would it be like? Describe it for me.

From this point on it is easier for Counsellor and Client to detail what a good promotion or change would look like for John and this in turn would lead to a discussion of how John might make it happen in this job or another. Since that retirement party John had been carrying his Quality World picture of his career development alongside a vague current perception that did not match that picture. By taking time to tease this out with a counsellor in a safe environment he can now see exactly where the discrepancy is and, once seen, he is in a better position to do something about it.

This process of homing in on the critical theme can take a long time in some cases. By seeking specific details the counsellor helps guide the focus towards the heart of the problem. Glasser once remarked that problems are never general, they are always specific. In my own experience of training counsellors, novices often make things very difficult for themselves by not getting sufficient detail about their clients. I sometimes suggest to them, "Imagine that tomorrow you will be asked to take on the identity of this person". Getting information to this level of detail is difficult but that's how hard a counsellor has to work.

In some forms of therapy, the "detail" they value is the client's past history or how the problem originated or how exactly the client describes his feelings. In Reality Therapy the details are always about the client's present perceptions. As in the previous example about John, if we explore the past at all it is to help clarify the present. We believe that the person is behaving now according to the perceptions of now. These perceptions are unique to the individual and have a logic and language of their own.

Logic, Language and Layers in The Quality World

The logic of any individual's Quality World can be remarkably complex but so too is the language a person uses. People have individual meanings for most of the words they use. If I tell you that my new watch was "very expensive", do you have the same understanding of "expensive" as I do? It is truly impossible to understand another human being. We can only do our best. For this reason it is wise to keep doubting our understanding as we explore another person's Quality World.

In a research project during my Psychology studies at university I found a group of school-girls frequently used the word "mad" to describe their friends and this puzzled me. Whatever it meant to me, analysis of the data revealed that it actually meant something positive for them. Eventually I discovered that the girls used the word in the sense of "mad about boys". Mystery solved! The teenagers I work with today use the word "mad" with an equally positive undertone but with a different meaning as in "fun-loving".

In helping the client explore the Quality World, we may need to peel back different layers of meaning in order to get a better understanding of what the client really wants.

For example, a client's statement that "I want my brother to stop drinking" could mean any one of several possibilities …

- This is bad for his health and I want him to be healthy.
- He gets more than his fair share of my mother's attention and I want exclusive attention from her.
- He looks like me and his behaviour is damaging my reputation, something I want to safeguard.
- He is engaging in light social drinking instead of playing tennis with me.

"I do not want to go to that interview" could mean …

- I feel more comfortable with the freedom I have now.
- I am very low in confidence for that job.
- The interview location is in a part of the city that is dangerous for me.

- I have been advised to wear a skirt to interviews but have never worn one in my life as I believe my legs are ugly!
- I do not really want the job

It is part of the counsellor's skill to help the client delve into the Quality World pictures and tease out their fuller significance and effectiveness for the client.

One structure I have found useful in exploring the different layers of the Quality World is to examine what the person says, what she means, what she wants, what she really wants and finally what she needs. (Figure 24.)

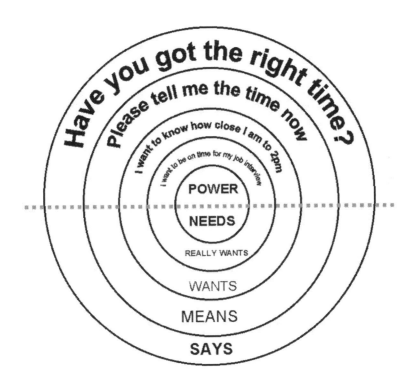

Figure 24

Sometimes what we think we want is not compatible with what we really want and, at the end of the day, is not really need-fulfilling. The example from Figure 24 together with two other examples are shown below in tabular form:

	1. THE TIME	2. THE WEATHER	3. THE PAINT-BRUSH
What the person **says**	Have you got the right time?	Isn't it a lovely day?	I want a paint-brush.
What the person **means**	Please tell me the time right now.	Please stop and talk to me.	I want a reasonably priced paint-brush
What the person **wants**	I want to know how close I am to 2.00 p.m.	I want to borrow your bicycle.	I want to paint my car.
What the person **really wants**	I want to be on time for my job interview and I want to get that job.	I want to get far away from my family who are nagging me a lot.	I want my car to look much better.
What the person **needs**	I need power	I need freedom.	I need power.

The Quality World, Interests and Obsessions

A strong image in my own Quality World is sailing. There are few things I like better than to be out on the sea in a boat under sail. Although this past-time is often described as a sport it is not such for me. I do love the thrust of a fair wind pushing six tons of boat through the water but I'm equally happy to be at anchor, reading the newspaper with a mug of coffee in my hand.

I now believe that my interest in boating has a lot to do with its symbolism, with how it fits into my inner logic. In my Quality World it is not simply a single picture but a series of intertwined pictures. For me boating represents independence and freedom. It is also a never-ending learning curve. Each time I go out on the boat it is a totally different experience. When friends are on board there is fun and excitement. The sea has a way of doing something for the spirit. These are all things that matter to me and one single activity feeds them all. There is more to sailing than meets the eye!

When someone has a strong interest I believe that a similar phenomenon is taking place. Somehow that particular interest meshes into the complexities of the individual's inner logic in a way that is intensely need-fulfilling. At least part of this satisfaction can come from the perceived symbolism of the activity. This, I think, is especially true of obsessions whether good or bad. The teenager with a fixation on a particular pop-star is usually infatuated by more than the musical talents of the star. Image makers and spin-doctors are well aware of the many factors than contribute to stardom.

Unfortunately, there are obsessions that are extremely dangerous. Whether it is those who abuse young children or the internet group that is interested in cannibalism I believe that somehow these obsessions all work in the same way. The activity as perceived by the obsessor fills a similarly shaped gap in that person's Quality World.

Part of the solution to such problems would be to understand the dynamic that is going on for the individual. Another part would be to avoid the general promotion of any images or symbolism that might feed into these strange logics.

It also follows from Choice Theory that so-called "needy" persons are more at risk. In desperation they are more likely to grasp at activities that appear to fill the gap in their Quality Worlds even if such activities are illegal or dangerous.

The Fantasy World

There is yet another type of layer that operates in the Quality World. I prefer to call it the "fantasy world" but do regard it as a component of the Quality World. Glasser alludes to something like this in "Choice Theory" but for a few years prior to its publication he had been speaking about part of the Quality World that "auditions" new pictures. When a good friend recommends a book to me, where does that suggestion go? Glasser believed that it went into an auditioning section of the Quality World and I believe that is very similar to the idealised or fantasy world he mentions in "Choice Theory".

Quality World pictures show up in our real behaviour because they drive it. We are likely to act on our Quality World pictures. What then happens to Fantasy World pictures? I believe they too show up in our behaviour but mainly in the thinking component. Any picture I put in my fantasy world is a picture I will enjoy thinking about though I might not do anything more than that! A round-the-world boat trip, a beach cottage in Hawaii, a private helicopter may all be pictures in my Fantasy World but I know I cannot afford them and do not even try to save for them. Whereas all the pictures in my Quality World are good, the pictures in my Fantasy World would be good if I could afford them! They do not emerge into my doing behaviours but that does not stop me "entertaining" the thoughts, which of course is a behaviour in itself. The "ideal self" referred to in the context of self-concept and self-esteem tends to be interpreted in ways similar to this Fantasy World rather than the Quality World. Indeed the "fantasy world" could be called my "ideal world". If the Quality World surfaces in our lives in the form of "wants", the fantasy world surfaces as "wishes".

Obviously, people can have problems if they confuse these two inner worlds. Counsellors sometimes ask clients, "What would you do if you won a fortune?" or "If you could wave a magic wand, what would you wish for?" Such questions can be useful but they do tap into the fantasy edge of the Quality World. When the client answers, asking her "which of these is in the realms of the possible in your life?" can move the focus into the more down-to-earth Quality World. Our aim would be to help the person move from the realm of wishes to that of wants and then into behaviour.

Social Aspects of The Quality World

When people work together in couples or in groups it becomes increasingly important for them to have clarity about the Quality World they share. For example, if two computer operators work in the same office, each will have Quality World pictures about how he wants the room to be. If one prefers general illumination and the other wants local reading lighting they could have a conflict. The fact that one likes sailing and the other is a ten-pin bowler is less likely to intrude in their working lives.

If each member of the group has a different understanding of the pictures that have a direct bearing on the shared behaviours of the group then there can be confusion and conflict.[91] The group will certainly not work as efficiently as it might had there been more consensus about the members' shared Quality World. Regular opportunities for the group members to meet formally or informally and ask "what are we as a group trying to do?" play an important role in clarifying the shared pictures.

In a similar way in the world of business it makes a lot of sense to check out the Quality World of the company's customers. What do

---

[91] The role of the Quality World in Relationships will be dealt with in more detail in the chapter on Relationships?.

they want from it? How do the products or services compare with the image customers have in their minds?

Education and The Quality World

The richness of our Quality World is important. If I have only one main picture about how to have fun, playing golf for example, then I will be frustrated when there is snow or when I have an arm injury. The more pictures I have the more options I will be able to consider in different circumstances. This is yet another reason why parents and educators should strive to give young people a very wide range of experiences. A healthy psycho-social life will need access to a rich and varied Quality World. So-called extra-curricular activities in schools are very important for enriching the Quality World, so important in fact that I believe schools should have a policy of openness to new activities at all times.

As people go through different life stages or even seasons, some pictures are more useful that others. It is important that education equip people for such changes by letting them sample many leisure activities.

Getting What We Want

Another important aspect of our Quality World is how we make pictures happen, how to get what we want. If I want to have restful nights instead of listening to my neighbour's trumpet practice how do I make the quiet nights happen? It becomes very important to communicate my wants clearly to the other person. At the same time if I also want to remain on good terms with my neighbour then my action plan needs to be worked out very carefully. I need a picture in my head for this complex piece of negotiation. Assertiveness training helps develop some of the relevant interpersonal skills.

Garth's Guitar

One day at school word was going around that one of the senior girl students had Garth Brook's guitar. The American singer had just visited Dublin and initially some of the staff members worried about how the guitar had come into the student's possession. Would Mr. Brook's Attorney soon be in contact?

We needn't have worried. The girl was glad to tell her story. She explained how she had gone to the concert with her little sister. The junior sibling got "sick" with the result that both girls got up to the front, right beside the stage and catwalk. Little sister hadn't counted on being hauled over the barrier and carried off to the infirmary but big sister's carefully thought-out plan was proceeding with military precision. She was now close to her idol.

"But how did you get the guitar?", I enquired. "I asked for it", she explained calmly and went on to describe how she held up a card she had prepared the night before. On it she had written the words "Mr Brooks, would you please give me your guitar, Sir?"

"What's with all this 'Sir' stuff?" I asked. "Oh, he likes politeness" she answered. She had even researched his Quality World! He spotted the notice, invited her onto the stage, sang to her, danced with her and gave her his guitar. This young lady knew a thing or two about how to make her Quality World happen ... and still does!

Getting what we want also requires careful attention to language. If you go to the hair-dressers and ask for a "short trim", do you believe that the person wielding the scissors has the same picture in his head as you for "short trim"?

Glasser rightly emphasises the central importance of the Quality World. The pictures that fill our heads drive our behaviours. Advertisers spend a lot of money offering us attractive new pictures in an attempt to influence our choices. A person's Quality World not only guides how that person behaves but, to know that Quality World is to know that person extremely well.

The Birthday Present

With a partner, ask the other what he or she would like as a birthday present. Ask for a simple answer such as "a brown brief-case". Then, based on the other's brief description, offer a detailed account of the gift you would buy for the person and check with them how closely that matches their Quality World picture. Notice how many differences there are and how many specific details you would need to buy a successful gift.

Alternatively, find out what your partner would like to do next week-end. Tease out the meaning of what he or she says, probe for the real wants.

Hidden Meanings

Read the following examples. The behaviours each individual will consider obviously depend on what he or she really wants, not simply on what she says or means. This exercise is simple but only because the real wants are explained.

Martin	SAYS:	I want a paint brush.
	MEANS:	I want a good well-priced paint brush.
	WANTS:	I want to paint my car.
	REALLY WANTS:	I really want something to give a smooth finish. (spray)
	NEEDS:	power and fun

Which of these two plans will meet this person's needs more effectively?

1. I will buy a small tin of car spray paint.
2. I will buy a brush because it is reasonably priced.

Chanelle	SAYS:	If only John would stop drinking.
	MEANS:	I want my brother to stop drinking.
	WANTS:	I want him to stop distracting my mother.
	REALLY WANTS:	I want my mother's undivided attention.
	NEEDS:	love and power

Which of these two plans will meet this person's needs more effectively?

1. I am going to give my brother a book on the evils of drinking.
2. I am going to watch a video with my mum at 9.30 tonight.

Michael	SAYS:	I want my son to keep his room tidy.
	MEANS:	I want him to make his bed and store his clothes.
	WANTS:	I want sense of order and some respect.
	REALLY WANTS:	I want the predictable loving child he was.
	NEEDS:	freedom and love

Which of these two plans will meet this person's needs more effectively?

1. I will do a deal with him tonight that he can do what he likes with his room but that he will tidy up any disorder he causes in the rest of the house.
2. I will just clean up his room and stop nagging him.

Quality World Mapping

This is an exercise developed by Jerry O'Sullivan from Cork[92] and can be very useful in counselling or even in self-development.

Give the client a blank page and offer instructions along these lines: "Imagine that this page represents everything that is important to you, people, places, events, things, ideas. Draw boxes or shapes that represent each of these making the box bigger the more important the item is to you." It can help to show the client an example such as in Figure 25:

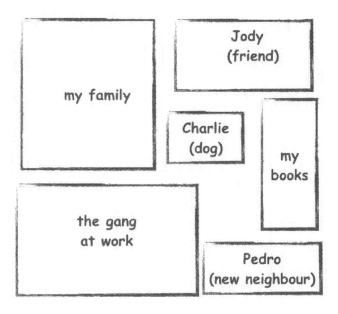

Figure 25

To this excellent original idea I like to add some variations. For example, the client may wish to represent items that are on the way into or out of his Quality World as in the example of the new

---

[92] O'Sullivan, Jerry. *A Technique for Exploring The Quality World.* Unpublished Reality Therapy Certification Presentation, Dublin, July 1991.

neighbour above. It can also be useful in counselling to ask, "Is there somebody or something that used to be very important to you and no longer is? Maybe you could draw this on the back of the page."

Obviously our aim in exploring a client's Quality World is to identify the main needs frustration that the client is concerned about. Using the Quality World map we could ask the client, "Where do you see problems here? Where are things not the way you would like them to be?"

An alternative application of this technique is to ask the client to draw boxes that represent his problems, varying in size according to the importance of the problem. This can be useful in helping the client decide which problem to focus on first. It can also be used at different stages of the counselling to evaluate progress.

Famous Quality Worlds

Practising Quality World exploration on fictional characters can provide a change of pace and some humour. The "client" in the role-play chooses a character such as one of the following without revealing the identity to the "counsellor":

   Robin Hood, Cleopatra, Dracula, Don Quixote, Albert Einstein

The role-play "client" begins "I want to have a holiday" and the "counsellor" helps the client explore his or her Quality World around the theme of holidays for this character. The "client" does not reveal his fictional identity until the end. At the end discuss how accurately we can (or cannot) guess about a person's Quality World pictures.

Your Own Quality World

Use the Quality World Mapping exercise from above to map out your own Quality World.

Next do a similar exercise mapping out how you spent your time over the last week. The more time you spent at a particular activity, the bigger the box.

Finally compare the two maps, the Quality World and the time usage. How do they compare? Does your life in the past week really reflect what is important to you?

Quality on the Move

Think back to certain important moments in your life and ask "what were the important pictures in my Quality World at the time?" (Sometimes an otherwise insignificant moment takes on great importance simply because one of our Quality World pictures is being challenged or changed!)

The Perceived World

In this chapter you will learn about:

- The importance of how we perceive our experience
- The perception of life as full of happenings or full of choices
- The role of the client's psychological strength in becoming aware of choice
- How we can examine the client's current choices in relation to the problem
- The need to attend to the total behaviour of the client
- Behaviours that are not normally explored in Choice Theory counselling

The ugly duckling's main problem was that he thought he was ugly. In the mysterious Quality Worlds of ducks there are obviously certain characteristics that all good-looking ducks have. When our hero peered into the water he could not see any of these in his reflection. All he saw was an ugly duckling and he didn't like it. We of the wiser species know of course that he was in fact a juvenile swan and not a duck at all.

But people do behave in a similar way. When they look at themselves and their world they do not always find what they want to find. Their perceptions and the logic they apply to them may be very inaccurate but it is what their sensory system presents to them as "real". It is all they have to compare with what they see in their Quality Worlds. In this chapter we examine in more detail this "perceived world" of the client and how we access it in therapy.

When a person seeks counselling it is safe to assume that at least one Quality World picture is not working. In other words, the perceived world (on the left of the scales in figure 26) does not match the Quality World (on the right of the scales); there is imbalance. The person has not got what the person wants!

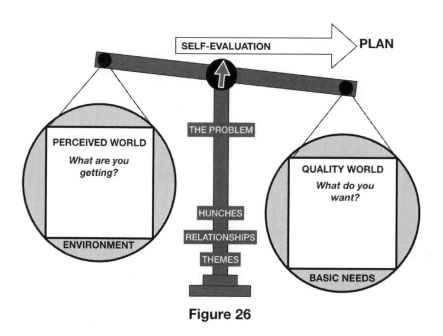

Figure 26

But this perceived world is not simply a one-dimensional entity. It is made up of experiences that happen to the individual as well as experiences that the individual controls. Many people think of course that almost all of what they can see in their lives is controlled by others.

Part of the counsellor's job is to help the individual explore the world as she (the client) sees it and learn just how much is in her own control and that means she can make choices about it.

Current Choices

The client is likely to perceive her world as one full of "happenings" whereas a central idea for Glasser is that we are always making choices. Whether we are being successful in getting what we want or not we are still making choices.

Of course, the therapist does not tell the client, "you got yourself into this mess, you are to blame for your own misfortune". When someone realises for the first time that they have been making choices all along it can be quite a shock for them. It is so easy to confuse responsibility with blame. Glasser's message is not one of criticising or blaming the client; instead he communicates a message of hope, something like, "You have been making more choices than even you realise up to now and so you can now make choices that may improve your situation".

The client, however, is more likely to begin by telling the therapist about everything that has happened to her, the client; she has bad luck, she has a disorder, a mental illness, it is her genetic inheritance, other people are the cause of her problems. Even if some things are in fact happening to her, she still has choices to make about how she deals with these experiences.

Sometimes I find it useful to begin talking to a client about what is "going on" in her life since that is usually how the client experiences it. Gradually I move towards the idea of choice pacing this shift in emphasis very carefully by observing how the client is coping with it. At the same time I am helping the client move from an external model of their lives to an internal one, from a life apparently determined by others to a life controlled by oneself.

For example, when a client says, "The people at work are not friendly to me", the Choice Theory counsellor may explore this in some further detail but will almost certainly move towards a question such as "And how have you been dealing with this so far?"

Psychological Strength and Awareness of Choice

I think it is important to pay attention to the client's psychological strength.   At the outset a person may feel helpless, lost and confused.   As I help him see that he has already made some choices in his life and that he probably could make some more, the client gets stronger.   Glasser does not specifically comment on this in his writings but I believe he is very aware of it in his counselling.

In his role-plays it is interesting to watch how he deals with the client's choices.   At the same time as he introduces the idea of choice he affirms the client by letting him see that the choices he has made so far were the best he knew.   This process of choice awareness is very much a strengthening one for the client.   It is not a debilitating accusation of blame.

When making a self-evaluation the client will be asking himself, "Is what I am doing getting me what I want?" or something similar.   It is vital therefore that the client is aware of the "I am doing" aspect, that he accepts ownership of his own current choices.

Before the self-evaluation and before planning new choices it makes sense for the therapist to check what attempts the client has already made to solve his problem.   In this phase of the therapy the counsellor usually helps the client realise just how many choices he may have made already, often with great courage and perseverance, and that new choices are a possibility.   As you can see, all of this means significant changes in the way the client perceives his world.

It is important to recall again that in his exploration of the client's current choices the counsellor looks for the theme or themes that are central to his problem. As counsellors we are not interested in all the choices the client makes, only those that have some bearing on his problem. This means that the review of current choices will go hand in hand with the examination of the client's Quality World.

Some of the advantages of checking the client's current choices are:

- The client realises that she has already made some efforts to solve the problem.
- The client is helped to see that earlier ineffective efforts were the best she knew at the time.
- The client becomes more aware of the extent of her own choices in her life.
- We can eliminate or re-adjust behaviours that did not work.
- We may get ideas for new behaviours.

Here is a portion of a counselling session with a fifteen-year old boy who has problems at school. Already counsellor and client have established what the boy wants and what he is not getting. Notice how the counsellor now keeps the focus on the boy and the boy's own behaviour. The right-hand column provides comments on the process.

REF	DIALOGUE	COMMENT
1 Counsellor:	Ken, you say you do want to get on better with Mr. Woods, your Geography teacher but you think he has a grudge against you? You say he is always "picking on you".	*The counsellor asks about something that 'happened' to the client.*
2 Ken:	Yes, if there is a noise in the room he accuses me. He doesn't seem to have noticed that I have been trying to change.	
3 Counsellor:	Tell me about that change, Ken. What have you been doing?	*Looking for more specific details about the "change". The question moves the emphasis to the client's choice.*
4 Ken:	Well, I am taking more care with my work. I actually like Geography and want to learn more about it but his constant nagging was making me sloppy about my work.	*Some external control language from Ken.*

5	Counsellor:	You started doing your work with less care than before?	*Offering a language of choice re-frame.*
6	Ken:	Yes and then he would give out more and things just got into a vicious circle.	*Note the very passive verb "got".*
7	Counsellor:	So in spite of all of that you decided to change!	*Offering a strong affirmation of Ken's decision to improve at school*
8	Ken:	Yes, I haven't been late for class or forgotten my books in over three weeks but a fat lot of good that has done me. He doesn't notice and doesn't care.	
9	Counsellor:	When you say you haven't been late, what time do you arrive for your nine o'clock class? Yesterday, for example, what time did you arrive?	*Checking on the meaning of "late", getting more specific details about Ken's new behaviour. Better to ask about a specific day!*

10 Ken: Yesterday? I think it was about five to nine. The latest I would ever be in recent times would be about two minutes to nine. But that makes no difference to him!

11 Counsellor: I suppose it's possible Ken that he hasn't noticed. Indeed, he might never notice! Have you done anything in particular to help him notice that you have changed?

Picking up on the "notice" theme, the counsellor examines behaviour relevant to this. The focus is on what the client can choose to do.

12 Ken: He must see that my work has improved. He must realise he hasn't had to give out to me for being late. What more can I do?

13 Counsellor: Ken, you have already done a lot and, in my experience, they are all very sensible things to do. But you yourself say things aren't getting any better. Maybe it's time to look at new things to try. What do you think?

Moving into self-evaluation and offering the idea of further change to Ken.

In this session the counsellor may have reached the personal conclusion that Ken's teacher is being unfair or is using pedagogical methods that are inappropriate for Ken. All of that is quite possible but it is Ken who is the client, not his teacher. In life he will encounter similar situations and it will help him now and in the future to learn what he himself can do about the problem.

Obviously if a child reports abuse of any sort we may then involve the teacher directly and, indeed, other authorities. Similarly if the child is very young it may be appropriate to have a chat with the teacher and the child's parents. Generally we try to help clients of any age control what they can control and we even encourage them to expand the areas over which they have control. At the same time we need to be realistic about the client's capabilities.

Here are some guidelines on how to explore the client's current behaviour:

- focus on the client's own behaviour
- focus on facts rather than on opinion or analysis
- examine the what, where, when, who of the behaviour
- explore the meanings of words used by the client, especially those that tend to have a more subjective meaning (e.g., "wonderful", "often", "fight")
- asking "why?" about the past tends to encourage excuses
- do not spend time processing excuses
- examine current behaviour rather than past actions.
- get the client's own perspective of his or her behaviour.
- emphasise the acting and thinking components rather than feeling and physiology.
- remind the clients that whatever they have been doing, it was their best attempt at the time.

- avoid any hint of criticism of the client's behaviour.

- get very specific details about the behaviour.

- ask about a particular day or time rather than a "typical" one.

- asking the client to role-play an incident can help clarify the details.

It is important that this review of the client's current behaviour should not become a litany of failures. The client has already done something about his problem. What he did was not effective (or he would not be seeking counselling) and it may even have been counter-productive. However, it was his best choice at the time. Even if he ignored the problem, hoping it would go away, that is still his best choice at the time. The counsellor can convey these messages in the conversation with the client. The counsellor can communicate a positive approach very simply in a straight-forward question such as "How have you been dealing with this so far?"

Total Current Behaviour

Given that counselling is essentially a verbal behaviour, a dialogue between two people, it is necessary sometimes to make a deliberate exploration of the non-verbal components of the client's current behaviour. In the counselling example earlier it is possible that Ken has been making all the improvements he says. It is also possible that occasionally the teacher asks innocently, "Are you listening, Ken?" and he replies, "I'm not the only one who is not listening. You're always picking on me! That's not fair!" This type of interaction does not show up in the counselling quoted earlier.

With experience of a given type of case the counsellor will know what situations to check out in greater detail and where to examine the tone of voice, the body language and other non-verbal communications. In other words, the counsellor attends to the totality of the client's behaviour and that includes the doing, thinking, feeling and physiology. Here are some sentences the counsellor might use with Ken if she suspected that some of his non-verbal communication could be worthy of some scrutiny:

> "Ken, help me see your situation better. Can you take me through yesterday morning, say from one minute to nine just as class was about to begin? Walk through my office door as if you were coming into the classroom and show me what you do. …. Did the teacher speak to you as you came in or later in the class? What exactly did he say? How did you reply? Say it to me the way you said it to him."

The counsellor is attempting to understand the total current behaviour as if she were present to witness it for herself. She probes to a point where she could almost become a double for the client. Ultimately, however, this knowledge is not for the counsellor but for the client. It helps him see what choices are effective and which ones are not.

Behaviours Not To Explore

There are certain behaviours the Choice Theory counsellor will not explore in great depth.

- blaming others or generally complaining about his life.
- excuses.
- getting involved in explanations of his behaviour, even psychological analyses of it.
- lengthy descriptions of feelings.
- Talking in detail about the client's "crazy" behaviour.

The last point merits further elaboration. If a person is choosing to wash his hands dozens of times every day because, he says, microbes are everywhere, then to argue about the omnipresence of microbes or discuss the use of different soaps is to join in the craziness.

In Choice Theory we see the crazy behaviour as the client's best attempt to satisfy his needs and that, in this case, he has dipped into his creative system for help. Working on the assumption, and it is an assumption, that this behaviour is probably ineffective overall (if only because it tends to scare friends away), if we discuss it too much we are helping maintain it since its only area of effectiveness is to attract other people's curiosity and advice. So what behaviour do we talk about?

As I have already indicated in the chapter on Theme Analysis, we go back to the underlying frustration the client is experiencing and we talk about current behaviours relating to that. The crazy behaviour will be one of these but there are probably more. If the counsellor has not been able to locate the focus of frustration so far and the client is not self-aware enough to talk about it then it can help to ask the client simply to describe his or her behaviour yesterday or today.

One of Glasser's favourite openings for a counselling session is "Tell me your story". It is an excellent invitation to the client to talk about his perceived world. Once he begins to tell his story, the counsellor can tease out the details.

Lunch-time

As a first step in practising an exploration of a client's perceived world, work with a partner and simply find out as much as you can about how he or she spent their last lunch-time.   Get as many specific details as you can.

A Happening

Working with another person, ask your partner to tell you about something that "happened" to them today or yesterday. Get specific details but gradually introduce the idea of "your choice" with questions such as "And then what did you decide to do?", "How did you deal with this?"

Unfamiliar Clients

This is a client-counsellor role-play.   It is important that the "counsellor" should not read the instructions for the "client".

Instructions for the Counsellor

Your task is to get as many specific details as possible about your client's perceived world. Do not read any of the client's instructions.

A Recent Experience

Before reading the rest of these instructions, write a summary of something you experienced today or yesterday. Use an event that has several different components. It is not necessary that it be a problem.

When you have finished writing, ask yourself the following questions about the experience:

1. Which of the events were things that happened to you, things totally beyond your control?

2. What choices did you make?

3. How certain can you be of the accuracy of your perceptions?

4. Think of a good friend of yours. If that person had the same experiences as you, would he or she have viewed them in exactly the same way? What would be different?

Further Details for the Unfamiliar Clients Exercise

Use the table that follows to find the details that correspond to the role you have chosen.

When the counsellor begins the session you may use the Role name below but not your secret identity.

You tell your story beginning as shown here. If the counsellor wants to know more continue the story in line with the real identity of your role.

Do not reveal your secret identity until the exercise finishes.

ROLE	CLIENT'S STORY	CLIENT'S SECRET IDENTITY
NICKY	I have to appear in a court in Dublin soon. The police accuse me of loitering on a roof!	Santa Claus
SCOTTY	People keep annoying me, dropping things on me. Others treat me as if I didn't exist.	Loch Ness Monster
IGGY	My brothers and sisters are always saying I look terrible and they tell me to go away.	Ugly Duckling
BILLY	My Dad is obsessed with apples and he sometimes gets very strange ideas about them. I don't like this.	William Tell's son

ROLE	CLIENT'S STORY	CLIENT'S SECRET IDENTITY
PADDY	I had been kidnapped and forced to look after animals. However, I escaped. Now my problem is that I'm hearing voices.	St. Patrick
KENNY	My girl-friend doesn't trust me. She thinks I'm meeting somebody else. Sometimes I dress a little funny.	Clark Kent (aka Superman)

The Language of Reality Therapy

In this chapter you will learn about:

- Helping the client become more aware of choice
- How we help a client focus on his or her personal responsibility
- How we use the idea of working together
- How flexibility is used and modelled in the counselling process
- How we communicate confidentiality to the client
- The value of metaphors, similes and other images in counselling
- Humour as involvement and as evidence of progress
- How optimism is built into the counselling session
- The advantages of affirmation over praise
- The value of reframing and different ways to use this
- The importance of specific details in counselling

In the last chapter we mentioned the gradual move towards talk of choice when processing the client's experience. Earlier we saw how the external control psychology used by so many people influences the very language we use. We tend to say "The way he treated his dog made me feel angry" instead of "I felt angry when I saw how he treated his dog". [93]

---

[93] There are lots of examples of external control language and sample choice theory alternatives in Glasser, William & Carleen Glasser. *Choice: The Flip Side of Control - The Language of Choice Theory*. Los Angeles: William Glasser Inc., 1998.

Glasser has always been aware of the importance of the words we use in talking about human behaviour especially the contrasting viewpoints found in the passive and active forms of the verbs as in "being depressed" and "depressing".   Some everyday phrases convey a strong sense of external control, not the sort of message we believe in projecting in Reality Therapy.   For example, "What happened to you?" or   "What made you angry?", both phrases implying outside forces at work.

There are other language considerations in Reality Therapy and in this chapter we examine eleven different examples of these. Although Glasser himself does not teach explicitly about all of them I believe they are to be found in abundance in his role-plays.

The Language of Choice

One of the core beliefs that a Reality Therapy practitioner has about his clients is   "You are responsible for your life.   At the present moment you can choose to go in a direction that may improve your life and you could choose to go in a direction that would probably worsen it.   In all likelihood you have more choices than you are aware of."

It would of course be very rare for the counsellor to use such a direct communication with a client.   Given the fragile situation and weakened state of so many of those who seek counselling, direct confrontation or challenge can appear overpowering and in most cases it would be inappropriate.

One valuable way to help a client gradually realise just how many choices she has is to use the "language of choice" in our exchanges with her.   This means using verbs such as "choose", "decide", "opt", "select".   These are introduced gradually and at the same time we cut down on our use of the language of external control as in "he made me mad", "I had to go", "I must", "I should".

Initially a client is likely to tell the counsellor general background information and much of this may be things that "happened to" the client. The counsellor can help the person become more aware of her level of control by introducing the language of choice very gradually. Reflecting back the client's external control statements in terms of personal choices is one way to do this. Obviously it is important to the counselling process if the counsellor chooses his words very carefully so that they do not come across as criticism of the language and concepts used by the client.

In the following sample extract from a counselling session where there is already a considerable level of involvement, I have used bold type to highlight the external control language and underlining to draw attention to the language of choice.

1	Christine	I have a wonderful husband and two beautiful kids and in fact it was Tom, my husband, who **made me** come to see you.
2	Counsellor	From what you told me earlier about Tom, (smiling) somehow I cannot imagine him dragging you here. It sounds as if you liked his suggestion and followed up on it by making the appointment.
3	Christine	Indeed. He was worried about me and I'm sick with worry myself. I work part-time and that's where my problem is. I have caught my colleague Judy taking money from the till on several occasions. I am going to **have to** tell the boss about it but I simply cannot handle this. I am very friendly with her.

4 Counsellor   So telling the boss is <u>one option you are considering</u> and it sounds as if that would be difficult for you. Maybe you can go into a little more detail for me about this whole situation and together we may be able to explore more options before you finally <u>decide</u> what to do about it.

It is quite common for clients to latch onto this new way of seeing their own behaviour and they will often begin to use the new language themselves, frequently accompanied with humour: "I had to catch the bus. OK, OK, I decided to catch the bus." What is happening is more than a simple change of vocabulary. As the person begins to recognise just how many choices she has she grows in the ability to take control of her own life again.

Throughout counselling and particularly in the early stages, the counsellor will be sensitive to just how much "choice awareness" the client is ready for at any given time. Certainly there must be a considerable level of involvement before the client is ready.

The Language of Responsibility

Here we are not talking about responsibility in the popular sense that implies blame or guilt. In therapy we think in terms of "who can do something about this?" rather than "who caused this?" or "who is to blame for this? From a Choice Theory perspective it is the client who can do something about the situation. The language of choice certainly helps move in the direction of the client's locus of control. Another relatively simple way we can achieve this is to keep the client at the centre of our focus.

Clients will often see others as responsible for their own problems. "My parents split up and it destroyed my life."   "I was sexually abused and it made me suicidal." Glasser recognises that in many situations we are in fact victims of external actions and events (e.g., an earthquake, an economic depression). But in all situations we have choices.

When a client claims that "my mother gives me too much housework and I have no time left to study" or "my boss keeps reminding me of my past failures and I find it hard to concentrate on my work", the therapist may think to himself that it is the mother or the boss who needs the therapy. That may well be true but the therapist's client is the person who has come to seek therapy. In Reality Therapy we will certainly listen to the client's story of what others have done to him but we will soon move to helping him examine how he has dealt with this situation up to now and what he could choose to do differently. People tend to blame others for their woes but, even where they are the cause, the only person who can change anything for the client is the client.

Helping the client talk less about other people and more about himself is one way to encourage this client responsibility:

1 **Client**	I really don't know what to do. My final examinations are at the end of the month. The people next door make more noise than ever. My "ex" keeps phoning me about money problems.
2 **Counsellor**	That sounds tough. What have you done so far to cope with all of these difficulties?

The locus of responsibility can be interesting to observe in counselling sessions. The counsellor, for example, by accepting a person as client, has undertaken a professional duty to help that individual to examine her life. Sometimes, however, the client attempts to alter the limits of that responsibility. For example, if a client says, "You are my last hope", in a sense he is shifting some of the responsibility for his life onto you, the therapist. An answer with a little humour can help clarify where the boundaries of responsibility lie: "Well, I suppose I am the hope you are choosing right now but of course you can choose more hopes if you wish!"

Glasser sometimes comments "remember who owns the problem". He believes that the client should be doing the bulk of the work, not the counsellor. Because of the respect that clients show their therapists it is very easy for the latter to assume too much responsibility. The client asks, "What do you think?" and the therapist can easily fall into the trap of assuming that he is supposed to know the answer to this question. It is interesting in this regard to observe how often Glasser says to clients, "I don't know".

When examining ways to deal with a problem in the client's life, counsellors sometimes feel that it is their responsibility to come up with options for the client. Certainly they have an ethical responsibility to share any possible options they know about with the client but it is the client's own responsibility to find and choose the most suitable option for them. The counsellor's job is to manage the structures that counselling can offer a person to solve the problems of his life.

The Language of Alliance

Using the pronoun "**we**" can be very powerful in counselling. A simple example is "Maybe if **we** look at the problem together **we** will find a better approach." In Reality Therapy, where we are highly aware of the responsibility of the client, we know too that we are working "with" the client. This collaboration becomes more effective when both sides are more aware of their quite different individual roles and responsibilities. Another advantage of using this collaborative approach is that it can contribute greatly to involvement.

Counselling is based on the notion that "two heads are better than one" and it can be helpful to remind the client of this without forgetting that each of the heads has a different job to do. I will sometimes remind my clients (and myself) "you are the expert in your life; my job is to help you look at it and see if you have better choices".

Of course, this is not a life-long alliance! It would be counter-productive for the client to become dependent on working with the counsellor. It is very much an alliance for a specific task, that of helping the client sort out his present problem.

The Language of Flexibility

Those who study Reality Therapy after learning other forms of client-centred counselling often have the impression that Glasser is very directive in his approach. It is true that he seems to give advice and sometimes even instructions. However, these always carry the vital ingredient of flexibility. The comment "A torch can help a child who is afraid of the dark" can sound like an authoritative piece of advice and a strong recommendation. If we preface the comment with the word "sometimes", it begins to sound more like an option for the client to consider but not to adopt blindly.

When there is a strong level of involvement between the counsellor and the client flexibility may be more implicit than explicit. It is probably better to err on the side of caution and sprinkle your dialogue with a lot of words such as: sometimes, frequently, usually, maybe, probably, may, might. Real life has a lot of maybes!

Whatever the means, it is important to communicate this flexibility to the client. We can share our own experience with the person but we know that it does not always apply in the same way to everyone.

We want to avoid any impression that this is something that the client "must" or even "should" do. Using a flexible framework allows us to share our own wisdom safely with another person.

This approach also serves as a model of flexibility to the client. Many people, when they have let their lives go somewhat out of control, adhere even more rigidly to certain beliefs or behaviours. After all it makes good sense to regress, to move back to safer territory. But the resulting lack of flexibility can seriously hinder their making changes in their lives. Unfortunately this can also encourage a similar degree of stubbornness in those around them. The relaxed and understanding approach of the counsellor is something they very much need and welcome. Even still it may take some time for them to feel safe enough to loosen up. This atmosphere helps them become more flexible themselves and goes some way towards teaching them the value of flexibility.

The Language of Trust

Although we normally spell out our policy on confidentiality early in the first counselling session it is something that we may need to underline frequently during the whole process. Even telling the client that we may have to refer certain matters to others is part of this trust. The client needs to have a clear picture of where he stands in relation to the therapist.

In a school context the reputation of the Guidance Counsellor as a trustworthy person is essential. Any departure or even apparent departure from confidentiality soon does the rounds on the school's bush telegraph and the value of the counselling service suffers.

Curiously the phrase "trust me" is not normally part of the language of trust. I would prefer to say to a client, "Don't trust me ... at least don't do it automatically. Tell your story in your own time. Check as you go along if I sound like someone you can trust. Talk to others about it if it helps." To be someone a client can trust means behaving in a trustworthy way and that in turn means respecting their need for caution.

Indeed, sometimes it can help to recommend caution. A client begins to talk about a very private problem and, once the flood-gates are opened, a lot of details can be disclosed. I might ask such a client, "are you comfortable talking about this?" I am also aware that such a client might have regrets later about opening up so much and so I might interject a reminder about how I treat the client's story.

Some clients may need a lot of ongoing reassurance about confidentiality. At the same time it is important to mention to them that they themselves can talk to whomsoever they wish about their problems and about what happens in counselling.

It can be helpful to inform clients that you will not discuss their problems if you meet them socially, and that you might even behave as if you did not know the client, all in the interests of protecting their confidentiality.

The Language of Imagery

By "imagery" we really include a wide range of possibilities: similes, metaphors, images, stories, parables, roles. Writers and musicians have always appreciated the power of images over concepts. When Wordsworth wandered "lonely as a cloud" and Simon and Garfunkel sang of a "bridge over troubled waters" I for one am glad they did not write about "a state of existential solitude" and "stress reduction resources" respectively.

Imagery has a special power of its own and can greatly enrich the communication between client and therapist. "If your life feels like a bundle of knots, where do we start to unravel them?" Authors sometimes refer to this as "therapeutic metaphor" and two useful references on their use in Reality Therapy is Robert Wubbolding's book[94] and Suzy Hallock Bannigan's article[95].

If I say "John is like a doormat" I am using a simile whereas to say "John is a doormat" is a metaphor. There is something immediate and powerful about this direct equating of person and image, something that gives the metaphor privileged status in counselling. Indeed many of the wonderful imagery techniques used in Gestalt Therapy rely on the power of metaphor.[96] Two films that celebrate the use of metaphor are "The Postman" ("Il Postino") and Peter Sellers' last film "Being There".

In fact concrete imagery was part of our earlier thought processes long before we developed the power to abstract and so it has greater immediacy for us. To shift our communication style too far away from the concrete has its problems for the would-be counsellor. Carkhuff and others found that the highly cognitive academic training of many counsellors reduced their ability to help others.[97] Learning to use more abstract language would not be a problem were it not for the fact that we often forget how to use a simpler more powerful language, one that our clients will generally feel more at home with.

Even in everyday speech we often compare people to concrete things:

- "John is as cool as a cucumber"
- "Jack is a doormat"

---

[94] Wubbolding, Robert E. *Understanding Reality Therapy: A Metaphorical Approach.* New York: Harper Perennial, 1991.

[95] Hallock Bannigan, Suzy. *Making Metaphors in Therapeutic Process.* Journal of Reality Therapy. 1989, 9-1, 25-29.

[96] Oaklander, Violet. *Windows to our Children.* Moab, Utah: Real People Press, 1978.

[97] Carkhuff, R.R. *What's it all about anyway? Some reflections on helping and human resource development models.* Counseling Psychologist, 1972, 3 (3), 79-87.

- "Mary is like a breath of fresh air"
- "Walter is a real butterfly!"
- "My lady's a wild flying dove."[98]

Sometimes we use ready-made comparisons, sometimes we make them up. The image may even become part of the person's identity as in nicknames.

- Boxcar Willie
- Rocky Marciano
- Elvis the Pelvis

In therapy the use of images, comparisons or metaphors has several advantages:

- A lot of meaning can be communicated in few words ("a breath of fresh air")
- The content is concrete rather than conceptual and so is more easily grasped
- Images chosen from the client's experience are extra meaningful to him/her
- Sometimes imagery can even suggest solutions ("Should you use the same golf club on the green as in the rough?")
- They can open up new perspectives ("I am in a hole and digging frantically to get out but I'm digging down. Come to think of it you can't dig up; you climb up.")
- Images can be developed during the counselling ("Do you think the breath of fresh air you are experiencing might need a little boost by opening a window?")
- They introduce colour and variety into counselling

---

[98] Song by US folk-singer Tom Paxton

- The same imagery can be returned to at different stages in the counselling. ("Are you still digging or have you begun to climb?")

Here are some ideas on how comparisons may be used in a therapy session:

- Ask the client for a metaphor or symbol representing his or her own life right now.
- Use Music - "If someone made a film about this part of your life what theme music would suit?"
- Use drawings - "draw how you feel right now".
- Stories, fairy-tales, legends – "Tell me your favourite. In what way is it similar to your life right now?"
- Certain objects have strong image value in counselling: kaleidoscope, jigsaw, weighing scales, hermit crab, muddle, car, boat, rosebush, log cabin, half-filled bottle of water, a tape measure.
- Take any object and ask the client in what way this object is similar to any aspect of his/her current life (or problem).
- Take ideas and language from the client's life experience:

  ‣ Golfer: "It's like trying to tee off with a putter instead of a driver"
  ‣ Sailor: "It's as if your boat's rudder is not working"
  ‣ Knitter: "It feels like you are knitting but someone is unravelling it as fast as you knit".
  ‣ Computer User: "It's as if the computer's mouse is plugged in but the buttons don't work!"

The Language of Humour

Humour may appear out of place in the serious atmosphere of counselling but in fact it is a very important addition to the counsellor's resources.

Glasser sees fun as one of the basic needs and he associates it with the experience of learning. It then comes as no surprise that moments of special learning during counselling will have a fun dimension.

Humour can be an important sign of progress. There are critical moments in the counselling process when a client takes a new perspective on his problems. This can be a moment of great relief and humour comes naturally at such a time. It is very often a sign that the client is now able to stand outside of the issue and see it from a distance. It may mean that he is now seeing it as past history or as something that is now solvable. It will very often occur just after an important self-evaluation or be the very expression of that evaluation. "I really am silly! The method I was using to talk to girls was actually scaring them off! I'm the Basil Fawlty[99] of romance!"

Humour can also be used pro-actively by the therapist to enhance counselling. Some very gentle humour at the outset can help the involvement atmosphere by relaxing tensions a little. On a rainy day the counsellor greets the client at the door and comments, "Now that's a day for the ducks!" There is no personally relevant content here and it acts as a light preface to the more serious business of counselling. To a client steeped in the problems of her life, a remark like this is also a gentle reminder of a normal life that is still there somewhere. (When you get home after all the stresses and worries of the day to see your pet dog lying belly-up in front of the fireplace without a care in the world, the effect is something similar!)

---

[99] Reference to the main character in the BBC's classic comedy series "Fawlty Towers".

Sometimes an individual remark can take on great therapeutic potential because of its humorous flavour. At one point a client talks about her behaviour as "banging my head against a brick wall". Noting the strength the client has gained even from this summing up of her behaviour the counsellor asks, "is head-banging something you do a lot of?" From this moment on the term "head-banging" becomes a light-hearted way of referring to ineffective behaviours for this client. Implied in the humour is the more serious message that the behaviour is a choice and therefore a different behaviour could be chosen.

It is not easy to teach a trainee counsellor when to use humour in a pro-active way but learning to tune in to the client's own humour would be a good first step. When a client adopts a lighter tone when speaking about her problems, the counsellor too can usually lighten up.

The Language of Optimism

It is easy to recommend optimism or hope but how does a counsellor convey this in practice?

In fact, neither hoping nor wishing are very effective behaviours. If we apply Glasser's idea of total behaviour we can see that the most effective form of optimism will have a strong doing component as well as the very active thinking one.

What we are talking about here is an active type of hoping, not simply sitting and wishing for the best but doing something about it. This requires a specific mind-set that predisposes the person to action: to think that "maybe we could make things better" is a much healthier hypothesis for living than to think "maybe we couldn't" or "maybe we will be lucky". Only the first of these "maybes" encourages us to look for new choices. Optimism is more likely to lead to positive change than is pessimism. You are more likely to wait for the bus you think "might come" than the one you believe "might not come".

The counsellor can model this active optimism in her approach to the client's problems. A calm confident professional air, attentive listening, the ability to break down problems into smaller more manageable components, the belief that we may find a better way, all of these convey a very real hope to the client. If as therapists we believe that most human situations can probably be improved and we have accumulated some learning about how to deal with a variety of human problems, this professional confidence transmits to the client as a really effective optimism.

The same is true of all professionals. Tell your garage mechanic that your new car is making a clanking noise. If she throws his hands in the air and starts shouting, it does not inspire a lot of hope for fixing the car. If she is all smiles and says that the car will be perfectly all right because she has read it in her horoscope, I certainly will not be impressed by her "optimism". If, on the other hand, she starts asking sensible questions in a quiet systematic way you get the idea that she knows what she is doing and that there is a reasonable chance of a solution.

A big difference in therapy of course is that the client is the person who fixes the client's problem. Still, the therapist's calm professionalism is important. Moreover the client will take away from the counselling the new skill of hoping, of not giving up too quickly when new problems emerge.

Some authors say, and I agree with them, that one of the roles of the counsellor is to help the client see the problem as more solvable than she first thought. This is very much the active optimism we are talking about here.

There is another aspect to Reality Therapy's optimism and that comes from the way it views a person's choices. Glasser recognises that we all make the best choices we can at any given time. If I choose to smoke a cigarette right now, even though I probably know how harmful it is to me, somehow in my inner scheme of things it is the best choice for me right now. If I knew of something better I would choose the something better!

So even the individual who is thinking about committing suicide is making the best decision she knows at the time. Almost anybody in the same circumstances and with the same knowledge and skills available might reach the same decision. This is not madness in any sense of the word. However, when the therapist acknowledges to the client that she was doing the best she could do at the time this affirms her strength and also the fact that there might be other options.

1 **Client:** I just can't take any more. I was a very happy person and now that monster has driven me to suicide.

2 **Counsellor:** What he did to you is so terrible that you now believe your life is not really worth living?

3 **Client:** It was worth living, it was really worth living. That animal has changed it all. How could he? He is sick, sick, sick!

4 **Counsellor:** You have decided to end your life. Is it possible for you to decide not to end it just yet, to give us a little time to see if there are other possibilities for you?

5 **Client:** What other possibilities could there be? He has destroyed my life. What else is there for me to do?

6 Counsellor: Right now I don't know. I do know that if you go ahead with your suicide plans we will never know if there was another way. If you can postpone your plans for a while it gives us a chance to look at other choices you might have.

7 Client: I know that makes sense but I don't know if I could do it. Everyday is just such a dark nightmare for me. You don't know what it's like.

8 Counsellor: No, I don't know but just from watching you and listening to you I get some idea. It certainly must be a horrible experience for you if you decide that death would be better than this.

9 Client: That's just it. I don't want to die but I want this even less. *[A change of tone in the client's voice suggests she is feeling more understood, safer.]*

10 Counsellor: *[After a few moments silence]* So you do want to live but not like this. Is it possible for you to give yourself a "stay of execution" just to see if there are other choices open to you. I will help you look for these choices.

11 Client: At this point in time I just cannot see any hope but I will give it a go. Somehow if I didn't, I feel I would be letting that animal win.

The Language of Affirmation

There is a difference between praise and affirmation. Praise is approval; it is an external value judgement. It can even suggest some form of superiority of the praiser over the praised person. It can appear as a reward and rewards so often belittle the very behaviour they are recognising.

Affirmation on the other hand is simply stating the obvious but focuses on the obvious positive rather than the obvious negative. There is no attempt to add anything but clarification to the process. It will of course be coloured by the belief system of whoever is making the affirmation. In Reality Therapy an important belief is that everyone is always making the best choice they know at the time. Reminding people of this is a great source of strength for them and is quite different from praise.

PRAISE	AFFIRMATION
It is wonderful that you made this appointment to help save your marriage. You are such a sensitive person!	You seem to have tried quite a lot of ways of saving your marriage. Right now you don't know what to do but you have taken the time to talk to a counsellor.
You are amazing! It was so intelligent of you not to cause further problems in the class.	In spite of feeling you were treated unfairly by the teacher you chose to come and talk to me about it instead of making a big fuss over it in class.

Self-affirmation can be an important skill for the client to learn. In my school counselling office I kept a bottle of coloured water (red food dye). It is half-full. When student clients are showing a lot of self-criticism or pessimistic thinking I sometimes use the bottle. "Is this half-full or half-empty?"

They soon reach the conclusion that both descriptions are perfectly true. "If every time you look at this bottle you remind yourself that it is half-empty, what effect might you create in your life?" They readily see the link between negative thinking and negative feeling. "Could you make a decision right now to use the 'half-full' approach more often?" They don't have to abandon the 'half-empty' view; it can remind them of things that need fixing. The important learning point is that they have a choice of different perspectives.

In ordinary everyday communication praise is quite natural and usually very welcome. In counselling however even such a hint of external control can be counter-productive. One important characteristic of affirmation is that it is usually more credible to the client than praise.

The Language of Reframing

A lot of what we have examined in other aspects of the language of counselling could be classified as "reframing". Indeed, in a sense counselling is very much about helping a client reframe his life, at least in the area of the problem.

Reframing means helping a person look at a situation in a different way. As such it is an important way of helping people re-evaluate their "pictures" and maybe change them. It can help them see hope where before they saw hopelessness. It is helping them take a fuller view of reality rather than only a partial view. Reframing is at the very heart of all therapy.

Here are some ways that we can help a client reframe ...

• using different words	"When you say it is half-empty, could you also say it is half-full?" "You say you are stubborn; maybe you are just being cautious!"
• changing the time perspective (e.g. from past to future)	"You say you have been feeling very down. Is there anything you can do to feel less down this afternoon, even if only for ten minutes?"
• checking out facts or contrasting facts and opinion	"You say that he hates you ... can you tell me exactly what he says or does?"
• using the language of choice	"So you decided to do something about it and you arranged this appointment!"
• using the language of alliance	"We will look at this together and I am sure that we will make some progress."
• asking for an evaluation	"What are your real chances of getting custody of the kids?"
• suggesting alternative strategies	"What would happen if you decided that you would only smoke at home?"
• pinpointing locus of control	"How much of this situation is within your own control? Can you change the other person?"
• offering any change of perspective	"Would you say this problem you have is a disaster or a hiccup?"

As counsellors we do not *make* people reframe. We can only guide and suggest but at least we can help the client choose from a broader spectrum of possibilities.

The Language of Specifics

Glasser once commented that all human problems are specific. "Being specific is very important. Life is lived specifically; generalities like 'I screwed up' are worthless in therapy. It's all the details that count."[100] Practically all of the counselling skills we have mentioned rely on the elaboration of specific details.

The client says he is worried sick and the counsellor begins to explore just what he is worried about and even what form this worry takes. The counsellor wants to know more about the client's life but instead of asking about a "typical day" she asks to hear about "yesterday, for example". The client talks about how he would like things to be and the counsellor seeks out the specific details of this. Counsellor and client have reached a point where they can work together on a plan and again this will be worked out in detail.

In conclusion, it is not surprising that students of Choice Theory and Reality Therapy soon find themselves becoming very self-conscious about the language they use even in normal conversation. Whatever you do it's probably not helpful to be too obsessive about this. And you certainly do not need to feel guilty every time you let slip an external control turn of phrase ... unless, of course, you decide you really want to feel guilty!

---

[100] Glasser, William. *Choice Theory*. New York: Harper Collins, 1998.

Language of Choice: Rephrasing

Discuss these phrases with another trainee counsellor and decide on an alternative way of saying each of them, a way that brings out the element of choice. How would you reply to a client who said each phrase, saying things in such a way as to help the client become more aware of the element of choice?

1. I had to answer the telephone.
2. My brother made me steal the money.
3. The boss's inflexibility caused us to go on strike.
4. I started smoking because my friends pressurised me into it.
5. The party on Friday will give me a massive hang-over on Saturday.
6. I can't study when the rest of the family are watching TV.
7. Michael's untidy room is really annoying me.
8. I react very strongly to being told what to do.
9. I haven't got time to cut the grass.
10. Remembering what she did to me gets me very depressed.
11. He is undisciplined because his father is alcoholic.
12. The weather really gets me down.
13. He calls me names and makes me angry.
14. It was her wearing sexy clothes that made him rape her.
15. My noisy neighbour really messes up my life.

Here are possible replies to the exercise above. There are of course more than one way of re-phrasing the client's statements. In these suggestions I have deliberately used the verbs "decide" and "choose" in most of the phrases to help underscore the element of choice. It would be equally effective and possibly more appropriate in a specific situation to use other verbs or phrases that carry the same meaning.

- You decided to answer the telephone.
- Your brother made a suggestion and you decided to do it.
- You decided to go on strike over the boss's inflexibility.
- You started to smoke because you wanted to please your friends.
- You got yourself a massive hang-over by going to the party on Saturday.
- You find it hard to study when you decide to do it where others are watching television.
- You fret about Michael's untidy room.
- You express strong opposition to being told what to do.
- You decide not to cut the grass now because you want to do other things.
- When you recall what she did to you, you are choosing what is a sad memory for you.
- He chooses his disorderly behaviour perhaps as a way of coping with a difficult parent or because he never learned other ways to behave.
- You choose to sit and mope when the weather is not the way you want it.
- You give considerable importance to the names he calls you.
- He decided to rape her.
- You say you are choosing a way of dealing with a noisy neighbour that is not really working for you.

Language of Imagery: Imagining

1. If you were a musical instrument, which one would you be and why?

2. If you could be an animal, which one would you be and what important aspects of your Quality World would it represent?

3. See how many objects you can pick from your immediate surroundings right now that represent some aspect of your life or personality.

Language of Imagery: Use of Objects Group Imagining

1. Form groups of 3 and choose an area of the room in which to work.

2. Each person should choose one object from the selection provided. (Or group members could be asked in advance to bring in an object each. Examples: pen, ruler, flower, stone, coin, fluffy toy, glass, toy boat, photo, compass, kaleidoscope.)

3. Your task is to work as a group to make up and write down as many comparisons as possible for each of the objects in your group. For example, "You are like this ruler - everything in your life seems well laid out and orderly."

4. Share general findings in full group.

Language of Imagery: Identification with Objects

All objects (from the previous exercise) are returned to the centre and people are told that a family shield is being designed for them. They should pick one object from the present selection to put on the shield and this will represent them.

Invite each to explain his or her choice ... allowing passing.

OR each person can talk as if they were that object using the present tense throughout, e.g., "I am a compass and ..." (Cf. the Gestalt exercise "Rosebush Fantasy"[101].)

Language of Imagery: Images for a Life-style

Identify comparisons, images you might use for a client who is:

- a golfer
- a medical doctor
- a typist
- a housewife
- a lorry driver
- a computer user

Reframing

Offer reframes of these statements from clients.

1. I am a stubborn person.
2. I nearly didn't get here today.
3. I am a perfectionist.
4. I let people walk all over me.
5. I get very worried about my exams.
6. I know I'm being very distrustful.
7. Eleanor never speaks to me.
8. I am very indecisive.
9. I was never any good at school.
10. I'm not very hopeful ... after all, you're my fifth "shrink".
11. I do like boys but I'm clueless when it comes to talking to them.

---

[101] Stevens, John O. *Awareness: Exploring Experimenting Experiencing*. Moab, Utah: Real People Press, 1971.

12. I don't think I've ever been able to carry out a plan in my life.
13. I cry too readily.
14. The French teacher is always picking on me.
15. Even my friends think I'm lazy.

Everyday Language

It can be interesting to examine the language we use to describe everyday experience:

I have to get up everyday at 8.00 and when I looked out this morning the Irish weather really got me down. The sight of a fried egg for breakfast made me sick as it brought back to my mind the thought of every egg I had ever known! When given food I do not like I tend to react quite strongly. On this occasion it made me sullen for the rest of the morning and nobody managed to cheer me up. The prospect of lunch-time livened me up a bit but when we were served fish in the canteen we began to discuss how much our attitudes to fish had been conditioned by centuries of a religious practice that made fish a penitential dish. If you really want to turn me off, just give me fish! When I got home in the evening pure boredom forced me to sit and watch television for several hours. I really don't know why we have to watch such total and utter rubbish suitable only for clots!

At this stage the reader should be able to re-write the above paragraph using the language of choice.

The Telephone

For many people the telephone is seen as one of the big external controls in their lives. They say "the telephone drives me mad!"

when in fact they could choose from a fairly wide range of optional behaviours for dealing with it:

- ignore it (or use a "do not disturb" feature)
- turn the ring volume down (or off!)
- leave the room
- remove the telephone
- use an answering machine with a message saying you will phone back
- use an answering machine with no promise to phone back
- use a caller identifier to choose which calls to answer
- answer the telephone and ask the person to call you back later
- tell people what times are best to call you
- ask people not to make business calls to your home
- tell people you prefer e-mail, letters, faxes or whatever
- use an ex-directory telephone number

In our modern world many people have bought cellular telephones for private use without thinking about how they will manage the potential intrusion in their lives.

Choosing Feelings

The RT/CT idea of total behaviour means that we even have a choice when it comes to our emotions.

- If you really wanted to feel angry right now, what could you choose to think about?

- If you wanted to feel more relaxed, what could you plan to do or think about?

- When you want a bit more fun in your life what are some of the things you can choose to do?

No-one can be made
to feel inferior
without their consent.

Eleanor Roosevelt

Self Evaluation

In this chapter you will learn about:

- The central importance of self-evaluation in Reality Therapy.
- The application of self-evaluation to the client's core problem.
- Different ways, verbal and non-verbal, to help a client make self-evaluations.
- How people always make the best choice they know at the time.
- How we shift our allegiance from one behaviour to another.
- The importance of involvement for self-evaluation

If one of the key tenets of Choice Theory is that a person can only control his own behaviour and cannot control that of other people then it follows that the person's system for monitoring his own behaviour is very important. In Choice Theory we refer to this as "self-evaluation" and we pay particular attention to this process in our counselling clients.

Self-evaluation is a very important transition point in counselling.

If I advise my client about what to do or if I openly evaluate my client's behaviour I am using external control procedures. By doing so I am undermining my client's sense of personal control. Indeed the client may then use his energy to defend his position against my external evaluation. In Reality Therapy our aim is to help the client take responsibility for his life and part of this means evaluating his own behaviour for himself. Our role is not to "force" a self-evaluation but to encourage and support it. In Reality Therapy there is a very strong awareness that the counsellor is standing outside the client's life and that the counsellor must at all times respect this different person.

Because we are all internally controlled, it is the client's internal evaluation that paves the way for the client's choice of change. The counsellor helps the client reach and cross these junctures but it is the client who makes the choices and every self-evaluation is an important movement forward in counselling.

By encouraging the language of choice (introduced in the previous chapter), we help the client become more aware of his own choices. We offer choices at every possible juncture: "Where would you like to sit?" "What do you want to talk about?" "Which of these problems do you think we should discuss first?" "When you scolded your daughter, how happy were you with the outcome?" It could be said that the Choice Theory counsellor aims to create an atmosphere of choice even when discussing the least significant aspects of the client's life.

The Core Self-Evaluation

There is usually at least one major self-evaluation in the counselling process, one that addresses the core problem for the client. In this the client will consider the issue that is really bothering him and ask, "Is my current behaviour getting me what I really want?" I refer to this as the "core self-evaluation" and this is the main focus for the rest of this chapter.

In a Reality Therapy session the counsellor will have created that friendly supportive atmosphere we refer to as "involvement" so that the client can open up his own inner world safely. He will also have explored what it is that the client really wants, something important he has not been getting and his reason for seeking counselling. In helping the client to see how much choice is involved, the counsellor will have invited the client to check on what he has been doing to get what he wants. At this point the "problem" should be fairly clear to both counsellor and client. By "problem" we mean the critical frustration, the discrepancy between what the client wants and what the client is getting. All the necessary components are now present for the counsellor to invite the client to self-evaluate.

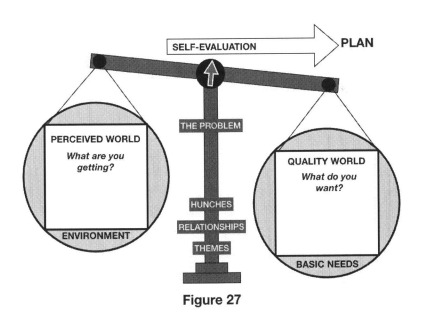

Figure 27

Referring once more to the scales diagram (Figure 27) we could say that client and counsellor now know what is on both sides of the balance. These two sets of information are necessary before the client can compare one side with the other and ask: "Is what I am doing getting me what I want?"

This is often a good moment in the counselling session for a short review of proceedings so far and here are some typical examples of summary plus invitation to self-evaluate:

Ben, you tell me that you want to come to a peaceful agreement with your neighbours about the new wall they are planning to build between your gardens. You already agree with the dimensions of the wall but you would prefer a different construction material. You have tried hinting at this; you have given them a catalogue of building materials; you have spoken to husband and wife separately. Have you got any closer to your goal with all of this?

Suzanne, your heart is set on passing this examination and doing well in it. You tell me you have bought two books on study techniques and have tried all their ideas. How much has the effectiveness of your study improved at this point?

Laura, it's obvious from what you say that your regular blushing is very embarrassing for you. You want to be able to control it. Did the relaxation exercises, the self-hypnosis or the tablets you have tried achieve any positive results?

It takes a lot of personal strength for a person to say, "No, what I have been doing is not working!" Indeed, the more aware the person is that they have been choosing their behaviour the more difficult such a self-evaluation can be. That is one of the reasons why involvement is so important.

This attention to the counselling environment is by no means a once-off process, something the counsellor "does" at the beginning of counselling. It must be on-going and subject to constant review. With experience and practice the counsellor will at all times be alert to the current level of involvement and how it compares with the counselling tasks in hand. There will often be times when the information gathering and evaluative aspects of counselling will be put to one side so that the counsellor can put extra work into strengthening involvement.

Typical Evaluation Invitations

1. Does that (what you are doing) help?
2. Is this what you really want to do?
3. How would your life be different if you chose to do the opposite?
4. Is this the road you want to go down?
5. What do you like and what do you dislike about your approach?
6. In what way does this help you?
7. Would you see yourself deliberately choosing that same strategy in similar future occasions?
8. You do not sound totally convinced that what you are doing is such a good idea!
9. Are you saying that you are not completely happy with what you are doing?
10. If you continue doing what you are doing now, do you think things will get better, get worse or stay the same?
11. What rating would you give yourself on a "Happiness Scale" from 1 to 100?
12. In that same situation my own tactic is to let both of us cool down a bit before continuing. What do you think of that?
13. Is what you are doing against the Law/rules?
14. Is your plan possible in its present state?
15. How much of your plan do you expect to achieve?
16. Which of these issues do you want to look at first?
17. Which issue is most important to you right now?
18. Would that work in your situation?
19. If you were doing this again, would you change it in any way?
20. Did that work?

In spite of the counsellor's preference for open questions over closed ones it is interesting to note that most of self-evaluative questions are closed. Self-evaluation is an important decision point in counselling and so short "yes/no" answers can be more appropriate here.

Alternative Examples of Self-Evaluation

Body language or just plain silence can invite an evaluation from the client especially when there is very good rapport.

"Chris, you are telling me you want to be a pilot. You are also telling me that you don't have the necessary qualifications and that you have a permanent eye-sight problem that effectively bars you from flight-training." The counsellor pauses and after a few moments Chris purses her lips and nods her head. Later when she speaks it becomes obvious that she has accepted that there is a major discrepancy between what she wants and what she has to offer. She is now more ready to consider alternatives.

The therapist has built up a very trustful relationship with Louise and on this occasion she is telling him about a "night on the town". After a few moments the therapist decides to jot down phrases on a note-pad while Louise continues with her narrative. About five minutes later Louise pauses and asks, "What are you writing?" and the therapist simply passes the note-pad to her without a comment.

She reads the summary notes quietly "parents refused permission, slipped out through window, four pints of beer, two vodkas, white tablet, sick in toilet, unable to stand, cursing club staff, thrown out, shouting on street, carried home by two friends, anything could have happened if they had not protected me". She sat silently for a while, no more narrative, and then she said, "I see what you mean".

The Best Choice We Know

Glasser's notion that we always choose the best we know at any given moment carries a very power message of optimism about human behaviour. At the same time it presents a huge challenge to the counsellor helping a client through the self-evaluative process. Nobody will choose a brand new behaviour unless they are convinced that it is better than the older behaviour.

For example, a person knows that smoking is bad for him but continues to smoke. Does this not contradict Glasser's idea of choosing our best at all times? In fact it does not because any given choice is the outcome not of one simple idea such as "smoking causes death" but of a complex series of thoughts and the linkages between them. The reason we choose a given behaviour is that the overall balance of our perceptions of that behaviour appears more need satisfying to us than any other behaviour at that moment. We may be acutely aware of some of these perceptions but many may be functioning at a pre-verbal level, an area of consciousness that many will refer to as "instinct" or "gut feeling".

The smoker, for example, may associate his habit with apparent relaxation, a variety of social situations, after-dinner chat, dreamy smoke, something to do with his hands. He may see a non-smoking life as stressful, rich in mood-swings, different from his peers, healthier but fattening. Even without sitting down and making a list of pros and cons, the smoker can have these associations with the construct of smoker/non-smoker and the balance in his internal world comes down in favour of smoking. Consequently he chooses to smoke.

The "Click"

It can happen that because of a series of information inputs we gradually shift the balance from one side of the scale to the other. One day a significant event happens, such as the death of a friend from lung-cancer, and suddenly the balance shifts to favour a non-smoking life. Something "clicks"; the penny drops. It is a moment of self-evaluation.

A friend told me how such a click happened for him just as he lit up what was to be his last cigarette. The match was still burning as his gaze fell on his new-born son, just back from the hospital with his wife. Suddenly it dawned on him that if he smoked he would be exposing his child to the fumes. In that split-second of realisation he took smoking out of his Quality World.

This important moment happens within the individual's own mind. No amount of external pressure, persuading, logic or rhetoric can ever guarantee that a person will make this shift in thinking, this moment when the penny drops, when some new view clicks into position. If counselling is about helping people to make changes in their lives it will be very important for us to understand this phenomenon as best we can.

I believe it is less likely to happen in the presence of external control. Preaching at the person, using heavy-handed persuasion techniques, bribing, criticising ... all are likely to have quite the opposite effect to that intended. In spite of this, parents who really love their children will often resort to these methods of persuasion when they see their offspring engage in potentially self-harming behaviour. This protective behaviour is understandable but it is also likely to be ineffective.

The problem is that the young person's resources are now occupied in self-defence. In a more relaxed and acceptant atmosphere such as that we aspire to in counselling, the individual is more able to think freely. It is in such an atmosphere that new ideas and viewpoints can more easily click into place.

It is only when clients become aware that their previous behaviour was not achieving what they want that they are likely to consider making new choices and new plans.

Involvement and Self-Evaluation

We have already referred to the importance of involvement in helping a client open up her inner world to the counsellor. There are other aspects to consider. When a critical self-evaluation point is reached the client will be reaching what can be a very painful conclusion. "I now know what I want and am beginning to realise that what I have been doing is not achieving it!" The combination of humility and strength needed to reach such a conclusion will in turn be greatly helped by the supportive atmosphere provided by a skilled counsellor.

A significant self-evaluation can be a big turning point in a person's life. As such it is very much an internal turning point. This is greatly helped by a counsellor who listens carefully, who does her best to understand, who is not critical, who respects the client's own choice and who offers to help the client search for alternative choices. All of this is what involvement is about.

Inviting Self-Evaluations

In each of these cases how would you help the person make an internal evaluation? Reply to their statements by saying "You say you want .... and what you are doing is ..... so is ..... getting you ..... ?"

- Helen: If I told Janice once I have told her a thousand times to tidy up her room but she still messes it up.

- Séamus: No girls want to go with me. When I walk up to a girl for the first time and ask her to be my girl-friend, she always says "NO".

- Katie: I used to be so involved in sports but now that I am depressed I simply cannot go out any more.

- Pat: I really do my best to improve my relationships with people but when they annoy me I just can't help myself. I get very agitated and I start throwing things at them.

- Michael: I really don't understand my wife. Our sex life just doesn't happen any more. And yet I always remember our anniversary and things like that. I got her a new toaster for her birthday, I invite her to all the golf-club functions.

Evaluating Evaluations

Which of the three replies in each case is closer to the Choice Theory principle of Internal Control?

Laurence: My wife expects me to do housework but I am out working all day.

COUNSELLOR A: When you don't do the housework what exactly happens?

COUNSELLOR B: Do you not think that husbands and wives should share the work equally?

COUNSELLOR C: Tell her you will do it but you need, say, an hour's rest just after you come in from work.

Joseph: If I talk in class the teacher picks on me but all the others are talking too!

COUNSELLOR A: I am sure the teacher had some reason for punishing you.

COUNSELLOR B: I suggest you start working better in class.

COUNSELLOR C: Whose behaviour would you like to talk about here?

More or Less Directive

Put these sentences in rank order starting with the one that is most directive (external control) and ending with the one that is most respectful of the client's internal control.

1. Would it help to talk to your friend about this?
2. Go and talk to your friend about this.
3. What would happen if you talked to your friend about this?
4. Will you talk to your friend about this?
5. I think it might help to talk to your friend about this.
6. Why don't you talk to your friend about this?

Self-Evaluative or Not

Which of these sentences are self-evaluative and which are more directive?

1. Whatever you do, don't give up the day job!
2. What was the effect on your life when you gave up the job?
3. How realistic is the plan you have in mind?
4. Did you not feel a bit stupid when you forgot about the plan?
5. You are choosing to depress, aren't you?
6. Wouldn't you be better off getting up an hour earlier?
7. You really have been doing very well in the last few days.
8. When you spoke to the boss like that, did it help?
9. What you really need to do is to help your girl-friend decide for herself.
10. Would you be able to do your job better if you had a new computer?

Reflection

Glasser suggests that we are more likely to be happy if we spend time evaluating ourselves rather than other people. Many people have the custom of spending time in "meditation" each day and, for some of these, the main purpose is one of self-evaluation, stock-taking, values clarification. A brief time each day considering what are the really important things in our lives and what we need to do about them today could be beneficial and help reduce major frustrations. However, it would be important not to try to solve everything in one meditation! Choosing one important topic per day might be more realistic ... and less scary!

Parental Evaluation

Teachers and parents might consider replacing the "I'm telling you what to do" approach with a self-evaluative one. It is an important part of a child's education to have many opportunities to practise this type of evaluation and to practise choices.

Ultimately how a person behaves as an adult will depend on their own internal evaluation of their lives so it makes sense to give children plenty of opportunities to develop this ability.

Here's how a parent might help her son evaluate his work.

1   Mum: Kevin, I heard your pals talking about an exciting project you are all doing about pollution in the locality. Are you involved?

2   Kevin: Ugh-agh (an almost unintelligible nasal grunt that means "Yes, I am and I'm not sure I'm glad you found out" in teen-speak.)

3   Mum: I'd love to have a look at it and hear how you are doing.

4   Kevin: Mum, you know I don't like talking about school. You will be picking out all my mistakes and things.

5 Mum: Kevin, I know I did that last week and I'm sorry. I promise I won't criticise any of your work but I would love to see it.

6 Kevin: OK, then. Here it is … but I haven't finished it yet!

7 Mum: You're the author! Tell me more about it. How happy are you with your work so far?

8 Kevin: Well, I don't like the layout of pages two and three and that last paragraph sounds all wrong.

9 Mum: Maybe you're being hard on yourself but then again you want to set high standards. If you want to revise those sections I'll help you if I can … and if you trust me.

10 Kevin: Mmm! Well, go on then! How would you write that last paragraph?

11 Mum: I thought you wanted to improve that section, not make it worse, the way I write! A friend of mine likes to read her written work out loud. You might like to try that approach. If you read the paragraph out loud you might see what you want to change. If you want me to have a look at your revised work, just give me a shout. I'll be in the garden!

In this example the mother avoids external evaluation including praise. What she gives instead is a lot of attention and genuine involvement. The son's responsibility for his own life is safeguarded and even nourished by the exchange. There is no criticism, no distancing in the relationship.

Technique: The Reality Choice[102]

Sometimes a person finds it difficult to make a choice and this is especially true when all the options are unpleasant. However, we cannot choose not to choose! The following is a structure for helping a client deal with the unavoidable choice. Needless to say these ideas should not be followed in a cook-book fashion.

What is the problem?

Although it sometimes takes a lot of time, there is a critical point in counselling when the clients become aware of how their life differs from their quality world, how what they have is not the same as what they want. The more specific this awareness the better. This is the starting point for this approach.

What are the OPTIONS open to the client?

The counsellor helps the client identify different approaches to dealing with the problem. This includes any ideas the client already has together with possibilities known to the counsellor. Depending on the seriousness and complexity of the problem it may be necessary to extend the list of options by consulting outside experts. It can also be helpful to include possibilities that appear far-fetched or even funny.

Add the "ZERO OPTION"

In all cases the counsellor will ensure that one option describes a "no change" or "do nothing" scenario. This is the "zero option". The counsellor might say, "One option is to do nothing at all about this. Let's include this!"

---

102 With special thanks to Lucy Billings Robbins for suggesting a name for this technique.

Establish the INEVITABILITY OF CHOICE.

It can be useful to introduce this with a remark such as, "When you leave this office you can choose to leave things as they are. You can choose the 'no change' angle or you can opt for one of the other plans. Is it possible not to choose? Would it be wise to have a closer look at each of the options before you choose?"

What are the possible CONSEQUENCES of each of these options?

Here we can ask about each option on our list: "What do you think might happen if you were to choose this option? If you choose this what else are you probably choosing? How might you feel once you make this choice? What would be good about it for you and what would be bad about it? How certain can you be about these outcomes?" We cannot foresee the future but good planning depends heavily on good anticipation. That's the best we can do.

How does the client EVALUATE each option bearing in mind its consequences?

"If you could award a satisfaction rating to each of these options where maximum score is 100%, what would you give to each option?" This helps the client compare the options and make an evaluation of each.

Which CHOICE will the client take?

"Maybe all your scores are between 90 and 100% but even if they lie between 10 and 15% you still have a choice and you can pick whichever seems best or whichever is least bad." Writing down the different options and giving each a score can help them see that, no matter how bad they may be, some choices are better than others.

We help the client PLAN to make that choice a successful reality?

This has to do with planning, teaching, rehearsing. "Would you like to look at plans for carrying out this choice? Do you need to learn new skills? Would you like to practise them now?" Suggestions about how to create good plans are listed in a later chapter.

FOLLOW-UP on the chosen plan

Plan a follow-up session to have on-going evaluation of the choices made and to refine them or create new ones.

Teaching Choice Theory

In this chapter you will learn about:

- The importance of teaching Choice Theory to our clients.
- That such "teaching" is not necessarily in academic terms.
- The ten axioms of Choice Theory psychology
- Examples of very different approaches to internal control

The more enthused Dr. Glasser became with Choice Theory the more important he saw the need to teach it to others and this included the clients of his counselling approach.

In "Counseling With Choice Theory"[103] he wrote, "An important difference between reality therapy and other therapies is that we teach choice theory to clients as part of their therapy".[104] He even recommended that a counsellor's clients might read "Choice Theory" or "The Language of Choice Theory". Alternatively the therapist could "teach them the choice theory they need to know as the counselling proceeds".

---

[103] Originally published in 2000 as "Reality Therapy in Action".

[104] Glasser, William. *Counseling with Choice Theory*. New York: Harper Perennial, 2012.

This is not to say that we sit our clients down and give them a little lecture about Choice Theory psychology. The fact that this was never Dr. Glasser's intention is evidenced in the many role-plays he has presented in written and recorded form in the years after his publication of "Choice Theory". There are no lectures in his role-plays.

Writing in "Choice Theory" about the fictitious client Francesca, Glasser states that, "after a few more sessions, I will start to teach her some choice theory - that no one can make her miserable; only she can do that to herself." What he wanted to teach was not an academic treatise about his ideas but very practical personal guidelines that arose from Choice Theory.

There was a core of Choice Theory that clients needed to grasp in some shape or form and the key idea here was that each of us can only control ourselves, the concept of internal control. Different people would grasp this central idea in different ways and it is this realisation that is at the heart of Choice Theory's power to liberate.

For some clients, reading the books would be a wonderful addition to the counselling process ... but not everyone is a reader! For others, some discussion about how we control our lives could be the best manner of learning the core of Choice Theory. For still others, an intuitive grasp of this central concept would be what they need. Whatever the method, to know the ideas without grasping their practical application would not be consistent with Glasser's intentions.

Most counselling, including Reality Therapy, tends to be based on conversation, essentially an exchange of ideas. As such it is structured in a linear way - from the beginning of the conversation to the end. However, it would be a mistake to assume that everyone thinks in this way. Not everyone has a mind that is trained in the ways of logic. Since most counsellors have a reasonable standard of formal education it means that some may struggle to communicate in a modality that suits other cognitive styles that are less linear.

One of our challenges is to explore these different modalities.

The Ten Axioms of Choice Theory

Glasser describes these axioms in the final chapter of "Choice Theory", a chapter with the title, "Redefining Your Personal Freedom". This was not intended to be an academic exercise of definitions but a personally liberating experience. In summary the ten points are:

1. The only person whose behaviour we can control is our own.

2. All we can give or get from other people is information.

3. All long-lasting psychological problems are relationship problems.

4. The problem relationship is always part of our present lives.

5. Revisiting the painful past can contribute little or nothing to what we need to do now: improve an important, present relationship.

6. We are driven by five genetic needs: survival, love and belonging, power, freedom and fun.

7. We can satisfy these needs only by satisfying a picture or pictures in our Quality Worlds.

8. All we can do from birth to death is behave. All behaviour is total behaviour.

9. All total behaviour is designated by verbs, usually infinitives and gerunds and named by the component that is most recognisable.

10. All total behaviour is chosen but we have direct control over only the acting and thinking components.

Although Glasser was keen for the members of his organisation to learn these ideas, his interactions with clients in role-play tended to focus on only a few of the axioms: internal control, the importance of relationships, the futility of returning to the past, the total nature of our behaviour and the importance of changing doing and thinking. He "taught" these more as attitudes to grasp rather than as concepts to understand.

In a role-play with a Dublin school-girl who had a little problem with ear-rings he gave a good demonstration of how he taught internal control to a child. A ring on her finger became a symbol of her own ability to take control of a situation. In another role-play with "Farrell", a psychotic client, he asked almost immediately, "What is your plan?", a direct appeal to the individual's own control. Glasser did indeed teach Choice Theory to his clients but not as a set of concepts.

Examples of different approaches

Here I show how a counsellor might begin to "teach" Choice Theory in a variety of different ways, each depending on what was appropriate for the client and, of course, depending on what they need to know.

- Louise, do you believe we can control other people? Are you able to control anyone? Can anyone control you?

- Ciaran, thanks for bringing in the photographs of your family. Which of these can you control? Which of them try to control you? Do they succeed?

- Conor, can you imagine your brother sitting on that chair? Let's pretend he is and you show me what you want to say to him about changing his ways! Tell him what you want to tell him. ... Now, you sit over there and pretend you are your brother. Guess what he might say back to you and let me hear it.

- Shanna, let's try something different. Relax on that chair and close your eyes when you wish. Breathe a little more slowly than before. Just think to yourself, "this is MY breath, MY body breathing". "This is ME". "Everything that is going through my mind is mine; they are my thoughts and pictures." If I mention a red car or a black hat you can decide whether to let that image into your head or not. It's your head and it's your life.

- JonJo, try this. Hold up your two hands with the palms facing me. I am going to do the same. [I push JonJo's hands back gently. He pushes back.] When I try to push you away, you defend yourself, you push back. When you try to control your son, what does he do?

- Sharon, instead of criticising your colleague for constantly using foul language you have decided simply to tell him that you prefer not to hear such language. Let me know how you get on. (By actually taking control, the person may learn about internal control.)

- Relate the Hans Christian Anderson story of the Emperor's New Clothes and how one person, a child, noted that the Emperor was not wearing anything at all. (The child is not swayed by the peer pressure around.)

Insight or Eureka moment?

A cognitive shift to a greater understanding of one's problem was believed central to progress in many therapies. Glasser has never given much importance to such an insight. For him, a solution was more important than an understanding. However, it is important that the client should learn Choice Theory in the sense of beginning to appreciate his or her own internal control. This is not necessarily a fully conscious awareness but it is an awareness nonetheless.

The therapist might not say directly to the client, "you are in control of your life" but the general procedures of Reality Therapy help foster the awareness. The Reality Therapy counsellor is constantly asking the client about what "you" are doing, about what "you" want and about "your" choices and plans. The awareness of internal control may be born before, during or after moments of self-evaluation but it may also take longer, maybe not appearing until the client has actually tried out a new behaviour.

No matter when it happens, it is a critical moment in Reality Therapy and it is an important lesson that will stretch well beyond the individual counselling sessions. It may be a moment of clear insight for some, a eureka experience for others or even an indescribable surge in the sense of personal power. However it happens, it is a moment of personal liberation.

Your Internal Control

Can you think of "internal control moments" in your own life, moments when you realised that you needed to take an initiative or that you could take an initiative? Which of these feelings were present? Excitement, fear, loneliness, liberation.

The Public and Private You

Peer pressure is not simply something that teenagers "suffer" from. We all do. Our behaviour and dress in different groups is not always the same as our behaviour in the privacy of our homes. However, according to Choice Theory it is always **our** behaviour. There may be external pressures but it is we ourselves who choose what to do. What choices do you make about how you present yourself in different groups? With your work colleagues, with in-laws, with neighbours, with club members? What are the choices you make about how you present yourself in different contexts?

Planning in Reality Therapy

In this chapter you will learn about:

- The general usefulness of dealing with planning.
- The need for planning to be appropriate.
- Ways to generate a range of options for planning including the past, experience and creativity.
- The qualities of good planning.
- The role of self-evaluation in the planning process.
- How to follow up on plans made in earlier sessions.
- How planning is grounded in Choice Theory.

Assuming that the client's central problem has been identified and he now wants to make a change in his life, the new behaviour needs to be planned carefully. Even when the main problem has not been identified in a particular counselling session the planning focus moves to what to do next.

Many clients have shortcomings in their planning skills over and above whatever central problem they bring to counselling. Indeed this skill shortfall might only appear in one section of their lives. A child who has no problem organising football matches on a Saturday may have a rather chaotic approach to planning study. A business-woman whom most would regard as a high-flier in her professional life may be a home-management nightmare.

We could say that planning follows in the Reality Therapy emphasis on specific details. We seek specifics in the client's story, in the client's Quality World, in the client's view of what she is doing about her problems and in her self-evaluation. When the moment arrives to consider new behavioural choices it is appropriate to deal with these in a very specific way.

As we shall see in more detail in a later chapter on relationships, Glasser now considers relationship problems to be at the heart of almost all unhappiness and he recommends that the counsellor check out a client's relationships.[105] He notes that the very important skill of relating to others is generally not taught in our educational systems.[106] Consequently clients often need help in planning around relationship issues.

Planning is an important component of therapy but it is also a general life-skill. The strategies that a counsellor facilitates can help clients make new choices in their lives but may also model good planning for them in a more general way.

Appropriate Planning

Before the details of a plan can be examined the client does need to have made a clear commitment to change. This will normally follow the major self-evaluation where the client becomes aware that previous efforts were insufficient. Premature or inappropriate planning is one of the traps many trainee counsellors fall into. They mistakenly think that because planning is a goal of therapy they rush ahead to make it happen before the groundwork has been completed. For this reason, when learning to be a counsellor it is very useful to avoid work on plans until all the other basic counselling skills are well established.

---

[105] Glasser, William. *Reality Therapy in Action*. New York: Harper Collins, 1999.

[106] Glasser, W. Keynote address to the Third European Reality Therapy Convention, Dublin, 7th July 2005.

During planning, if the counsellor is working on something really relevant to the client's problem situation the individual will normally show considerable interest. She may appear to anticipate many difficulties (for example: "But I couldn't say that", "My friend just won't listen!"). This active engagement in the planning process is usually a good sign that it is relevant.

When a client shows little interest in a plan proposed by the counsellor there can be several reasons:

- The plan may be totally irrelevant to the client's real problem.
- It may appear difficult, impossible or naïve.
- The client may not understand what the counsellor is saying.
- The client may have already tried this option.
- The client may be choosing to give up, not try.
- The plan may sound like external criticism rather than collaborative help.

Whatever the reason, client lack of interest means that the counsellor needs to self-evaluate his own approach and decide whether or not he needs to change it. It is generally neither accurate nor helpful to think that the client is "being awkward", "blocking", "in denial"; if a plan appears useless or threatening then the client naturally will not show much interest in it.

Decisions

Before considering a plan of action, the client will need to choose the action. We can really divide planning into two important stages: choosing what to do and then devising a strategy to implement it. We need to attend both to the WHAT and to the HOW.

Considering Options

Somewhere between the identification of the problem to be addressed and the detailed planning stage there is usually time spent on examining options. Obviously it is to the client's benefit to have several different choices to consider but the actual source of these does not really matter a great deal. Even the past can provide ideas. One of the situations where Glasser atypically advocates turning to the past is where the client might learn from past strengths to deal with the present problem.

> Whether we work in therapy or in the schools, we must work with the present failure, utilising the past only as it relates to past success or to the possibility of present success.[107]

In this regard Solution Oriented Therapy[108] has many ideas to offer that fit the Reality Therapy model very well.

---

[107] Glasser, William. *Schools Without Failure.* New York: Harper & Row, 1969.

[108] O'Hanlon, Bill. *Do One Thing Different.* New York: William Morrow Paperbacks, 2000

Related to the past strengths idea is what we might call current strengths. The shop manager who is having difficulties at home with her sixteen year-old son could be asked: "If you had similar difficulties with a customer in your shop, how would you deal with it?"

It is perfectly compatible with Reality Therapy for the therapist to propose some plans for the client. These should not take the form of advice or recommendations; instead they should be presented as tentative suggestions. If the therapist has some potentially good ideas it makes sense to share them with the client for the latter's approval.

For example, a parent is concerned about his child's fear of the dark. Leaving lights on all night has helped a little but gives rise to other problems of long-term dependency. The father wants to find a better way of dealing with the child's fear. The counsellor might approach this in several ways:

- Client's own ideas: "Have you any ideas of other ways to deal with this?"
- Client's past solutions: "Did you ever have a similar problem in another area of your life and found a solution?"
- Client's current solutions in other areas of life: "Let's suppose you had a fear yourself, maybe a concern about your health. How might you deal with it ... and does this suggest any possibilities for dealing with your child's fear?"
- A role-model: "You admire your best friend's parenting skills. How would he deal with this?"
- Consultation: "I have a colleague who is very familiar with children's fears. Would you like me to ask her for ideas?"
- Research: "If we look on the Internet we might find some useful ideas."

- Therapist's experience: "Sometimes giving the child a torch is helpful. Would this work for your child?"
- Creative solutions: "Let's do a brainstorm on dealing with fear of the dark!"
- The counsellor's own experience: "When I get an unwelcome worry in the middle of the night I often listen to the radio for a little while."

Whatever the method, the bottom line is that the client chooses the plan. To a child and even to some adults, a counsellor's suggestion may be seen as a strong recommendation and so the counsellor must be careful about how he offers these. At the same time it is natural for a counsellor to have useful ideas and it could even be unethical at times not to share these with a client.

Over the years a counsellor will amass many "organised behaviours" relating to his area of expertise. So, for example, the counsellor specialising in child therapy may have the torch suggestion in his repertoire for children who fear the dark. The experienced couples and relationship counsellor will know the strengthening value of enquiring about how the couple first met.

Reality Therapy itself is a process, not a collection of techniques but its practitioners will want to accumulate as many useful techniques as possible for their chosen area of interest. With the exception of methods based on any form of external control, the therapy can work effectively with a very wide range of strategies.

The least bad option

As in the "Reality Choice" approach mentioned in a previous chapter, sometimes all of the client's options are a rather unattractive lot. One of the better least bad options is that of not making a situation any worse. This may seem somewhat negative but very often it is the only practical option available ... apart from making things worse, of course.[109] I find it helpful to process this option by first looking at what the person could do to make the situation worse.

1	Counsellor:	Gráinne, your friend won't forgive you for forgetting about her birthday. We have come up with three possible strategies for you. Which do you intend to choose?
2	Gráinne:	Well, to be honest, I don't think I could do any of those. I just know they wouldn't work. I'm really stumped!
3	Counsellor:	Do you know how to make the situation worse?
4	Gráinne:	Now that would be easy. Last night I felt like picking up the phone and telling Liz that she was being childish. Fortunately I didn't. If I said that to her then forgetting her birthday would be the least of my worries.
5	Counsellor:	So you decided not to make the situation worse. Sometimes, Gráinne, that's all we can do, not make the situation worse. If you like we can spend some time planning that approach for future use.

Generally negative planning is not very helpful but I have always found this discussion of how not to make the problem worse to carry a strong positive charge. In a situation where neither client nor

---

[109] If all politicians would swear an oath never to do or say anything that would make life worse for people, the world would be greatly improved.

counsellor has any idea about how to improve the situation the idea of choosing actively not to make things worse can be a positive ray of hope. Frequently I find that the client is already making that choice and it is empowering for him to become more aware of this.

Creative Solutions

Unlike the vehicle mechanic or the brain surgeon, the problems brought to the counsellor's office cannot be catalogued in a fairly finite list. The frustrations that people experience are as infinite as the variety of human experience itself. For this reason it is to the counsellor's advantage to be able to suggest creative solutions. Books on creative thinking[110] can help us build organised ways of tapping our creativity and here are a few suggestions.

Keep an open mind: When looking for solutions it is very easy to dismiss an option too quickly. Being able to say "It's mad! It's impossible! It's never been done before! It sounds illogical! I'll consider it!" helps keep creativity alive.

Take a broader view: Reality Therapy already encourages this when we step back from the presenting problem to examine the underlying needs frustration. So, for example, when dealing with a person with anorexic behaviour we would not necessarily focus on eating or physical self-image issues. If it emerges that this person's behaviour is her desperate attempt to deal with a life that is seriously out of control then planning suggestions would be in the area of regaining that control.

Seek alternative views: Considering different or unusual views of a situation can suggest new angles. "If William Glasser were in this situation what would he do?" "If my car was behaving like this what would I do?"

---

[110] Von Oech, Roger. *A Whack on the Side of the Head*. London: Thorsons' Publishing Group, 1990.

Brainstorm: This is a well-tried and tested technique for creative ideas. Central to its success is the rapid jotting down of all ideas without any discussion or criticism. When a sizeable list is ready, discussion can focus on making a shorter practical list.

Random words: Pick a word at random from a book and see does it suggest any ideas. The advantage of this method is that it cuts across our own mental habits and helps establish a new perspective on the problem.

An ability to tap his or her own creativity and a willingness to consult with others are assets to any counsellor who is helping a client come up with better pictures for controlling his or her life.

Evaluating the options

Once counsellor and client have created a list of the different possibilities it is usually helpful to write down the list of available options. Then the counsellor might say: "Would it help for us to examine each of these in turn, writing down what you regard as the good and bad points for each?"[111] This deliberation about pros and cons is often overlooked and people tend to judge an issue based on one salient feature instead of considering all aspects of the problem.

Once all available options have been evaluated in this way the client still has one important self-evaluation to make: which path to take. Once this is determined counsellor and client can work together to plan how to do it.

---

[111] See the "Reality Choice" exercise in the earlier chapter on Self Evaluation for a more detailed approach to evaluation of options.

The Qualities of Good Planning

Hard-nosed business people know the importance of risk in their professional lives. In a counselling situation, however, clients are generally in a debilitated state and the amount of risk they can bear is reduced. Part of the professional expertise that the counsellor can make available to the client is help in elaborating a plan that has a high chance of success. Glasser wrote, "Never make a plan that attempts too much, because it will usually fail and reinforce the already present failure. A failing person needs success, and he needs small individually successful steps to gain it."[112]

Here are some of the qualities that tend to enhance a plan's chances of success.

Possible   Beware of the client making a plan that is so big or difficult that she does not have much chance of carrying it out successfully. It is better to choose something she definitely can do. Success in each small step helps her build her own strength to continue with the next step. What are her chances of succeeding? If less than 90% then what can she change in her plan to make it more likely to work? Absolutely anyone can tear a telephone directory in two ...
if they tear out one page at a time!

Precise   Make the plan as specific as possible. Check out all the details: what? Where? when? who with? how? For example: "What is the best time to talk to your friend about this?", "Where will you meet?", "How will you open the conversation?"

---

[112] Glasser, William. *The Identity Society*. New York: Harper & Row, 1972.

Positive   It is better for the client to say what she is going to do, not what she is going to stop doing! It is easier to do something than to stop doing something. If necessary she could choose a positive action that is incompatible with the behaviour she wishes to stop.

Prompt   She should set the plan in motion as soon as possible even starting during the counselling session itself. The counsellor could ask, "Would it help to make that phone call from my office now?" A prompt start maximises the fallback time available if the plan needs to be adjusted and tried again.

Practice   The counsellor should help the client rehearse the planned activity if possible. For example: "Tell me what you will say to your friend, just as if I were your friend. Let's hear how it sounds." Practising and perfecting the same thing several times can boost confidence a lot.

Promise   The counsellor should encourage a strong commitment (not "I might", "I'll try" but "I will") from the client. When the client says "I'll try", the counsellor might ask, "How can we change the plan so that you could say 'I will do it' instead of 'I will try it'?"

Persistent   Keep trying. In the follow-up do not spend time on excuses or criticism but advance to changing the plan so that it will work. Many people believe if they try something and it is not successful then they have failed. They may need to learn the value of perseverance.

Some other qualities of good planning:

Preparation	check the details, rehearse words and actions
Prioritised	tackle first what the client wants first
Practical	focus on doing rather than thinking, feeling or physiology
Pleasant	make the plan as attractive as possible
Partnership	with others but not by others, use reminders
Precautions	check for sabotage, conflicts, threats to the plan's success
Perceptible	use measurable results, goals
Prize	acknowledge your own progress in some way
Progressive	keep the plan alive, adjusting on an ongoing basis

We can also improve our knowledge of planning skills by dipping into resources used by the business community. A fine example of this is the book "Simply Brilliant" by Fergus O'Connell.[113] This author emphasises the importance of seeking simple solutions first, of allocating time and resources to the tasks and of having good contingency plans.

Here is a sample dialogue where the counsellor is moving from a client's self-evaluation into a planning episode.

---

[113] O'Connell, Fergus. *Simply Brilliant*. London: Pearson Education Limited. 2001.

DIALOGUE	COMMENTS

1 Pete:

Are you saying that all my efforts to impress the boss and get promotion were wrong? I mean the extra hours, those courses in computing that I did in the evenings. I really did improve and even my colleagues were surprised I didn't get the position.

2 Counsellor:

I didn't say that Pete! It sounds as if you did a lot of very sensible and even difficult things and your customer feedback supports what your colleagues think. However, did it bring you the promotion you are so keen to get?

The counsellor makes it clear that the evaluation must come from Pete.

3 Pete:

It should have! Everybody thinks it should have.

Pete's answer is strong with a hint of anger in his voice but he has avoided the answer, and the responsibility.

4 Counsellor: Yes, it probably should have but did it?

The counsellor using a quiet voice invites a self-evaluation again.

5 Pete: No!

Pete's short answer is followed by a few moments of silence as he painfully accepts his own verdict.

6 Counsellor: So all this excellent work you put into improving your capabilities was not enough. Do you think all that work, those courses, everything, was a waste of time?

The counsellor affirms Pete, helping him recognise that he was not wasting his time.

7 Pete: No, I don't suppose it was. No, I couldn't say it was. At least I have it behind me and maybe it will help when the next promotion comes along in the new year.

8 Counsellor: Pete, do you want to do something else to improve your chances even more or do you think that what you have already done will be enough?

This is where planning begins. The counsellor is checking if Pete wants to change.

9 Pete: It might be but I suppose the evidence is that it's not. I have a few months and maybe I could do something extra, something new.

10 Counsellor: One thing you mentioned on Tuesday, Pete, might give a lead. You said your boss was not aware of how you had averted a strike through some very sensitive negotiation you carried out with your staff leaving both sides very happy.

The counsellor decides to suggest one from something Pete already said.

11 Pete: That's right. Actually he is not aware of a lot of the things I do. As a matter of fact he's not too well tuned into most things that are going on at work.

12 Counsellor: Would it help to tell him about some of these activities of yours?

13 Pete: I suppose it would but I just can't storm into his office and start to sing my own praises.

Notice Pete's perception of such a visit to his boss.

14 Counsellor: Maybe not like that but we could look at some options. If you knew how to let your boss know more about you without appearing vain, would you go for it?

The question, "if you knew how, would you?" can be very useful in planning.

15 Pete: You bet I would, but what can I do?

16 Counsellor: Has there ever been a time when you told him something you hadn't expected to tell him or something that was awkward?

Here the counsellor looks for past strengths that might be called on for the present situation.

17 Pete: (Laughing) The time I crashed my car! I needed to get out early to go to the garage and I just had to tell him the full story. I was as embarrassed as hell! The accident had been my fault.

18 Counsellor: How did you do that, talk to your boss I mean ... not the accident?

19 Pete: Well he always comes in half-an-hour earlier on a Friday morning so I did the same and asked him if I could have a private word with him. He even offered me a cup of coffee in his office.

20 Counsellor: Is this something that might work again?

Here is another self-evaluation, this time about a future possibility.

21 Pete: It probably would ... but what would I say? That's the problem! I wouldn't have a clue what to say.

22 Counsellor: First of all tell me what you would want to tell him if you knew how. Later we can look at the "how" bit.

23 Pete: Well I'd tell him .. or at least I'd like to tell him about the strike negotiations. There's also the new rostering arrangements I brokered with the servicing department. In fact I have new plans for my own department ...

The safe environment of counselling helps the client test out new and possibly risky behaviours.

24 Counsellor: Is that something you would include also?

25 Pete:

Actually that would be an excellent idea. I think I have hit on the solution of a security problem we have had for a long time and it would make sense to share that with the boss.

26 Counsellor:

Pete, we've almost run out of time but I think it might be a good idea to take up all of this next day. Would you like that? It doesn't sound like something you have to do right away so spending a little time on working it out could be helpful.

Here the counsellor introduces a different plan, one for the next session.

27 Pete:

Yes, I'm getting to like the idea. I have more to tell than I thought.

28 Counsellor:

OK, suppose you write down all your ideas. Fill them out a little so that they will make sense to me. Bring the notes along next day and we will work you how you could present them to the boss.

We already have a time and place, early Friday morning at the factory. Next day we focus on the "how" of it all. What do you think of that?

This helps the client see that it is his life, his plan, not the counsellor's. The counsellor proposes a structure and the client welcomes it.

29 Pete:

That is perfect. I might even think of a way to express it all to him before our next session.

30 Counsellor:

And that would be even better. I'll see you on Tuesday.

Self-Evaluation and Planning

Self-evaluation, where the client is encouraged to judge the effectiveness of her own behaviour and to make her own choices on that basis, is included in every aspect of Reality Therapy work. During planning it has its own special usefulness:

- whether to carry out a particular plan
- to prioritise plans or problems
- to process and choose from a list of options

- to check on potential "sabotage"
- to appraise a plan's effectiveness
- to adjust or replace a plan

As always in Reality Therapy we work from the side-line of a client's life. We are constantly checking the choices made by the client and how the client is evaluating her own life.

Follow-Up to Plans

In a follow-up session the counsellor will want to check on the success or otherwise of the plan but it is important how this is managed. It must not be or appear to be some sort of external inspection of the client. The counsellor could ask, "How did you fare out with your plan?" or "Was there anything about the plan you want to talk about today?" Focus on the client's satisfaction with the outcomes rather than the counsellor's. "How happy were you with what you did?" in preference to "Were you successful?", "Did it work?"

When a client returns and you find that the planned action has not been carried out there are several possibilities:

- The plan was inappropriate. (See the section on Appropriate Planning at the start of this chapter.)
- The plan was too difficult or too complex. Adjustment is needed.
- Unexpected circumstances made it impossible to carry out. That's life! Does he want to try again?
- The client simply forgot.
- The client conveniently "forgot" or tolerated sabotage of plan - it may in fact be too difficult or may be off-target.

Whereas it is useful for the counsellor to find out the source of any difficulty it is not normally a good idea to ask the client a direct "why" about this. Such an exploration may be wasteful of time and may encourage excuses rather than progress. A more positive approach such as "what do we have to change to get this plan to work?" is better.

Remember always that it is the client's evaluation of the plan's success that matters, not yours. This may mean tuning a plan down to an extremely simple level in some cases. In a high proportion of cases the client needs to learn the importance of trying again and again instead of relying on a doomed one-shot approach to planning.

> It ain't no disgrace for a man to fall but to lay there and grunt is.
>
> Josh Billings

In general there are some things Glasser suggests we avoid when helping a client process a plan that did not go as expected:

No Excuses
- Do not encourage excuses.
- Avoid asking why the plan was not carried out.
- Do not be dismissive of apologies.
- Do not make up excuses for the client.

No Criticism	• Do not complain or argue about the unfinished plan.
	• Aim at finding a "better way", improving or replacing the plan.
	• Do not dwell on real or imagined client "weakness".
	• Move forward.
	• Criticism can hurt the client's needs further.
	• It can also add to the sense of failure.
No Punishment	• Allow reasonable consequences of the inaction.
	• Maintain a high level of involvement.
	• Punishment does not teach a new approach; it tends to alienate; it is an external control technique.
No Surrender	• Do not give up easily.
	• Plans will often need multiple adjustments and re-attempts.
	• This does not exclude the possibility of referral to another.

The Choice Theory Perspective on Planning

The practicalities of planning in Reality Therapy are firmly based in the Choice Theory explanation of human behaviour.

Basic Needs/Homeostasis

A person's plan should ease need frustration, not aggravate it. Therefore plans should have a good chance of success not simply in the area of major frustration. A good plan will not remedy one need deficiency whilst generally upsetting the other needs, something that can easily happen.

The over-zealous student who has finally seen the writing on the wall and decided to study four hours a day (previously did 10 minutes on a "good" day) may get into difficulties. In a short space of time the resulting reduction in time with friends becomes very hard to take. The danger in this is that the client "pendulums" back to a no-study pattern. (Don't bore a second hole in the boat to let the water out!) If a person's problem can be likened to an imbalance in need satisfaction, then a good plan will restore balance gently, bearing in mind all the repercussions of any simple change.

Total Behaviour

According to Glasser, doing, thinking, feeling and physiology change together. However doing is the easiest behaviour to change and so planning will normally focus on this action component. Thinking plays an important role too as it carries the strategy and the motivation.

Phenomenology: Internal Control

The client's self-evaluation is essential. If he or she does not see a need to change then planning is premature. If the plan is not fully accepted by the client as his own then it is less likely that he will make real changes in his life. If the counsellor is "telling" the client what to do then chances are that there is an attempt at external control. The client's commitment to the plan is essential. This does not rule out the counsellor sharing his or her experience and expertise with the client.

How to Stand Up

This can be an interesting exercise in convincing a group of people that making plans is not always as easy as it looks. One volunteer lies down on the floor. The role of the rest of the group is to give single clear instructions, one at a time, explaining to the volunteer how to get up to a standing position. These instructions must be very specific such as "bend your right arm to a 90 degree angle with your hand sticking upwards" not general instructions such as "lift the top half of your body". (It soon becomes clear that it is almost impossible to help another person plan how to get up off the floor.)

On Your Knees

This requires a group of about 10 people. Ask them to find a way in which everyone in the group can sit on someone else's knees at the same time ... and then do it! This is a fun exercise that requires some planning with the added dimension that it is a group plan. Afterwards it is interesting to discuss:

- How the group dealt with the idea of "impossible" if it came up

- How people tried to meet everybody's needs

- The importance of specific details in a plan

- The importance of practice

- What assumptions were made

- Did people look for external control?

Problem Plans

Identify the weaknesses in these plans and suggest ways of improving them:

1. I am going to try harder from now on.
2. I am going to stop smoking.
3. I intend studying 15 minutes extra each day but I'll start next week.
4. I promise I will not drink again.
5. From now on I will make my bed every morning, wash the breakfast dishes, make a list of housework and then do it all every evening.
6. I intend enjoying myself a lot more from now on.
7. I will be careful about how much television I watch starting tomorrow evening.
8. From now on I will keep all the school rules.

Following-up on Plans

Comment on these remarks made by a counsellor as she processes the follow-up to a planning session:

1. We spent a lot of time yesterday working this out.
2. Don't worry about forgetting. I often forget things.
3. Well, there is not much else we can do about this.
4. You have made your bed so you'll have to lie on it.
5. If you haven't got the plan done I'm not going to see you.
6. You are just going to have to go back and try again!
7. The man who made time made plenty of it.

Practice Plans

Here are ten client statements. Assume that they are made after about 40 minutes of counselling and that the client now has a better idea of what he needs to change and wants to change. Role-play counsellor and client focusing exclusively on developing and fine-tuning the plan initiated here.

1. All right, I do need to change something and a short walk every day would be a good first step.

2. I can see now that my wife and I just left fun out of the picture when the kids arrived. But we can't afford the time or money to join a golf club or anything like that so what do we do?

3. At work I have about 20 jobs pending, at home the rooms are in a mess, I've not seen my friends for ages ... where do I begin?

4. Since I moved out into the country it's true that I have practically no friends at all. The problem is that I don't even know where to begin. If I were in the city I would have a better idea of how things work there.

5. I really have been neglecting myself since the kids arrived. I have almost forgotten how to enjoy myself. Maybe it would be good if I did something for myself this weekend! Part of my problem is that I don't have a lot of money.

6. When I try to study I keep thinking about how far behind I am. I end up doing nothing. What can I do?

7. I always was shy but it wasn't a big problem until I changed my job. I don't know anybody in the new office and I really feel left out.

8. My neighbour plays loud music after midnight. I have tried doing the same myself but he doesn't get the hint. I accept that talking to him is probably the best option but I don't know how to do it.

9. It really is important for my wife's career that I accompany her to this gala dinner but I'm afraid that I'm just not ready to have alcohol around me yet. If somebody offers it to me I'm worried that I might say "yes".

10. My cousin will be very disappointed if I'm not at her wedding but the flight will cost €200 and I am hopeless at saving money.

Changes

For a counselling client to carry out what we perceive to be a "simple plan" can in fact represent a massive leap in her life. This exercise is intended to help the trainee counsellor become aware of how changes can impact on his life.

Make twelve cards and write one phrase per card from the list below.

Give each trainee a card.

Give them the following instructions:

Read the card.

In what ways will these changes affect your life?

How might these changes affect people who are close to you?

Trainees could then share their answers with one or more fellow-trainees.

1. Due to a failure to pay bills, you will be without electricity, telephone and water for the next month.

2. As a result of a skiing accident both of your arms will be in plaster for about a month.

3. You have registered for a computer class you will attend every Wednesday evening for the next four weeks.

4. New government legislation requires you to do military service. You will spend the next six months in an army base 500 km from your home.

5. You have gone to stay for a month in a foreign country. You soon discover that physically you are like an identical twin of the country's most hated television presenter.

6. Your next-door neighbour celebrates her birthday just two days after you. Suddenly you receive startling news, that all those years ago you were both taken home by the wrong parents.

7. Your doctor discovers an error in your birth certificate and you now learn that you are in fact ten years older than you had believed up to now.

8. Because of a minor throat operation you are unable to use your voice for a month, not even to whisper.

9. You have developed a very rare disease. One of the side-effects is that over the next month most of your sexual characteristics will change to those of the opposite sex.

10. You realise that you are homosexual (or, if you are homosexual, you realise that you are heterosexual).

11. Starting tomorrow, you will be travelling to work by train, leaving your nearest station one hour earlier than your usual rising time.

12. Immigration officials call unexpectedly at your home and you discover from them that as a child you were illegally adopted from a foreign country and are to be deported back there in one week.

Everyday Planning

When I wrote earlier about the qualities of good planning I really could have called the section the "qualities of effective behaviour". Even when we carry out routine everyday tasks, normally without a great deal of awareness, those qualities are present. Conversely, when there are areas of our life that are not working out too well, one or more of these qualities is often missing.

There are tasks we want to do but for one reason or another we put them in the "mañana" file, a no-go area for the qualities of good planning. When we really want something we start planning how to get it straight away. So, if you want it, plan it.

Take some example from your own life, something you have been putting off for some time. (Be gentle with yourself by taking one of the easier items from your list. After all, in good planning we aim for what is "possible".) Start working on a time slot for this project, when you will start it, what exactly you will do, how you will do it. Do not write down anything you are not prepared to do.

Integrating The Skills

In this chapter you will learn about:

- How Reality Therapy can help empower the clients
- How the trainee counsellor can develop skills with confidence.

Here's a challenge that children enjoy – although it might be too difficult for adults. Sit down and lightly tap the upper part of your left thigh with your left palm. Next change to the same part of your right leg and rub it towards the knee and back with the palm of your right hand. Finally do both activities at the same time. Tough ... but don't worry! This particular skill is not often required in real life.

If you have been practising the different modules presented in Section Two of this book it is now time to ensure that you can do them all together and at first this will be difficult, almost as hard as the exercise above. It may be a cliché to say that the total is more than the sum of the parts but it is very true about counselling. It is true about the counsellor's learning process and it is true about the effects of counselling on the life of the client.

As the counsellor gradually incorporates more and more of Choice Theory and Reality Therapy into his method, he also gives the method his own personal style and flavour. That is why the advanced stage of Reality Therapy training emphasises the individual needs and style of the trainees.

Before detailing some exercises to help trainees integrate the skills it is worth pausing to examine the total effect of Reality Therapy on clients. This very often goes far beyond the problem the client brought to counselling. People can learn about internal control, about focusing on what they can do about their situation, about the power of choice in their lives.

Understanding how this happens will serve as a brief revision of some of the components of Reality Therapy.

Empowerment in Reality Therapy

The Reality Therapist provides a gradual and sensitive process of helping clients become aware of the choices in their lives and a parallel process of strength-building in clients so that they can take their responsibilities on their own shoulders. This psychological strength of the client is a very important component of effective counselling.

Almost always a significant portion of a counselling session is given to helping clients feel stronger, fortifying those personal resources they will need to regain control of their lives. Self-evaluation is one of Reality Therapy's key strategies but to invite a client to make such an evaluation too early in the counselling process could be detrimental. For these reasons I believe that an effective counsellor will constantly check on levels of involvement: How well is the counsellor-client relationship developing? Closely linked to this, he will check on empowerment: How strong is the client?

Strength is needed to be able to talk about problem areas in his life, to be able to trust the counsellor, to evaluate the effectiveness of his current behaviour and to consider the possibility of change. The counsellor can observe different signs of growing strength in the client: less tension and anxiety,   more optimism, sometimes excitement, smiles and humour.

Recalling the different components of Reality Therapy it becomes apparent that this strengthening or empowerment is happening in many different ways:

- **Involvement**

    Absence of threat, ridicule etc. provides safety for openness, realistic self-evaluation and planning.   Removes coercion and fear.

- **Drawing on the past for strength.**

    "When was the last time you laughed with your Dad?"
    "Where did you first get to know your spouse?"
    "Where you ever in a situation like this before where you handled it differently?"

- **Drawing on other experience of the client.**

    "If one of your customers had this problem what would you do?"
    "How often would you keep replacing a fuse in your car if it blew each time?"

- **Allowing fun and humour in the counselling relationship.**

    Offers alternative pictures of what is happening.

- **Acknowledging difficult choices.**

    "What you intend doing will not be easy."
    "I can see you really are having a tough time but you keep working."

- **Offering help – the language of alliance.**

  "I will help you work it out."
  "Let us have a look at this together."
  "Do you want me to phone you to remind you?"

- **Offering Hope.**

  "We will help you look for better options."

- **Affirmation.**

  "You are speaking kindly about people who have been unkind to you."

- **Reframing.**

  "When you call yourself 'stubborn', do you mean that you have carefully thought out beliefs that are important to you?"

- **Changing in small but successful steps.**

  "So you are determined to spend ten minutes extra at study tonight!"

- **Teaching or Rehearsing new skills.**

  "Will we practise what you want to say to your teacher?"

- **Explain basic human psychology.**

  For example, how our needs work and the signal value of feelings.

Empowerment of The Trainee Counsellor

It makes sense that those learning how to use Reality Therapy should do so in a way that progressively strengthens their counselling skills. Attempting too much too soon can have a powerful discouraging effect.

Sometimes trainees approach counselling training as if it would proceed in the same way as learning Mathematics or History. The set of skills, knowledge and expertise that contribute to effective counselling is much more complex than any academic subject and so the learning process will be more complicated.

The trainee needs to keep a constant eye on the target by studying and re-studying the theory, by observing as much good role-play as possible and by practising the approach with the help of an instructor or supervisor. Progress, as experienced by the trainee, will be more akin to that of a garden gradually maturing than to a building rising layer by layer.

The remainder of this chapter gives ideas to help the trainee advance with confidence even when learning how to integrate all the different strands of Reality Therapy. These exercises assume that the trainee has already practised each of the components outlined in earlier chapters in this section.

Foundations

The "client" role-plays a person with a relatively straight-forward problem, although it might not be the presenting problem. The "counsellor" should have a quick read through the set of questions below before beginning the role-play. After the standard pre-role-play briefing the counsellor will proceed to work with the client. It is important not to be self-critical. If you are not sure what to do just chat and get more information (or stop and have a look at your notes). After approximately twenty minutes stop and answer the set of questions.

Only when the counsellor has answered these (self-evaluating) should there be any discussion of the role-play with the other trainee. The main focus of training is the trainee counsellor, not the role-playing client nor the real case. By making a detailed self-evaluation, the counsellor is becoming more aware of the processes she is using. Notice that in this role-play we are not interested in self-evaluation or planning with the client.

Questions

1. What have you done that fostered an atmosphere of involvement?

2. What themes did you detect in the client's story?

3. Which theme seems to carry the major frustration for the client?

4. How does the client want things to be (Quality World) with relation to this theme?

5. What is actually happening?

6. What is the client doing about it?

If possible do this role-play a second time with the same participants in the same roles.

Repeat this type of role-play as often as necessary with different partners and cases to gain confidence in foundation work.

Full Session

Again using a case that is not complex, role-play with a partner. This time allow about thirty to forty minutes. Where relevant, encourage self-evaluations in the client. If possible help the client elaborate a plan for changes in his life. After the role-play, the counsellor uses the questions from the previous exercise to self-evaluate and then adds the following questions.

7. What self-evaluations did the client make?
8. At what points did the client show a wish to change his behaviour?
9. What options for change were discussed?
10. What plan was worked out (give details)?
11. What estimate of success would you place on the plan (as a percentage)?
12. What do you know about the client's needs?
13. If you get the chance to repeat this role-play with the same client, what variations would you like to try?

Complex Session

Role-play with a partner but in this instance the client will deliberately present several problems and, if left to her own resources, will tend to ramble on about each problem. The task of the counsellor is to help the client focus on one problem to deal with.

Creatively Crazy

In this role-play the client should play the part of a person who is displaying what others regard as "crazy" behaviour, for example, obsessive hand-washing. The counsellor's task is to help the client look at his life in general and identify major frustrations he has been trying to solve with his crazy behaviour.

Chosen Clients

Using a small card or note each trainee writes down some introductory details about a client he or she can role-play.

These notes are displayed for all the members of the group.

Each then gets a chance to be counsellor to the client of his choice.

After the role-play, the counsellor self-evaluates before having a brief discussion about the role play with other trainee.

As always, it may be helpful to repeat the role-play using a different approach.

Mixed Role-Plays

Only when the trainee counsellor has gained some confidence in what we might call structured role-plays should he move to the unstructured area, taking "unseen" role-plays. The set of questions in the first two exercises can still be a useful guide to self-evaluation.

Relaxed Role-Play

This plays an important role in the integration of skills. Every so often the trainee is invited to do a role-play without thinking very much about the processes; just let it happen. Trainees tend to worry about how well they are doing, what they might have forgotten. This is all part of the enthusiasm to learn but it can get in the way at times.

The relaxed role-play helps them integrate the skills painlessly! This fits in best when the trainees have been introduced to all the standard procedures of Reality Therapy and after they have practised these in modular form. At the end of the relaxed role-play the counsellor can self-evaluate in the usual way.

Incorporating Other Techniques

In this chapter you will learn about:

- A framework for incorporating ideas from other therapies
- Examples of using ideas and techniques from a selection of therapies

As I hope the reader will have grasped by now, Reality Therapy bases itself on a very specific understanding of how the human being functions psychologically. I would find it hard to believe that any therapy could be truly effective unless the therapist's work is grounded in some specific explanation of human behaviour. There are some who believe it is impossible to understand human behaviour and consequently they give up trying to do so. I too believe it is impossible to understand a human being fully but I am not prepared to give up on it. I started the book with this very belief. I am convinced that we must always give it our best shot, always attempting to understand better and better how people function.

Reality Therapy uses Choice Theory psychology as its underlying explanation of human behaviour. Arising directly from this perspective are a number of core processes such as "involvement" and "self-evaluation" that are central to Reality Therapy. These will always be present in some form in the practice of Reality Therapy. At yet another level are a whole series of techniques that a given therapist may or may not use. This is an ever-expanding area where the practitioner develops her own new methods or learns them from other therapies.

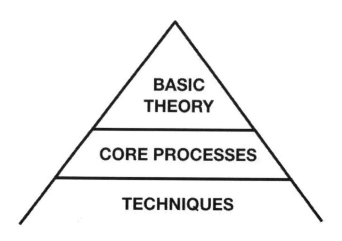

Figure 28

My understanding of an effective "eclecticism" is based on this model (Cf. Figure 28). If I use techniques from many different sources, I will still use them according to my own implicit or explicit understanding of human psychology. I will apply these techniques in the context of the core processes that stem from my basic theory. Another therapist might use the same technique as myself but rely on a totally different theoretical sub-structure. Indeed, I might "borrow" what is a core process in one therapy and use it as a technique in my own approach. I see this as a valid and even recommendable way of developing new techniques to help our clients.

On the other hand, when "eclecticism" refers to a haphazard thrashing around taking techniques from somewhere, anywhere, without basing their use on some underlying theory, the resulting therapy is unlikely to be very effective or efficient. The result may be an interesting patch-work quilt but it lacks the lining that holds it together and gives real depth and warmth!

In this chapter it is my intention to provide a few examples of how a practitioner of Reality Therapy might use processes and techniques from other therapies in the context of Reality Therapy and Choice Theory. What follows is not intended to be an exhaustive list of all possible borrowed techniques.

Adlerian Therapy

The Adlerian[114] emphasis on encouragement fits very well into the Reality Therapy focus on affirmation as does Adler's belief that all human behaviour is purposeful. Even pathological states are seen as ways of coping with difficult life situations. The use of Socratic questioning is very similar to the self-evaluative style of Reality Therapy and is fully respectful of the client's own control of his or her life.

Art Therapy

The term "art therapy" covers a range of different practices and theoretical bases. Here I am referring especially to what might be described as the interactive approaches rather than the use of art and craft activities as an aid to relaxation or physiotherapy.

The counselling client may be invited to make drawings or paintings, to use clay or other materials to represent an aspect of his or her life. Alternatively the invitation may be to work in a freeform way, producing whatever comes into the client's head. Later the client may be asked how this piece of creativity is similar to his or her life.

---

[114] Adler, Alfred. *Understanding Human Nature*. Trans. from the 1927 edition by Colin Brett. Oxford: Oneworld Publications, 1992.

At this level the activity becomes one of helping develop awareness of one's own life and awareness too of the choices the individual is making. This increase in awareness fits perfectly into a Reality Therapy context and with it comes the possibility of self-evaluation. "Is my life going in the direction I want?" A question such as this may be offered by the counsellor or may take the form of an emerging awareness for the client.

Although we use the word "art" in a very loose sense in this context it sometimes happens that the client's work achieves a truly artistic dimension. The end result can communicate a lot more about the client's life than any mere verbal explanation could accomplish. It can become a truly "total behaviour" communication about the client's life and experience.

The client could be invited to make a further drawing or work that expresses how he would like his life to be different, an opportunity to explore the Quality World in a more plastic way.

Behaviour Therapy

From a behavioural perspective if a person has a fear of social encounters, the cause may have been conditioning that taught him to avoid such situations. One solution to such a problem is to condition the person gradually to cope with situations that are increasingly like the social interactions he wishes to be able to confront. This technique is called "systematic desensitisation" developed by Joseph Wolpe.[115]

From a Choice Theory perspective the person is not being controlled by external events. Instead we see this client as choosing behaviours that in some way satisfy or protect his basic

---

[115] Wolpe, Joseph. *The Experimental foundations of some new psychotherapeutic methods.* In A.J. Bacharach (Ed.), Experimental foundations of clinical psychology. New York: Basic Books, 1962.

needs. If he has a problem with his choice of social avoidance then it is because this behaviour is frustrating other needs. For example, he may feel safer (need for survival) by staying away from other people but this choice may cause problems in his daily work (need for power).

In spite of these very different interpretations of the social avoidance behaviour in the two therapies, a strategy very similar to the behaviourists' systematic desensitisation can be employed in Reality Therapy. If a student, for example, perceives his survival need to be in danger when he is in a classroom full of fellow students, then it may be useful to help the student interact in smaller groups first, starting with just one other student.

However, it is worth noting that Reality Therapy will explore other angles. What appears to be a frustrated survival need is just as likely to be a frustrated love and belonging need. The student who has no friends in the classroom will feel uncomfortable there and will probably choose to avoid it. Rather than helping the student desensitise to large groups, we might focus on helping him learn friendship-making skills. Even here the desensitisation approach can be useful in that we begin with very basic skills and gradually move to the more complex.

Brief Psychotherapy

In this approach[116] there is a strong pragmatic sense and a general lack of interest in probing the past. Techniques which reflect these emphases will fit well with Reality Therapy. Speed of working is valued as it is in Reality Therapy. Reality Therapy practitioners do not attempt to influence clients directly as some brief therapists might but will use their knowledge of Choice Theory psychology to

[116] Haley, Jay. *Uncommon Therapy: The Psychiatric Techniques of Milton H. Erickson, M.D.* New York: W.W. Norton & Co., 1993.

probe specific aspects of the client's life. This reliance on a theoretical underlay tends to be avoided in Brief Psychotherapy.

Client-centred Counselling

There is very little in Rogerian[117] counselling that is not compatible with Reality Therapy. The high value placed on empathy and congruence is something we share. Guidelines about how to listen well are equally important for Reality Therapy. Where we do differ is in being more pro-active in helping a client process his or her life and when we attend to the client's feelings it is normally as a window to his or her total behaviour.

Cognitive Behaviour Therapy

The cognitive component of this therapy focuses on the impact of thinking on behaviour. As such it offers many techniques which fit into Reality Therapy's idea that thinking is one of the components of total behaviour that is easier to change. Beck's[118] idea of "automatic thoughts" feeds nicely into Glasser's idea that our choices are not always at the level of awareness and the CBT techniques can help challenge these unprocessed choices.

Construct Theory

George Kelly realised at the beginning of his career as an educational psychologist that people's behaviour was very much dependent on their perceptions. His two volumes[119] about Personal

---

[117] Rogers, Carl. *On Becoming a Person: A Therapist's View of Psychotherapy*. London: Constable. 1961.

[118] Beck, Aaron. *The Past and the Future of Cognitive Therapy*. Journal of Psychotherapy Practice and Research 1996, 6 (4): 276–284

[119] Kelly, George. *The Psychology of Personal Constructs (2 vols)*. New York: W.W.Norton & Co. 1955.

Constructs details the inner workings of our perceptions and outlines a therapeutic approach based on his ideas.

His repertory grid technique provides a way of exploring a person's inner logic very well although some mathematical or computer skill is a decided advantage. His definition of constructs as distinct from concepts, his "creativity cycle", his analysis of constructs as tight or loose, all of these ideas can greatly enrich our understanding of how a person's inner logic works. This of course has important implications for understanding the Quality World of our clients.

Gestalt Therapy

One of the great strengths of the many techniques of "Gestalt Therapy" as taught by its founder Fritz Perls[120] and applied by authors such as Violet Oaklander[121] is that they enable a client to deal with her life in a more holistic way. Most counselling tends to be based on talking and this can very easily become quite rational. This is perfectly appropriate for many clients but not for all. For some clients or for some aspects of their lives a more concrete way of dealing with their experiences can be more powerful.

Questions such as "What do you think is going wrong in your relationship with your girlfriend?" or "What guidelines could you follow in your relationship with her?" are operating at a very conceptual level. It is much more concrete to say, "Speak to me as if I were your girlfriend. Use the same words and tone of voice." Subsequently the therapist might suggest, "Now, imagine you are your girlfriend. Put yourself in her place. Sitting on a different chair might help. How would she answer what you said? Speak as if you were her."

---

[120] Perls, Fritz. *Gestalt Therapy Verbatim*. Utah, Real People Press, 1969.

[121] Oaklander, Violet. *Windows To Our Children*. Utah, Real People Press, 1978.

The use of such role-playing techniques can be very effective. In Reality Therapy the core process of self-evaluation could then be applied to what the client's role-play has revealed. "How does that feel?" "Is this the way you want your relationship to develop?" "Would you like to repeat this conversation with your girl-friend but doing things differently this time?"

In this technique we deal with real chunks of behaviour rather than conceptualised analysis. Any form of role-playing or drama-based therapy uses similar methods.

Human Givens[122]

As the "givens" in question are "needs", this approach can give alternative views of the basic needs although its approach to dreams would not fit comfortably into Reality Therapy.

Mindfulness

With its origins in the east this path to personal well-being can provide a refreshingly different approach to our more logical forms of therapy. Meditation and awareness become important and mindfulness provides ways to become more aware of the present, of the self and of personal responsibility.

Neuro-Linguistic Programming

One of the techniques offered by Neuro-Linguistic Programming (NLP)[123] is that of helping a client without knowing what the problem is. This could be useful if a client finds it extremely difficult to talk about the problem or is not sure what it is.

---

[122] Tyrrell, Ivan; Joe Griffin. *Human Givens*. Human Givens Publishing. 2004.

[123] Bandler, Richard and John Grinder. *Frogs into Princes*. Utah: Real People Press, 1979.

The same technique can be applied in a Reality Therapy structure but without relying on any form of external control. A client may not have had time to establish sufficient involvement with you to tell you her story or she may be unsure about where to begin. If a solution is required urgently this approach can be helpful.

I can ask my client, "was there ever a similar situation in your life, one that you were able to deal with reasonably well?" If there is, the client can be asked, "Is there anything you can learn from what you did then, something you could apply to the present situation?" Obviously a counsellor normally prefers to deal with the known in a client's life, carefully establishing a climate of involvement that helps the client talk openly about the problem area. But if the client does not wish to disclose the problem this technique can be helpful.

I still recall the first time I used this technique borrowed from NLP. The client in question was so upset that she barely wanted to stay in my office when a concerned friend brought her in. She was obviously very upset but she was not in a talking mood. I acknowledged this and asked if she would mind if I spoke. There was a little relaxation in her body language and I interpreted this as some form of agreement. Then when I asked if there was a similar situation she had dealt with effectively there was a delay before she grunted an answer, a grunt I interpreted as a "yes".

On asking if there was any part of that past solution that she could apply to the present problem she couldn't hold back the wry smile that gradually spread over her face. Later that day she was back to her usual cheerful self and even to this day I have never found out what the problem was.

Psycho-Analysis

Those who adhere closely to Freud's original techniques often use the client's dreams and symbols in therapy. In Reality Therapy I might use these as metaphors or similes. The client's dreams and symbols come from her own mind and, if they have any meaning at all it is in the context of the client's own perceptual world. This would certainly not be my first choice of techniques for use in Reality Therapy but sometimes a change of direction can be useful, especially if the underlying problem is not so easily identified.

My client might tell me about a recurring dream where her teeth are falling out. I ask her if this is in any way similar to her present problem with Ivan. Is she afraid that he too will fall out of her life? Or does she feel less secure in his presence? Only the client can answer questions like this. She might say there is simply no connection at all.

Glasser himself does not use client's dreams or fantasies but I believe they can provide useful and creative ways to probe a client's experience especially when it is proving difficult to find out what the problem really is. They offer an alternative route into the client's mind, no more and no less.

Rational-Emotive Behaviour Therapy

It is not surprising to know that Glasser and Ellis[124] developed a strong mutual respect in the last years of Ellis' life. They had both challenged the psycho-analytic model of therapy and had both moved towards a total behaviour explanation of human conduct. In challenging a whole series of cognitive myths, Ellis provides useful ways of investigating the thinking component of a client's behaviour.

Solution-Oriented Therapy

Glasser is not a great believer in exploring a client's past but there is one important exception that he makes and this is when we look for past strengths. In a similar way he looks for strengths in other areas

---

[124] Ellis, Albert. *A Guide to Rational Living.* Englewood Cliffs, N.J., Prentice-Hall, 1961.

of a client's present life.   Tapping these valuable resources is exactly what Solution Oriented Therapy does extremely well.

Bill O'Hanlon writes, "Problem-oriented and explanation-based theories focus on what is wrong with a person or what went wrong in the past. Solution-oriented therapy highlights what is right with the person, what has worked or been helpful in the past, and what the person can do right now to change things."[125] This is very close to a Choice Theory approach and the Reality Therapy practitioner will find lots of useful ideas in O'Hanlon's writings.

Transactional Analysis

In a book originally published in 1970 as "The Book of Choice", we could expect to find some useful ideas for Reality Therapy. By 1973 a catchy title helped popularise the book as "I'm OK – You're OK".[126] The simple but very powerful analysis of human interaction outlined in the book is very useful where a client needs to evaluate her interactions with others. The layer that a Reality Therapy practitioner will add is to invite the client to self-evaluate asking, for example, "which of these four hidden messages do you want your own communication to carry?"

Another interesting idea from TA is that of the child, parent and adult voices. I might adapt this idea to a Reality Therapy context where it could be useful for self-evaluation.

I could present the ideas to the client in these words: "Sometimes we all want to behave the way small children do; we want to say 'I'll do whatever I want to' or 'I want fun and I want it now'. At other times we want to be very proper, to follow all the rules, to be the same as everybody else, not to stand out.   Then sometimes we want to judge each situation on its merits, look at things in a

---

[125] O'Hanlon, Bill. *Do One Thing Different*. New York: William Morrow & Co. Inc.,1999.

[126] Harris, Thomas A. *I'm OK – You're OK*. London: Pan Books. 1973.

balanced way." Subsequently we could use these ideas as a basis for the client's self-evaluation of her own behaviour. I might use a series of questions: "Which of these methods do you use at a party?" "Which have you been using with your current problem?" "Which approach would you like to use with your problem?"

Extending Reality Therapy Techniques

This book's main focus is on the acquisition of basic Reality Therapy knowledge, skills and techniques. As the counsellor gains experience he or she will develop or acquire special applications or techniques of Choice Theory for new situations.

The present author includes a number of examples of such approaches in the companion volume to this one, "The Practice of Choice Theory Psychology"[127]. These include anger, difficult choices, relationships, conflict, bullying, school refusal, sexual abuse, suicidal intentions and stress. A range of similar topics is included in the "Choice Theory in Action Series" listed at the end of this book.

Each counsellor is encouraged to develop new strategies for specific situations.

• How can I introduce the idea of choice into this issue?

• Are there some frequently used options I should be able to offer to clients?

• How can I best demonstrate to the client the range of options available?

• How can I process this issue with different clients, those who prefer a rational approach, those who need more concrete examples, those for whom artwork might be more appropriate?

---

[127] Lennon, Brian. *The Practice of Choice Theory Psychology.* Amazon, 2019.

Influences

In your current work reflect on the different influences you have chosen to incorporate into your work.

1. What is your own basic theory?
2. What would you regard as core processes arising from this theory?
3. What other techniques do you use and what were their origins?
4. What plans do you have to enrich your approach?

Creating New Techniques

Every "technique" we use in helping others was created at some point in time by an individual and then possibly improved by others. It is good to remain open to the possibility of creating new techniques yourself.

Can you think of ways of using any of the following when helping other people?

- Music or a person's musical preferences
- Advertisements
- Story-telling
- Doodling
- Toys

Conclusion

There are of course some authors in the fields of counselling and psychotherapy whose writing is essential reading for anyone working in these areas. They helped lay the foundations of counselling and their ideas continue to be important today. Here I refer to people such as Alfred Adler, Carl Rogers, Arnold Beck and Albert Ellis. These authors have all given a central role to the person's own responsibility for his life and learning from them will also enrich our ideas in Choice Theory and Reality Therapy.

Fortunately, this chapter could end up bigger than the entire book as there is such a wealth of therapies in the world today. Just as each counsellor develops his or her own area of expertise so too people are attracted more to particular techniques that suit their own personal styles. It is probably equally true about the underlying explanation of human behaviour that each counsellor adopts ... including my belief in Choice Theory. We choose an explanation that fits into our Quality World, that makes sense in our own inner logic.

For almost twenty years I have found Reality Therapy and its related theory to enrich my own counselling work greatly. It is very firmly based in common sense and has strong face-validity with young people in particular.

What I and many others have found particularly beneficial is that there is a strong sense of a guiding structure for the counsellor. This can help make the process very efficient in time and energy. In the introduction I claimed that the purpose of counselling is to help the client achieve a happier life and I firmly believe that Reality Therapy achieves that purpose very well.

My final recommendation is to try the ideas and the approach. Above all read the original works of William Glasser and, if you can, watch recordings of him in role-play. I hope that this book succeeds in helping you in your own work and life.

Bibliography

Books by William Glasser
(in chronological order)

Glasser, William. *Mental Health or Mental Illness?* New York: Harper & Row, 1960.

Glasser, William. *Reality Therapy.* New York: Harper & Row, 1965.

Glasser, William. *Schools Without Failure.* New York: Harper & Row, 1969.

Glasser, William. *The Identity Society.* New York: Harper & Row, 1972.

Glasser, William. *Positive Addiction.* New York: Harper & Row, 1976.

Glasser, William. *Stations of the Mind.* New York: Harper & Row, 1981.

Glasser, William. *Control Theory.* New York: Harper & Row: 1984.

Glasser, William. *Control Theory in the Classroom.* New York: Harper & Row, 1986.

Glasser, William. *The Control Theory - Reality Therapy Workbook.* Los Angeles: William Glasser Inc., 1986.

Glasser, William. *The Quality School.* New York: Harper & Row, 1990,1992.

Glasser, William. *The Quality School Teacher.* Chapel Hill: New View Publications, 1992.

Glasser, William. *The Control Theory Manager.* New York: Harper Business, 1994.

Glasser, William. *Staying Together*. New York: Harper & Row, 1995.

Glasser, William. *Choice Theory*. New York: Harper Collins, 1998.

Glasser, William & Carleen Glasser. *Choice: The Flip Side of Control - The Language of Choice Theory*. Los Angeles: William Glasser Inc., 1998.

Glasser, William. *Creating the Competence Based Classroom*. Los Angeles: William Glasser Inc., 1999.

Glasser, William. *Reality Therapy in Action*. New York: Harper Collins, 1999.

Glasser, William. *Every Student Can Succeed*. Chula Vista: Black Forest Press, 2000.

Glasser, William & Carleen. *What is this thing called Love?* Los Angeles: William Glasser Inc., 2000.

Glasser, William and Carleen Glasser. *Getting Together and Staying Together*. New York: Harper Collins, 2000.

Glasser, William. *Counseling with Choice Theory: The New Reality Therapy*. New York: Harper Collins, 2001.

Glasser, William. *Fibromyalgia: Hope from a completely New Perspective*. Los Angeles: William Glasser Inc., 2001.

Glasser, William. *Unhappy Teenagers: A way for parents and teachers to reach them*. New York: Harper Collins, 2002.

Glasser, William. *Warning: Psychiatry can be hazardous to your mental health*. New York: Harper Collins, 2003.

Glasser, William. *Defining Mental Health as a Public Health Issue*. Los Angeles: William Glasser Inc., 2005.

Glasser, William and Carleen. *Eight Lessons for a Happier Marriage*. New York: Harper, 2007.

Glasser, William. *Take Charge of Your Life*. Bloomington: iUniverse, Inc., 2011.

Many of the above are available from wglasserbooks.com

Other Reality Therapy Titles

Glasser, Naomi (Editor). *What Are You Doing?* New York: Harper & Row, 1980.

Glasser, Naomi (Editor). *Control Theory in the Practice of Reality Therapy.* New York: Harper & Row, 1989.

Lennon, Brian. *The Practice of Choice Theory Psychology.* Amazon Publishing, 2019.

Palmatier, Larry. *Crisis Counseling for a Quality School Community.* Washington DC: Accelerated Development. 1997.

Rice, Michael. *A Choice Theory Approach to Drug and Alcohol Abuse.* Madeira Publishing Company, Mesa, Arizona. 2009.

Rice, Michael. *Choice Theory with Addicted Populations.* Madeira Publishing Company, Mesa, Arizona. 2011.

Robey, Patricia A., Robert E. Wubbolding & Jon Carlson (Eds). *Contemporary Issues in Couples Counseling.* New York: Routledge Taylor & Francis Group, 2012.

Wubbolding, Robert. *Reality Therapy (Theories of Psychotherapy).* Alexandria, VA: American Psychological Association (APA), 2010.

Wubbolding, Robert. *Reality Therapy for the 21st Century.* New York: Routledge, 2000.

Wubbolding, Robert & John Brickell. *A Set of Directions for Putting and Keeping Yourself Together.* Minneapolis: Educational Media Corporation, 2001.

Wubbolding, Robert & John Brickell. *Counselling with Reality Therapy.* New York: Routledge, 2017 (2nd Ed).

Wubbolding, Robert E., *Reality Therapy and Self-Evaluation.* Alexandria, VA: American Counseling Association, 2017.

Wubbolding, Robert E. *Understanding Reality Therapy.* New York: Harper Perennial, 1991.

Wubbolding, Robert E. *Using Reality Therapy.* New York: Harper & Row, 1988.

The Choice Theory in Action Series Titles

A Choice Theory Psychology Guide to Addictions: Ways to Overcome Substance Dependence and Other Compulsive Behaviors - Mike Rice

A Choice Theory Psychology Guide to Anger Management: How to Manage Rage in Your Life - Brian Lennon

A Choice Theory Psychology Guide to Depression: Lift Your Mood - Robert E. Wubbolding, Ph.D.

A Choice Theory Psychology Guide to Happiness: How to Make Yourself Happy - Carleen Glasser

A Choice Theory Psychology Guide to Parenting: The Art of Raising Great Children - Nancy S. Buck Ph.D.

A Choice Theory Psychology Guide to Relationships: How to Get Along Better With The Important People in Your Life - Kim Olver

A Choice Theory Psychology Guide to Stress: Ways of Managing Stress in Your Life - Brian Lennon

The Choice Theory in Action Series is available
from Amazon as e-books or paperbacks
and may be obtained through bookshops
including wglasserbooks.com

See wgii.ie/choice-theory-in-action-series/

Research

A listing of research relating to Choice Theory and Reality Therapy may be found at:

www.wglasserinternational.org/research/

Biography of William Glasser, M.D.

Roy, Jim. *William Glasser: Champion of Choice*. Phoenix, Arizona: Zeig, Tucker & Theisen, 2014.

William Glasser International

The body that Dr. Glasser approved to continue teaching and developing his ideas is William Glasser International.

This organisation helps coordinate the work of many member organisations around the world.

If you are interested in training in Reality Therapy, Choice Theory psychology or any of its applications, you are recommended to contact WGI or your nearest member organisation of WGI.

www.wglasserinternational.org

The Author

Brian Lennon has worked as both a guidance counsellor and psychologist over almost thirty years. He has been using Reality Therapy as his main counselling approach since 1985. He is a senior faculty member of William Glasser International, the official body representing Choice Theory psychology and Reality Therapy on behalf of their creator, Dr. William Glasser.

In dedicating his book about psychiatry to Brian in 2003, Dr. Glasser wrote, "Since we met many years ago, I have felt your mind is a mirror of mine."

Brian is a Fellow of the Irish Institute of Guidance Counsellors, a Fellow of the William Glasser Institute Ireland and Chairman Emeritus of William Glasser International. He has produced several books and software in the Guidance & Counselling area and has presented on the topic of Choice Theory psychology in many countries around the world. He was a close associate of Dr. Glasser and, with his approval, founded William Glasser International. He lives in Co. Dublin, Ireland.

The author may be reached at dystraxia@gmail.com

INDEX

guidance counselling IXf.
guidance counsellor 4, 200, 203f., 306, 417
guilt 302
gut feeling 93

H

Haley, Jay 397
Hallock, Suzy IX, 308
happiness VIII, 7, 40, 137, 225, 229, 412
Harris, Thomas 403
Harshman, Linda IX
homework 50
Human Givens 400
humour III, 98, 214, 219, 280, 299, 302, 304, 311f., 385
hypothesis 54, 70, 90, 312

I

identification 53, 181, 262, 322, 356
Imagination 106, 261
immediacy 308
impulsivity 226
incident analysis 37
indirect 204
infancy 112
inner logic 21, 30, 73, 76, 85f., 88, 98, 100f., 229, 253, 271, 399, 407
Institute of Guidance Counsellors IIX, 417
intelligence 45, 68
internal control 13, 17, 40, 70, 337, 345f., 348ff., 376, 384
interpersonal problems 44
intervention 1, 59, 112, 161, 163, 234

involvement V, VIII, IIX, 23, 121, 125, 129f., 137, 140, 147f., 167, 169, 173, 176, 199ff., 206ff., 212, 214f., 218ff., 241, 259, 299, 301f., 305, 311, 327, 330f., 335, 340, 375, 384f., 388, 401
Ireland IXf., 25, 34, 68, 160, 204, 207, 234, 240, 324, 417
isolation 170

J

justice 256

K

Katz, Al IX
Kelly, George IX, 81, 187, 398
knots 307

L

leadership VII
leisure 65, 141, 214, 274
Lennon, Brian II, VII, IX, 404, 411f., 417
linguistics 400
love and belonging need 19, 143, 226, 397

M

management 13, 70, 353, 412
marijuana 252
marriage 43, 316, 410
measurement 66, 93
medication 62ff., 90, 92, 191
meditation 339, 400
memory 56f., 68, 88, 140, 321
mental health 13, 32, 44, 51, 59f., 64, 91, 137, 409f.
mental illness 32, 91, 136, 228, 285, 409
metaphors 260, 299, 307ff.,

Printed in Poland
by Amazon Fulfillment
Poland Sp. z o.o., Wrocław